American Poetry *as* Transactional Art

MODERN AND CONTEMPORARY POETICS

American Poetry *as* Transactional Art

STEPHEN FREDMAN

THE UNIVERSITY OF ALABAMA PRESS TUSCALOOSA

The University of Alabama Press
Tuscaloosa, Alabama 35487-0380
uapress.ua.edu

Typeface: Scala and Scala Sans

Cover image: Untitled pigment print, 2018, by Faiya Fredman,
from her *Graffiti Goddess* series; courtesy of the artist
Cover design: Michele Myatt Quinn

Cataloging-in-Publication data is available from the Library of Congress.
ISBN: 978-0-8173-5981-2
E-ISBN: 978-0-8173-9294-9

For Gerald L. Bruns and Marjorie Perloff
Treasured Partners in Conversation

Contents

Figures

Preface

In *The New York Trilogy*, poet and novelist Paul Auster asks a question that reverberates for American poetry: "How to get out of the room that is the book?" This is a question about hermeticism, about self-enclosure, about solipsism, and it has been answered in many ways by poets writing since World War II. Much of the poetry of this period is characterized by its pragmatist cast, by how it finds new ways to encounter changing circumstances and to solicit, in turn, engaged responses from outside it, refusing to stay confined in "literature." I use the word "transactional" to signal poetry's existential interactions with the outside world, something more dynamic than the concept of subject matter. In lyric poetry, as it has often been understood, the poet controls the point of view and aims for a timeless, intransitive utterance. The work treated in this book amounts to something different: a poetry of conversation, of talk, of correspondence—one dependent on transactions at a variety of registers. By exploring American poetry's relationships to spirit, to its historical moment, to the other arts, and to prose, I hope to demonstrate some of the dimensions of its interactional dynamism.

I want to add a word of caution about the term "transactional." It has lately been extracted from economics and used as a metaphor for a cynical, quid pro quo politics, where I'll give you what you want if you give me what I want, and we need never agree about underlying principles, goals, or ideals. This is not the sense of the term I wish to invoke. Instead, I mean something like the notion of art as transactional that Hannah Higgins invokes in her wonderful study, *Fluxus Experience* (2002). She adopts John Dewey's definition of experience as "active and alert commerce with the world . . . complete interpenetration of self and the world of objects and events," to propose experience in art as a "transactional, interpenetrative framework" for creating "a sense of continuity with the world" (xiv). By "transaction," then, I mean interaction, interchange, conversation, correspondence, translation—activities that involve a give-and-take based on mutual respect and shared goals, rather than on the desire for cynical gain. Like Higgins, I use "transactional" in a pragmatistic sense, in which poetry is situated in actual occasions of relationship, whether they are spiritual, political, artistic, or heuristic, and the goal is not control but what David Antin calls "tuning." Tuning is the term he substitutes for understanding, in which the emphasis is placed on transactional relations in motion, as in the mutual adjustment of the strides of two people to walk along together for a while.

This book, more than any other I've written, has grown out of conversations over the course of many years, and thus my memory will not be sufficient to thank everyone I should. For those who recognize in these pages ideas we have discussed, please accept my heartfelt appreciation.

First, I want to thank the dedicatees, Gerald L. Bruns and Marjorie Perloff, for countless hours of conversation, of reading one another's work, and of joining together in imagining ways to understand modern poetics. My intellectual life would be so much poorer without your example, your encouragement, and your friendship.

At the University of Notre Dame, I have had the good fortune to explore poetics with a marvelously responsive group of faculty and graduate students. Among the faculty, I would like to thank, in particular, those who have participated directly in our Poetics Program: Francisco Aragon, Jacqueline Brogan, Gerald L. Bruns, Cornelius Eady, Maud Ellmann, Johannes Görasson, Romana Huk, John Matthias, Joyelle McSweeney, Orlando Menes, Henry Weinfield, John Wilkinson, Ivy Wilson, Ewa Ziarek, and Krzystof Ziarek. Among the many graduate students to whom I am grateful for outstanding contributions to poetics, I will confine myself to thanking by name those who have entrusted me with the direction of their dissertations: Brian Conniff, Linda (Taylor) Kinnahan, Sharon LaBranche, Feng Lan, Grant Jenkins, Ranen Omer-Sherman, Kaplan Harris, Craig Woelfel, Chris Chapman, Kristina Jipson, Todd Thorpe, Yugon Kim, Joel Duncan, and Semyon Khokhlov.

I have benefited greatly from critical readings of the manuscript of this book, as it formed during a two-year period, by Semyon Khokhlov, Henry Weinfield, Peter Middleton, Nick Fredman, Hank Lazer, Charles Bernstein, and two anonymous readers for the University of Alabama Press. I owe a special debt to Kate Marshall, who graciously organized a symposium to celebrate my retirement, which presented the occasion to write much of the material that ended up in the introduction and epilogue to this book. Dan Waterman has offered a great deal of helpful advice on the making and production of this book, which has aided materially in its completion and publication. As always, Barbara Black-Fredman has been one of my closest, most critical, and engaged readers; this book, and my life, would be much duller without her sharp wit.

Many of the essays have appeared, usually in substantially different form, in journals and books. Chapter 1 was first published in *A Concise Companion to Twentieth-Century American Poetry*, edited by Stephen Fredman (Oxford: Blackwell, 2005). Portions of chapter 2 appeared in *Reading Duncan Reading*, edited by Stephen Collis and Graham Lyons (Iowa City: University of Iowa Press, 2012). A shorter version of chapter 3 appeared in *The Poetry and Poetics of Michael Heller: A Nomad Memory*, edited by Jonathan Curley and Burt Kimmelman (Madison, NJ: Fairleigh Dickinson University Press, 2015). An earlier version of chapter 4 was published in *The Objectivist Nexus*, edited by Rachel Blau DuPlessis and Peter Quartermain (Tuscaloosa: University of Alabama Press, 1999). Shorter versions of chapter 5 appeared first in "Charles Olson at the Century: A Projective and Archival Reconsideration," edited by Steve McCaffery, special issue, *Open Letter* 15, no. 2 (2013), and then in *Contemporary Olson*, edited by David Herd (Manchester, UK: Manchester University Press, 2015). Chapter 7 is a revised version of the introduction to Robert Creeley and Marisol, *Presences: A Text for Marisol*, a critical edition, edited by Stephen Fredman (Albuquerque: University of New Mexico Press, 2018). Chapter 8 is a revised version of the introduction to *How Long Is the Present: Selected Talk Poems of David Antin*, edited by Stephen Fredman (Albuquerque: University of New Mexico Press, 2014). The germ of chapter 9 was published in 2013 by Rachel Galvin on *Feedback*, the weblog of Open Humanities Press. A much earlier version of part of chapter 10 was published by Donald Wellman in "TRANSLATIONS: Experiments in Reading," issue 3 of *O.ARS* (1983). Earlier versions of chapter 11 appeared online in *Postmodern Culture* 6, no. 3 (May 1996), and in *Paul Auster*, Bloom's Modern Critical Views, edited by Harold Bloom (New York: Chelsea House, 2004). An earlier version of chapter 12 was published by Miriam Nichols in *West Coast Line* 35, no. 3 (2002). Many thanks to all of these editors for their conversations about the essays and for having the faith to publish them.

Finally, I have the pleasure of thanking my mother, Faiya Fredman, for providing the cover image, "Untitled pigment print, 2018, from the *Graffiti Goddess* series," which was exhibited in *The Steel Goddess: Works by Faiya Fredman, 1998–2018*, Oceanside Museum, September 1, 2018–January 13, 2019.

Introduction

HOW I CAME TO SEE POETRY AS TRANSACTIONAL ART

Poets are interested in everything. One of the defining qualities of poetry is its sheer ambition, its intellectual reach. Poets read promiscuously. They look for ways to bind together what they read, what they experience, and what they hear about into big pictures of the world. Many people think of poetry as a hermetic art, as though poets write only about themselves (or those they wish to seduce) or as if the subject of poetry were finally only poetry, its forms and traditions. These partial truths obscure so much. Poets I have known are among the most intellectually curious, socially inquisitive, and culturally conversant people I have ever met. For them, poetry affords a means to draw together images, ideas, practices, rituals, and verbal techniques from around the globe and across time—not to equate them but to establish dialogue, to invite as many guests as possible to the World Party, which Robert Duncan has called memorably the "symposium of the whole."

My thinking of poetry as an art of transaction began in conversation. I feel remarkably lucky to have listened at length to poets speaking, usually informally, and to have been able to join in the give-and-take. Early on, I aspired to be a poet, which took me as a college student to the Bay Area, where I ended up living for ten years during the 1960s and 1970s and participating in aspects of the birth of Language poetry, which is what many of the poets of my generation were up to in that time and place. During those years, I met three of the most voluble and immersive talkers I have ever known: Robert Duncan, Robert Creeley, and David Antin. Animated exchanges with these elder poets and with others of my own generation always felt consequential for learning what poetry could be and what we wanted to do with it. Often the subject of conversation would be new work, and the game of situating it would take all our faculties—to describe it and then to place it in relation to other ideas, inquiries, and art practices going on at the time.

In the early 1970s, when I first met Antin in San Diego, his talk poems were roiling the waters of the poetry orb. People worried he was "anti-poetic"—wondering what that might mean. He had stopped composing verse as a written art and was the first person to propose the poetry reading as an occasion to stand in front of an audience and think out loud, without a text. His method was designed to issue a challenge, and it provoked energetic reactions, from excited approval to downright hostility. He would begin a talk by ruminating about the details of preparing his tape recorder to capture what he said, then he might casually remark on circumstances leading up to his being in that particular room, and slowly it would dawn on the audience that *this* was the poem. His presentational style blended equal parts roving art critic, language philosopher, and wise-guy storyteller from Brooklyn. After the event, he would transcribe the recording into unpunctuated units of utterance—separated by spaces and without justified margins—that graphed the movement of his thinking. Duncan, whom I'd met several years before Antin, saw these spontaneous talk poems, with their rigorous disavowal of the efficacy of form, as a disturbing experiment in probing the limits of poetry. Duncan also valued spontaneity in composing a poem (in *writing*), but he was obsessed with form both in the poem and in the cosmos, and he was always looking for ways to embed the rhythm of the one in the rhythm of the other. Like Antin, he pushed against the boundaries of poetic order, in his case by exposing his intricate sound play to the structural disruptions of collage. In the heavily populated solar system of California poetry during the early 1970s, Duncan and Antin were large planets, although they seemed to orbit each other more like matter and antimatter.

Oddly, one of the gravitational attractions between them was that each claimed a heritage from Romanticism, although their definitions of it diverged substantially. This was the time in which postmodernism was first being proposed, and it provoked disputes centered around the relationship of contemporary work to that of modernism and the early-twentieth-century avant-garde. Both poets found these terms of discussion too narrow, arguing that the inventions setting the horizons for contemporary poetry had occurred at the end of the eighteenth and the beginning of the nineteenth centuries. For Duncan, Romanticism inaugurated the primacy of imagination in poetic thinking, leaving behind a narrow rationality in favor of the full range of human consciousness. Furthermore, he saw imagination as the faculty for apprehending cosmic or natural forms that organically underlie poetic intuitions and poetic forms. For Antin, on the contrary, Romanticism marked a new historical epoch in which human beings can invent their own phenomenological realities, without the guardrails of common sense terms for experience—realities that in turn make existential demands on their inventors. He saw the existing forms of poetry, like the accepted terms for emotions, as instances of false consciousness that shield us from confronting unexpected situations or from joining someone in the risky act of thinking aloud and trying to figure out what is not understood.

When Duncan came in 1972 to read at UC San Diego, where Antin taught in the Art Department, it seemed the moment for each man to decide if his sense of poetry might have room for the other's. Each had a conception of poetry as a comprehensive way of being in the world, a transactional mode that could include any type of knowledge but would be guided by only one overriding perspective (his own). Duncan read that afternoon mainly from new, post–Black Mountain work, which eventually would become *Ground Work: Before the War* (1984). In this poetry, he expanded his projectivist working method to include further explorations of music and rhythm in verse, placing himself in conversation with poets from the past, such as Dante, Baudelaire, and the Metaphysical poets. Antin had already staked out his position with regard to "music" in poetry: he thought it was a bad metaphor for the speech rhythms and the phonemic and syntactic repetitions that mark the lines and stanzas of verse. He likened its impact on poetry to the impediment of skipping rope while trying to tell a story.

The night before the reading, I found myself alone with the poets in the house David and Eleanor Antin were renting on the bluffs overlooking the Pacific Ocean in Solana Beach. Eleanor, a multimedia artist obsessed with narrative, excused herself and went off to the bedroom to watch soap operas. In the longish, somewhat narrow living room, Robert and David seated themselves at opposite ends. I sat in the middle, to one side, like a line judge in a professional ping pong match, in which players stand far back from the ends of the table and let fly fearsome volleys. This was combat among two of the most uninterruptible and unpredictable talkers I had ever heard. I felt my head whip back and forth as though watching grenades lobbed across the net and saw, once and for all, that poetry is for real and is played for keeps.

Across their careers, these poets championed a view of poetry as a mode of thinking that can include *everything*. For Duncan, this conviction was based in part on a faith, inherited from Freud, that every cognitive event is meaningful —even slips, mistakes, dreams, the childish, the everyday, the occult, the perverted—and that anything human beings are capable of thinking or doing must be brought on board and measured within poetry. In Antin's pragmatist belief, the poet develops an ability for confronting whatever is going on and thinking with it as it does. Rather than driving to resolve an occasion into accepted categories, the poet is willing to let it interact promiscuously with other facts, attitudes, circumstances, to see what happens. Duncan was a maximalist, a formidable metaphor machine, setting everything in relation to everything else along what he called "an absolute scale of resemblance and disresemblance."[1] Antin was a minimalist, intent on extending the avant-garde project of making ordinary language and everyday happenings strange and newly alive, a project inaugurated in the early twentieth century by Russian Futurism, Ludwig Wittgenstein, and Marcel Duchamp and renewed in the postwar era by John Cage, Allan Kaprow, Fluxus, and conceptual art.

The interchange I witnessed between the "poet's poet" (Duncan) and the "philosopher poet" (Antin) has remained vivid. As a heuristic device, it makes sense to think of the poetry that matters to me as stretched between two poles: on the one hand, a mystical faith that poetry penetrates and sets in relation every level of the world and, on the other, a conviction that poetry is the artful use of language to participate meaningfully in an unforeseen present event. Mapping this territory, though, requires being cognizant of what these two poets have in common as much as of their disagreements. I have already mentioned that both see themselves as inheritors of Romanticism, which is as much a philosophical as a poetic affiliation. More specifically, they both value highly pragmatism, which has roots in the American Romanticism of Emerson. Duncan proclaims in a letter, "A true child of Dewey and James I am a pragmatist and the poem is my practice."[2] In *Experience and Nature* (1929), Dewey claims that science and art partake of the same method of engaging a situation—whether it is called "experiment" or "experience"—and in their own ways, both Duncan and Antin regard this notion of participatory learning as essential to poetry. In an essay on Kaprow, the originator of Happenings, Antin quotes approvingly a paragraph from Dewey's *Art as Experience* (1934) and then translates Dewey's definition of "*an* experience" into the terms of his own theory of narrative: "For Dewey all experiences have a common form, a narrative form, because, as he sees it, *an experience* is not continuous or instantaneous, but an articulated whole with a beginning and end that enclose a sequence of engagements between a desiring subject and a resisting object that comes to some kind of definite resolution."[3]

There are many consequences of this mutual regard for pragmatism. One is an avowal that composing the poem or talk is an experience in itself, one that retains its primacy as a fully rounded moment regardless of the "subject matter" invoked. Another is to ground poetry resolutely in the domestic and the everyday worlds, refusing to cordon off the mundane from "high" art or the historical past. No matter how far Duncan flies into the realm of imagination or how deep Antin goes into the minutiae of science, both affirm allegiance to the intimate life of a household, with its primary persons, its extended family, and its friends. Another consequence of the pragmatist influence is profound admiration for Gertrude Stein, the prize student of William James. Antin is famous for quipping, "From the modernism you choose, you get the postmodernism you deserve," and the modernism he chooses is one for which Stein's linguistic innovations are crucial. Duncan, likewise, cared so for Stein that he spent years writing imitations of her work. The various transactions each poet undertakes with Stein are also emblematic of their extensive interactions with other artists and forms of art. At the most intimate level, Duncan's networks of artistic exchange begin with his husband, Jess, a painter, collagist, and sculptor, and Antin's begin with his wife, Eleanor Antin, a multimedia artist, filmmaker, and storyteller. These collaborations with partners spread outward to encompass a surprisingly extensive scope of poetry, art, and music. Finally, just as pragmatism insists on not resting on prior formulations that would preclude new discoveries, Antin and Duncan dedicate their arts to holding open the radical potential of not-understanding, in order to allow new ways of making sense to appear.

SCOPE OF THE BOOK

In this book, I explore some of the kinds of exchanges in which American poets engage. For many of the chapters, Antin and Duncan serve as points of reference, and even when they are not mentioned specifically, their ways of thinking about poetry and art may inform what is said. The book is divided into four sections, each of which contains essays about how poetry looks beyond itself, drawing from and addressing other realms: "Poetry & Spirit," "Poetry & Its Time," "Poetry & the Arts," and "Poetry & Prose." This adds up to a transactional view of poetry. Instead of embracing the model that prevailed when I began to read poetry in my teens—of a poem as intransitive and lyrically self-contained—I want to emphasize how it interacts with other entities. Here, I discuss its transactions with spiritual traditions and practices, with social and political realities of its historical period, with other artists and other art forms, and with its categorical "other"—prose. The epilogue looks briefly at another crucial transaction: teaching American poetry in the classroom.

"Poetry & Spirit: Against Orthodoxy" contains three chapters. The first, "Why Mysticism in Twentieth-Century American Poetry?," seeks to provide handholds for a reader coming to the poetry with no knowledge of its spiritual affordances. American poets have studied spiritual, religious, and mystical traditions for a variety of purposes, but a new reader may be surprised at the sheer extent of poetic interactions with these traditions. Although reasons for delving into the spiritual are often personal, many American poets share an adversarial relationship with American society that primes them to employ mystical materials to counter or protest economic and political values they see as inimical. The second chapter, "Jerome Rothenberg's *Technicians of the Sacred*: Transactions between the Indigenous and the Avant-Garde," discusses Rothenberg's groundbreaking anthology *Technicians of the Sacred* (1968), which makes connections between poetry, songs, chants, rituals, and visual art from across the world and into deep time, especially placing tribal and archaic pieces in dialogue with antinomian poetry and art of the contemporary era. Rothenberg's definition of the sacred insists on an erotic core at the heart of the spiritual, and in this way, he continues the egalitarian "symposium of the whole" evoked by Robert Duncan. Just as Duncan sought "a poetry of all poetries" through collage methods in series such as "Passages" (written from the mid-1960s until his death in 1988), Rothenberg has created an assemblage on a different scale in *Technicians* and his other anthologies. The third chapter, "Judaism as Loss and the Buddhist Element in Michael Heller's *Eschaton*," discusses the original blend of Jewish and Buddhist perspectives in one of Heller's recent books. For Heller, a poet writing in the objectivist lineage, Judaism acts as locus for some of the most advanced European thought as much as it signifies a religion. While his writing records the personal and familial loss of Jewish faith and tradition, it also celebrates the Jewish impetus behind secular writers such as Walter Benjamin and Paul Celan. Heller's readers have been slow to notice that the ongoing "loss" of Judaism he recounts also opens a transactional space in his poetry for Buddhist virtues such as silence and emptiness.

Of the three chapters in "Poetry & Its Time: Revising Literary History," two concern Charles Olson, who was himself consistently immersed in historical research. The first, "'And All Now Is War': George Oppen, Charles Olson, and Literary Generations," places Olson in conversation with Oppen to argue that the concept of literary generations often obscures significant historical realities. Although Oppen and Olson are commonly assigned to two consecutive generations—the objectivists (1930s) and the Black Mountain poets (1950s)—these attributions overlook how the poets, born two years apart, share philosophical views and stylistic qualities that arise from experiences of World War II. Continuing to explore how poetry interacts with its historical milieu, "'The Lordly and Isolate Satyrs': Charles Olson's Contemporaries" discusses Olson's affinities to Beat poetry by looking at the presence of popular culture in one of his most successful poems. "The Lordly and Isolate Satyrs" recounts the dream appearance of a motorcycle gang on the beach at Gloucester Harbor, and it shows the poet's multidimensional, lyrical interactions with the world of his contemporaries. Another poet intent on speaking directly to her times is the performance artist Laurie Anderson. Her poetic uses of language, including the subtle upending of clichés, have made possible a devastating critique of American imperialism. "Laurie Anderson in the Reagan Era" explores in particular the many poetic, artistic, and spiritual affiliations of the angels in her album *Strange Angels* (1989). Summoning them at the close of the Cold War, she creates verbal collages and works of appropriation that make pointed political statements about "the end of history," questioning whether the ethical imperatives that arise at this time come from the angels invoked by Walter Benjamin or Wim Wenders (in his film, *Wings of Desire*) or rather from ourselves.

The third section, "Poetry & the Arts: Multimedia Exchange," looks at transactions between poetry and the other arts. The first chapter concerns *Presences: A Text for Marisol* (1976), one of the most successful collaborations between a poet, an artist, and a designer. "Robert Creeley, Marisol, and *Presences* as Transaction Network" discusses the genesis and reception of this carefully integrated work composed of prose poetry and photographs of sculpture. By examining materials found in Creeley's own copy of it and in his personal library, which includes illuminated correspondence between Marisol, Creeley, and the designer, William Katz, the essay shows how *Presences* functions as a transactional network. The next chapter examines the ways David Antin's talk poems occupy a complex site where poetry, fiction, philosophy, criticism, conceptual art, and performance art come together. "The Language Art of David Antin's Talk Poems" discusses how Antin opens poetry outward onto the total field of what he calls "the language art." The final chapter, "Audio File Audiophile: Listening for Ambient Poetry," takes off from the amazing fact that millions of poetry readings are downloaded annually. It stands to reason that most are listened to not with rapt attention but as a form of ambient music, heard while other activities take place. Likewise, an ambient writing, often with musical qualities, has emerged as a transactional form in the work of a number of poets, including that of Gertrude Stein, John Taggart, Nathaniel Mackey, Pamela Lu, and Tan Lin. The ambient writing, in turn, illuminates the minimalist operas of composers such as Philip Glass and Steve Reich.

The final section, "Poetry & Prose: Intimate Opposition," amplifies and extends issues broached in my earlier book, *Poet's Prose: The Crisis in American Verse*.[4] The first piece, "Translation and Not-Understanding," consists largely of a manifesto, "Not-Understanding: An Abecedary for Walter Benjamin," along with an introduction discussing the place of not-understanding in the theory and practice of translation. Written in poetic prose, the manifesto presents the case for not-understanding as a primary poetic virtue—for both poet and reader—as, in fact, *the* creative state. The impetus for it arose from thinking about my own practice of translation and from reading Benjamin's essay, "The Task of the Translator," in conjunction with George Steiner's *After Babel*.[5] Symbolically equating prose with understanding and poetry with not-understanding, this chapter prepares for considering transactions between poetry and prose in the next two. "Paul Auster's Solitude in the Room of the Book" looks at early works of prose by a former poet and translator. In his memoir, *The Invention of Solitude* (1982), and his meta-detective fiction of *The New York Trilogy* (1990), Auster imagines a room of the book in which a tense struggle takes place between poetry and fiction. Within this claustrophobic setting, Auster meditates on themes of memory and redemption after the Holocaust, wondering in particular how the son as writer might rescue the father. The third chapter concerns Lyn Hejinian's *My Life* (1980, 1987), a sterling example of the "New Sentence" and probably the most consistently read and taught work of Language poetry. "Lyn Hejinian Becomes a Person on Paper" traces the development of Hejinian's concept of the "person" over the course of the autobiographical poet's prose in *My Life*. Comprising forty-five chapters of forty-five sentences (one for each year of her life at the time of writing), the book dramatizes the growth of a writer as, in pragmatist terms, the situated experiencer. In the transactions within and between her discontinuous sentences, Hejinian investigates the essential building block of prose—the sentence—to release its full poetic potential.

The epilogue discusses how interactions with poetry and with individual poets can be transformative for university students. In addition to relating anecdotes about poets visiting with students, it presents the outline of a course I have taught, "American Culture as Collage," which draws students into specific conversations between poetry and other art forms as these have taken place over the course of the past two centuries.

POETRY & SPIRIT: AGAINST ORTHODOXY

1

Why Mysticism in Twentieth-Century American Poetry?

INTRODUCTION

This essay was written as a chapter for *A Concise Companion to Twentieth-Century American Poetry* (2005), which I edited for Blackwell Publishing.[1] The volume's purpose is to provide, in twelve chapters, some pathways for reading twentieth-century American poetry. This was a tricky goal because the chapters present not the usual history of literary movements but a variety of specific cultural contexts for the poetry, such as feminism, the academy, the queer city, the blues, and science and technology. It is envisioned especially as an aid for readers unfamiliar with many features of American poetry or even of American culture. I was asked to edit the book while teaching in Notre Dame's London Program in the spring of 2003, when the invasion of Iraq took place. The timing of the volume's inception helps explain why it opens with a chapter by British critic Peter Nicholls called "Wars I Have Seen" (using a title from Gertrude Stein), and why several other chapters are written by critics from the United Kingdom. After attending conferences overseas, though, I had already come to see the advantage of having voices from outside the United States participate in framing ways to look at its writing and culture. These critics suffer from neither the tendency to national self-justification nor the insider's sense of exclusive possession that can narrow horizons when discussing one's "own" literature. I also learned from European critics of American culture that slicing the fruit from different angles allows whole new segments to appear.

The chapter that fell to me is on mysticism in twentieth-century American poetry. This made a certain amount of sense because I had a long-standing interest in meditation and also because my first poetic mentor, Robert Duncan, had made mystical research a signal component of his poetry and poetics. Beyond these personal connections, though, reading American poetry and listening to what poets had to say about it had convinced me that mysticism—or spirituality, as it is now called—is a recurrent feature, from Emerson and Whitman to the present. I also knew that digging into the poetry in the classroom requires devoting significant time to summarizing kinds of spiritual material on which poets rely. The essay offers an introduction to varieties of mysticism, as employed by poets, and also extends a tentative hypothesis about why American poets have found themselves attracted to this material. In accounting for some of the many ways that mysticism obtrudes on the poetry, I began to see that it has important social and political functions and is for many poets as much a matter of group formation or protest as it is of belief. The topic of this chapter is truly vast, so let me reiterate that what follows is meant as an introduction for readers expert neither in religious studies nor in twentieth-century American poetry.

"Mysticism" is an inexact term that covers a broad range of religious and spiritual phenomena. Loosely conceived, mysticism refers to knowledge or experience gained by an individual that effects a direct relationship to absolute reality or divinity. In practice, mysticism erases boundaries that enforce a limited conception of the self, and, by so doing, gives rise to a pervading sense of unity, ecstasy, or love. As so defined, mysticism can be found within monotheistic and polytheistic religions and in nontheistic Buddhism. It also appears in less orthodox movements, such as the tantric sects of Hinduism, Buddhism, and Taoism, the gnostic sects of early Judaism and Christianity, and the occult sects in European culture beginning in the Renaissance. To highlight the importance of mysticism for twentieth-century American poetry, it is useful to evoke three traditions in particular: neo-paganism, Buddhism, and Christian mysticism. In terms of impact upon poetry, the most prevalent of the three is neo-paganism, which comprises a number of non-Christian occult movements, such as Hermeticism, alchemy, Theosophy, and Primitivism. Buddhism gained a surprisingly strong foothold in American poetry of the second half of the century—especially the schools of Zen and Tibetan Buddhism. The most prominent strains of Christian mysticism have been the incarnational, which can encompass nature mysticism, and the *via negativa* (or apophatic theology), which approaches the ineffable by stripping away all conceptions of the divine and of the self. It is also noteworthy that these three traditions contain overlapping ideas and practices, and many poets have been attracted to more than one.

Before looking at how particular poets and poems interact with these forms of mysticism, it might be helpful to think about why they appeal to American poets and about what sorts of effects they have on poetry and poetics. Since spiritual movements are often esoteric and thus at odds with dominant ideologies, the first thing to notice about mystical literature is its countercultural status. Although such beliefs and experiences have contributed to literary masterworks such as the Chinese and Japanese poetry arising from Zen, the Sufi poetry in Persian of Rumi and Hafiz, the Christian mystical poetry of Dante's *Paradiso* and St. John of the Cross, and the American Transcendentalist works of Emerson, Thoreau, and Whitman, each of these literary monuments was arguably countercultural when created. For twentieth-century American poets, mysticism also bears a countercultural weight. Rather than speaking for liberal, mercantile values, poets often address through spiritual means moral and political shortcomings in ideologies, such as capitalism and consumerism, that they find at variance with both individualist and communalist ideals of American democracy. For instance, many poets have criticized a spiritual blindness that accompanies both national self-promotion and individual acquisitiveness. If Emersonian individualism has led to two kinds of self-realization in American culture—the mystical and the entrepreneurial—poets may well view these as diametrically opposed. It's true that spiritual individualism may contribute to self-aggrandizement (and fame and fortune)—and poets are not immune to this tendency—but American poets more often undertake self-exploration as a route not to ego inflation but to erasing the boundaries of self and opening onto social virtues of love, compassion, and solidarity.

Paradoxically, though, poetry promoting solidarity and compassion can sometimes do so through exclusionary means, and this too may be traced to the influence of mysticism. For instance, one of the most pronounced qualities of the avant-garde wing of twentieth-century American poetry is its initiatory stance. Like heads of mystical brotherhoods, poetic gurus (usually men) propound esoteric, countercultural doctrines that, although often trumpeted as virtually self-evident, require initiation into specific ways of thinking to be intelligible. Doctrines like Ezra Pound's Vorticism, Louis Zukofsky's objectivism, Charles Olson's projectivism, Robert Bly's Deep Image, and Charles Bernstein's Language poetry are purposefully obscure, asking prospective followers to accept a set of intuitive or nonrational propositions in an apparently mystical leap. The esoteric quality of American avant-garde poetics acts as a gate, inviting "believers" into the fold while holding at bay those deemed obtuse or wrongheaded. Adherence to a doctrine can involve more than an aesthetic decision, for the adept may receive an esoteric key that ties the poetry and poetics to celestial, political, or erotic realms. In this sense, there is a mystical style surrounding many movements in twentieth-century American poetry, which accounts in part for grandiose claims to philosophical or quasi-religious stature.

NEO-PAGANISM

The twentieth-century American poet who most knowingly and effectively set up as master of a poetic cult was Ezra Pound. Through his close association in London (where he lived from 1908 to 1921) with Irish poet W. B. Yeats and several other occultists—such as G. R. S. Mead, A. R. Orage, and Allen Upward—Pound became convinced of the need to fold a series of historical occult movements into the worldwide poetic pantheon he convened. This intertwining of poets with pagan and neo-pagan figures allowed him to claim that each poem he admired was in some way an embodiment of a mystical doctrine or illumination. Likewise, from the London occultists Pound borrowed, at least in part, the oracular, at times pontifical, style that dominates his poetry and prose. Pound's aesthetic, social, and economic pronouncements in *The Cantos* and his prose are delivered as though from the mouth of a "master," whose direct access to knowledge (gnosis) guarantees their authority. As a result of this spiritual stance, Pound acquired a threefold influence upon later poets. First, he became the exemplar of the poet-as-guru, offering a spiritual doctrine that ties poetry to other realms, including politics, economics, religion, nature, and the erotic. Second, he assembled a tradition of "illuminated" writers who partake of what he called the "Spirit of Romance," such as Ovid, Apuleius, the Troubadours, Guido Cavalcanti, and Dante, who also become touchstones for poets after him.[2] Likewise, Pound bequeathed the habit of erecting such a countercultural tradition. Third, he gave a powerful example of how to write a modern poetry in which spiritual and factual intersect—a practice that originated in the American Renaissance with Emerson, Thoreau, Melville, Whitman, and Dickinson and flourished during the twentieth century.

Spiritual tendencies were in full flower as the modern arts developed in the West at the beginning of the twentieth century, contributing, for example, to pivotal breakthroughs into abstraction in painting, sculpture, and cinema.[3] Occult movements arose at this time (and then returned periodically throughout the century), advocating two interlocking investigations aimed at uncovering hidden truths: the rediscovery of "ancient wisdom" and the conduct of modern experiments in expanding the senses—through meditation, contemplation, trance, divination, magic, drugs, and so on. The ancient wisdom was exhumed from classical pagan and "primitive" sources, while the experiments carried on by psychic pioneers in the modern era laid "'claim to knowledge of a scientific nature which is inaccessible to the accepted methods of positive, objective scientific research'" (G. R. S. Mead).[4] The ultimate object and source of these mutually reinforcing forms of knowledge was the divine, but at a more instrumental level the two ways of knowing derived their authority from opposing social institutions: tradition and science. The occult tradition consists of texts and artifacts strung out in a long and loosely connected history that begins in classical Greece and the Hellenistic period, although many of its texts posit an even earlier pseudo-source in ancient Egypt (Tryphonopoulos 24–25). Practitioners of the experimental component often adapt scientific terminology, inventing fields such as "psychic research" to overcome the restrictions of a positivist epistemology by using its vocabulary for magical knowledge. As a practice placed between science and normative religion—often borrowing the vocabulary of one to counter the arguments of the other—the modern occult can be characterized as "a neo-pagan piety that is polytheistic, fleshly, erotic and ecstatic rather than a Christian or Jewish piety that is monotheistic, otherworldly, ascetic and revealed."[5]

For Pound, the Eleusinian Mysteries of Athens, the most renowned religious cult of the classical world, represents one of the two basic poles of culture—which he sees as residing "Between KUNG and ELEUSIS" (*Canto* 52), that is, between the ethical order, epitomized by Confucius, and the spiritual order, exemplified by the Athenian Mysteries.[6] The myth behind the rites of Eleusis is that of Demeter, the Earth Mother or Grain Mother (Ceres in Latin), and her daughter Persephone (Proserpine), or Kore, who is carried off to the underworld by Hades (Dis). During her disconsolate wandering in search of her daughter, Demeter finds her way to Eleusis, outside Athens, where she has a temple built and then retreats inside it—with devastating consequences for the fertility of the natural world, including human beings. Demeter petitions Zeus and ultimately wins the release of Persephone, but because the girl has eaten several pomegranate seeds, she must return to Hades for part of every year. With Persephone set free, Demeter restores fertility and reveals the rites of the Mysteries. Scholars remain uncertain about the actual content of the rites, but we know there were two major rituals at Eleusis, one of initiation and purification, the other of revelation and mystical union.[7]

In "Persephone's Ezra," Guy Davenport argues that Pound's career from beginning to end takes guidance from Persephone, the goddess of springtime clarity, beauty, and purity, who appears in his writing in many guises but always signifies direct experience of the nature and beauty of living things.[8] The speaker of "The Tree," the poem Pound places at the inception of his poetic career (it opens *Personae*, his collected shorter poems), says that he "stood still and was a tree amid the wood" and that he learned "the truth of things unseen before"—in other words, knowledge such as that granted at Eleusis. During the rites, the gods were thought to provide the initiate with an expanded state of consciousness, granting a sense of identification with nature and especially with natural fertility. As a result of this identification, the speaker says, "I have been a tree amid the wood / And many a new thing understood / That was rank folly to my head before."[9] The figure of Persephone as embodiment of a neo-pagan connection to the gods and nature recurs many times throughout *The Cantos*. In *Canto I*, for instance, Pound recounts the moment in the *Odyssey* when Odysseus, seeking counsel on how to get home, slaughtered sheep as a sacrifice and "Poured ointment, cried to the gods, / To Pluto the strong, and praised Proserpine" (*Cantos* 4). In *Canto XLVII*, Pound's Odysseus is advised, "First must thou go the road / to hell / And to the bower of Ceres' daughter Proserpine" (236). In his endeavor to navigate the chaos of the war-torn modern world, Pound sees Persephone as a welcome signpost of the release from hell and the promise of regeneration through natural/divine forces.

Alongside the Eleusinian Mysteries in ancient Greece, there were also Orphic and Pythagorean cults, which likewise had mythical underpinnings and involved rites of initiation and salvation. Orphic and Pythagorean cults attracted Pound's followers Robert Duncan and Charles Olson, who in turn saw their Black Mountain movement as a modern-day version of such a cult, transposed to the realm of poetry. Olson, for instance, takes the Pythagorean sect as a model for a new initiatory cult of poetry in his poem "The Praises."[10] Both poets also embrace the classical myths as primary poetic material. Duncan employs the myth of Cupid and Psyche—a tale with quest features similar to that of the Demeter and Persephone myth—as the backbone of his "Poem Beginning with a Line by Pindar."[11] All three poets were also invested to varying degrees in the occult tradition that succeeded the Greek mystery religions—a pagan tradition developed in the philosophies of Gnosticism and Neoplatonism, which in turn gave birth to a long succession of occult movements from the Middle Ages to the nineteenth century: Catharism, alchemy, Kabbalah, Hermeticism, Rosicrucianism, Freemasonry, Swedenborgianism, and Spiritualism (Tryphonopoulos 31–48). Near the end of the nineteenth century, these occult strains were brought together and cross-fertilized with Hinduism and Buddhism by Helena Petrovna Blavatsky. The movement she founded, Theosophy, had a striking influence on the arts of the early twentieth century and was the principal form of the occult to reach Yeats and Pound.

Pound resembles Blavatsky in his belief that there is one principle of knowledge, available at all times and places, that the initiated can receive both through synthesizing clues hidden in prior occult thinkers and through direct experience. Responding to a challenge from his friend T. S. Eliot to succinctly state his beliefs, Pound declares allegiance to the neo-pagan tradition: "Given the material means I would replace the statue of Venus on the cliffs of Terracina. I would erect a temple to Artemis in Park Lane. I believe that a light from Eleusis persisted throughout the middle ages and set beauty in the song of Provence and of Italy."[12] Eliot's own relation to mysticism is very different but equally complex and extensive. Over the course of his career, Christian mysticism takes pride of place, although both early and late, Eliot sets it in dialogue with Hinduism and Buddhism.[13] In *The Waste Land*, however, neopaganism dominates, although Eliot uses its symbols in strikingly ambivalent ways. Its impact stems particularly from his reliance on Jessie Weston's *From Ritual to Romance*, which he says provided him with "not only the title, but the plan and a good deal of the incidental symbolism of the poem."[14] Unlike *The Waste Land*'s other primary source, James Frazer's anthropological treatise, *The Golden Bough*, Weston's book is a work of Theosophy, which helps account for the myriad occult images populating the poem (Surette 73–96).

Notwithstanding Eliot's ambivalence toward occult symbols in *The Waste Land*, many other poets have found an occult synthesis attractive because it creates a symbolic language that invests the images of poetry with a spiritual potency. Not only do the symbols have a multi-layered and multivalent quality, but they can be seen as magically efficacious in their own right: "The occult image is not merely a symbol, but in a transformation that is the poet's dream the symbol creates what it signifies."[15] H.D. (Hilda Doolittle), a poet personally and aesthetically close to Pound when young, takes belief in the mystical potency of poetic symbols farther than perhaps anyone but Yeats. In her *Trilogy*, for instance, written during World War II, H.D. presents the artist as a spiritual healer capable of restoring a dying civilization to health. Out of her experience living through the Blitz in London, she depicts a symbolic transformation that she believes will effect an actual regeneration of the gravely wounded world. *Trilogy* is shot through with occult maneuvers and with syntheses of religious symbols from many times and places. In one section, for example, the poet's work is deemed analogous to that of the alchemist:

> Now polish the crucible
> and in the bowl distill
>
> a word most bitter, *marah*,
> a word bitterer still, *mar*,
>
> sea, brine, breaker, seducer,
> giver of life, giver of tears;
>
> now polish the crucible
> and set the jet of flame
>
> under, till *marah-mar*
> are melted, fuse and join
>
> and change and alter,
> mer, mere, mère, mater, Maia, Mary,
>
> Star of the Sea,
> Mother.[16]

In an alchemical alembic, compounds are distilled over a flame, provoking a sequence of transformations that culminates in the *prima materia* or philosopher's stone. In *Trilogy*, the alchemical transmutation is not of literal elements but of linguistic ones, so that the mixing of *marah* (Hebrew: bitter) with *mar* (Spanish: sea) results in a series of multilingual puns that tie the sea to the maternal through bitterness. The linguistic mutations link the bitter memories of H.D.'s brush with death when giving birth to her daughter, Perdita, to the alchemical breakdown of compounds into salty and bitter elements. Applying an imaginative heat to the crucible containing divine figures from different religions (Maia, Mary) and words from different languages (French, English, Spanish, Greek, Latin, Hebrew), H.D.'s alchemical punning confers on words a mystical potency beyond their everyday usage and effects a linguistic synthesis that mimics and calls forth a synthesis of figures from various myths and religions. In content, this spiritual conjunction of the sea with bitterness and maternity is similar to Walt Whitman's conjunction of the sea with death and maternity in "Out of the Cradle Endlessly Rocking." They differ, though, in that Whitman personifies the sea as an "old crone rocking the cradle," who whispers "the low and delicious word death,"[17] while H.D. treats the words of her poem as if they were themselves occult symbols, made capable, through her patient ministrations, of provoking psychological and spiritual change.

The foremost inheritor of H.D.'s poetic and occult sensibility was Robert Duncan. In his vast, unfinished study of twentieth-century poetry, *The H.D. Book*, Duncan casts American poetry in an occult key, with H.D., rather than Pound, Eliot, Frost, or Stevens, as central figure. *The H.D. Book* explores the spiritual world behind modern American poetry, mainly in H.D.'s generation but also in Duncan's. His ability to unravel the role of the occult in poetry and poetics is so skillful because Duncan himself grew up in a family that believed in and practiced Theosophy. As he writes in *The H.D. Book*, the mystical and magical investigations of his parents, grandmother, and aunt afforded the lore that haunted his childhood:

> [I]n the inner chamber, the adults, talking on, wove for me in my childish overhearing, Egypt, a land of spells and secret knowledge, a background drift of things close to dreaming—spirit communications, reincarnation memories, clairvoyant journeys into a realm of astral phantasy where all times and places were seen in a new light, . . . of most real Osiris and Isis, of lost Atlantis and Lemuria. . . . Egypt was the hidden meaning of things, not only Greek things but Hebrew things. The wand of Hermes was the rod of Moses, and my grandmother studied hieroglyphics as she studied Hebrew letters and

> searched in dictionaries for the meaning of Greek roots, to come into the primal knowledge of the universe.[18]

As an adult, Duncan remained an active investigator of the occult, not as a believer, in the manner of H.D. or Yeats, but as a kind of anthropologist of exotic psychic states, exploring the most far-flung realms of human meaning-making for the poetic, psychological, and even social powers they could release. "Although he did not literally believe in occult doctrines, they were so natural to him that he has employed them with complete assurance. In this confidence he resembles many intellectual Christians and Jews in mainstream culture who are imbued with the spirit rather than the letter of their religions" (Materer 108). Duncan was so at home with the occult that in "The Architecture: Passages 9," a poem that describes the house he inhabits with his husband, the painter Jess (Collins), he sets the scene by invoking not only the architecture, the furnishings, and the music playing but also the books:

> from the bookcases   the glimmering titles arrayed   keys
> Hesiod · Heraklitus · *The Secret Books of the Egyptian Gnostics . . .*
>
> *La Révélation d'Hermès Trismégistes*
> *Plutarch's Morals: Theosophical Essays*
> *Avicenna*
> *The Zohar*
> *The Aurora*
>
> (*Collected Later* 319–20)

These "keys" to a hidden mystical tradition comprise Greek mythology and philosophy, Gnosticism, Hermeticism, Hellenistic Theosophy, Islamic Sufism, Jewish Kabbalah, and the Christian mysticism of Jacob Boehme. For Duncan, these keys open up not literal truths but rather the truths of reading. He probes the occult much as Freud works with dreams—to tease out correspondences among levels of reality and to lay bare psychic structures.

As a "born" Theosophist, Duncan had a level of comfort with outré doctrines that other poets setting out in the 1940s and 1950s did not share. One of the threads woven into his theosophical upbringing, for instance, was Kabbalah, which Duncan references when he mentions the hidden meanings in Hebrew letters and when he points to the most renowned of all Kabbalistic texts, *The Zohar,* among his books. Although the Jewish mystical tradition of Kabbalah had been incorporated into Christian occult circles during the Renaissance, it didn't begin to have an influence outside those circles until Gershom Scholem published his first scholarly treatment of the subject, *Major Trends in Jewish Mysticism* (1941), made available in English in 1946.[19] Many concepts from Kabbalah inform Duncan's work, and an entire volume of his poetry, *Letters* (1958), is undergirded by Kabbalistic conceits.[20] It is not surprising that Kabbalah would appeal to a poet, because it is a kind of alchemy that engages the materials of writing: the word, the letter, and the book. Kabbalah contains the various levels of spiritual "work"—magical practice, meditation and contemplation techniques, visionary excursions, and self-transformation—all carried forward by investigations of language and writing. From his occult background and Kabbalistic explorations, Duncan in turn instigated lifelong research into Jewish mysticism by a number of Jewish poets, such as Jerome Rothenberg, David Meltzer, and Jack Hirschman. Meltzer, for instance, who edited *Tree*, a journal devoted to Kabbalah and poetry, and *The Secret Garden*, an anthology of Kabbalistic texts, calls Duncan "my exemplar" in Kabbalah studies and credits Duncan with introducing him to the works of Scholem.[21]

Curiously, Charles Olson, whose poetry, like Duncan's, draws from many strands of neo-paganism, was not enticed but threatened by his friend's occult proclivities. In "Against Wisdom as Such," Olson accuses Duncan of being deceived by the false "wisdom" (the secret doctrines and symbols) of the occult and thereby relinquishing responsibility for his own acts of meaning-making: "The poet cannot afford to traffick in any other 'sign' than his one, his self, the man or woman he is. Otherwise God does rush in. And art is washed away, turned into that second force, religion."[22] As soon as "wisdom" is separated from individual experience and formulated in a general statement, it becomes false, for "wisdom, like style, is the man," rather than the doctrine or the symbol (261). At base a pragmatist, Olson insists that value can be found only in individual people and their attempts to gain experiential knowledge of the world and of themselves:

> There are no hierarchies, no infinite, no such many as mass, there are only
> eyes in all heads,
> to be looked out of[23]

By finding truth through experience, Olson counsels, one remains an "artist" rather than being fooled by "religion." As was pointed out previously, modern mysticism encompasses two ways of knowing: exploring recondite texts and engaging in mind-expansion through experiential knowledge. Olson combines the two in his active definition of "history": citing the first Greek historian, Herodotus, Olson claims, "'*istorin* in him appears to mean 'finding out for oneself' instead of depending upon hearsay."[24] Olson devotes his writing life to such historiography, probing deeply into recondite texts to locate primary instances of human experience. In *A Bibliography on America for Ed Dorn*, he offers this advice to the young poet:

> PRIMARY DOCUMENTS. And to hook on here is a lifetime of assiduity. Best thing to do is *to dig one thing or place or man* until you yourself know more abt that than is possible to any other man. It doesn't matter whether it's Barbed Wire or Pemmican or Paterson or Iowa. But *exhaust* it. Saturate it. Beat it. And then U KNOW everything else very fast: one saturation job (it might take 14 years). And you're in, forever. (*Prose* 306–7)

For Olson, the sorting of historical documents becomes an occult practice, whose ultimate purpose is to chart varieties of experience in order to have a complete measure of human capacity. To do this, Olson chooses the early history of Gloucester, Massachusetts, as his "*one place*" and spends twenty years exploring every aspect of it, writing *The Maximus Poems* to report his research, his breakthroughs, and resultant new cultural principles.

BUDDHISM

Olson makes a good transition figure to the subject of Buddhism because his two most famous essays, "Projective Verse" (*Prose* 239–49) and "Human Universe" (155–66), espouse a philosophy with many affinities to Buddhism, especially to Zen as it was received in the United States in the 1940s and 1950s through the writings of D. T. Suzuki. In "Projective Verse," several aesthetic points align with Zen values: the focus upon breath as a central component of poetic composition, as in meditation; the admonition to move from one perception to the next without stopping to cogitate ("in any given poem always, always one perception must must must MOVE, INSTANTER, ON ANOTHER!" [240]); and the countering of egotism with "objectism," which is "the getting rid of the lyrical interference of the individual as ego, of the 'subject' and his soul, that peculiar presumption by which western man has interposed himself between what he is as a creature of nature . . . and those other creations of nature which we may, with no derogation, call objects" (247). In "Human Universe," Olson likewise decries self-centeredness, idealism, and any thought process that creates or depends upon an isolated self or ego. He insists that "the skin itself, the meeting edge of man and external reality, is where all that matters does happen, that man and external reality are so involved with one another that, for man's purposes, they had better be taken as one" (161). He also mirrors the Buddhist emphasis on radiant awareness in the here and now, stressing that active alertness is the highest form of human endeavor: "If there is any absolute, it is never more than this one, you, this instant, in action" (157).

With such views on the proper disposition needed for writing poetry and the proper relationship of the individual toward the world, Olson joins contemporary Buddhists in taking a resolutely countercultural stance on core American values. If American culture bases many of its ideals upon the furtherance of individual self-interest—lauding an ability to "take charge" and encouraging the "pursuit of happiness" and the American Dream of getting ahead financially—Buddhism stresses letting-be, nonattachment, the cessation of desire, and the illusory nature of the self. The one value that American culture and Buddhism both esteem is freedom, although Buddhism interprets it more radically than as lack of governmental control and the ability to do as one pleases, for Buddhism seeks freedom from suffering and desire and the cognitive liberation that comes with enlightenment. American poets have embraced Buddhism for its opposition to many values of the culture at large, adopting its complex and demanding philosophy and practices in surprising numbers. An early anthology of Euro-American poetry influenced by Buddhism, *Beneath a Single Moon* (1991), edited by Kent Johnson and Craig Paulenich, prints work by forty-five poets, including Olga Broumas, John Cage, Diane di Prima, Allen Ginsberg, Susan Griffin, Sam Hamill, Michael Heller, Robert Kelly, Jackson Mac Low, George Quasha, Leslie Scalapino, Andrew Schelling, Armand Schwerner, Gary Snyder, Lucien Stryk, Nathaniel Tarn, Anne Waldman, and Philip Whalen. Snyder maintains that the poetry of this extremely diverse group shares a set of qualities: "They are unsentimental, not overly abstract, on the way toward selflessness, not particularly self-indulgent, wholehearted, nonutopian, fluid (that is, able to shift shapes), on the dry side, kindhearted, unembarrassed, free of spiritual rhetoric and pretense of magic, and deeply concerned with the questions of knowing."[25] Likewise, many Asian American poets not included in the anthology, such as Theresa Hak Kyung Cha, Arthur Sze, Myung Mi Kim, and Mei-mei Berssenbrugge, have drawn on Buddhism in complex and inventive ways, and their poetry exerts a growing influence on their Euro-American confreres.[26]

The three most well-known mid-century poets associated with Buddhism are Cage, Ginsberg, and Snyder. For all three, Buddhism was a shaping element, both aesthetic and philosophical, through much or all of their mature work. The most orthodox of the three, Snyder gives a succinct list of some central tenets of Buddhism: "The marks of the Buddhist teachings are impermanence, no-self, the inevitability of suffering, interconnectedness, emptiness, the vastness of mind, and the provision of a Way to realization" (Johnson 7). While most mystical philosophies and practices promise to unite the self with the divine, Buddhism turns mysticism inside out by asserting that there is no self and no divine. For Buddhism, the absolute is a void and all forms that exist, including the self, are inherently empty, interconnected, and without permanence. In a world characterized by impermanence and shackled with suffering caused by desire for what are ultimately unreal objects and states, Buddhism contends that the proper way to act is to let things happen, instead of trying to direct them, and to cultivate an attentive stillness and silence.

For Cage, who divided his life into periods before and after meeting the Zen philosopher D. T. Suzuki, cultivation of silence and nonintervention constitute not only spiritual but also ethical, aesthetic, and even political principles. Cage's first and most influential book, *Silence* (1961), explores the implications of attending to silence for a new understanding of music.[27] Interspersed with Zen and Zen-like stories, a number of which are spoken in his famous ninety-minute musical composition, *Indeterminacy* (1959), *Silence* includes poem-lectures with Zen-inspired topics, such as "Lecture on Nothing," "Lecture on Something," and "Where Are We Going? and What Are We Doing?"[28] As in much of his music, he composes these poem-lectures using chance operations (often involving the *I Ching*, the classic Chinese book of divination), to circumvent personal preference and ego control. In addition to relying on chance, Cage often writes indeterminate works that are realized uniquely each time they are performed, with the object of sharpening attention in both performers and audience. Cage's penchant for welcoming the unforeseen and for heightening attention culminates in his most renowned piece, *4′33″*, during which a pianist plays no notes and signals the succession of three movements by opening and shutting the keyboard. The audience hears ambient sound both inside and outside the concert hall, which Cage refuses to separate from the concept of "music." Subsequent poets have taken his example in two directions. Jackson Mac Low composed poetry for half a century using chance operations and indeterminate means, with Buddhist texts and poetic forms prominent among his materials. David Antin has converted the poem-lecture composed by chance into the spontaneous talk poem delivered without notes to a unique audience. Like Cage, he believes in the crucial importance of the present moment and debunks the American faith that "experts" can solve problems of individual and social life—a faith satirized in the title of Cage's *Diary: How to Improve the World (You Will Only Make Matters Worse)* and in many of Antin's talk poems.[29]

For Beat writers of the 1950s and 1960s, such as Allen Ginsberg, Jack Kerouac, Diane di Prima, Joanne Kyger, and Philip Whalen, Buddhism was a central preoccupation and Gary Snyder was its American avatar. In his reportorial novel *Dharma Bums* (1959), Kerouac enshrines Japhy Ryder (the Snyder character) as an ascetic, studious, free-loving, anarchist, ecstatic mountain man.[30]

Snyder's pursuit of Zen included extended stays in Japan, where he learned the Japanese language and studied under several roshis in traditional monasteries. No matter how orthodox his Japanese Zen training, his poetry always presents Buddhism as a natural human birthright, at home in the American West as much as in Asia. In an early poem, "Hunting," he rhapsodizes about the birth of a baby, "Baby, baby, noble baby / Noble-hearted baby," and then switches gears abruptly:

> One hand up, one hand down
> "I alone am the honored one"
> Birth of the Buddha.
> And the whole world-system trembled.[31]

The most natural occurrence, the birth of a child, can also evoke the most miraculous occurrence, the birth of the Buddha. Suddenly assuming the iconographic posture of a Buddha, the "Noble-hearted baby" represents the utter freshness, benevolence, fearlessness, and contentment of "natural mind," the enlightened state.

Allen Ginsberg also cultivates "natural mind" in his poetry. He asserts that writing poetry and sitting for meditation have much in common: valuing the "process" rather than looking for a "product"; learning to let go of predictable thought patterns; cultivating a direct, "purified" perception of the objects of the world; and recognizing that the mind is larger than the thoughts within it (Johnson 94–100). Ginsberg's slogan for this spontaneous, attentive mode of composition is "First Thought, Best Thought," and it corresponds closely to Kerouac's principle of "spontaneous bop prosody." Ginsberg first discovered Buddhism in 1953, led to it, like many artists and thinkers, by the writings of Suzuki.[32] In 1962 he traveled to India in search of a guru, stopping on the way in Israel to see if Martin Buber might fit the bill (he didn't). In India, Ginsberg met many holy men and visited many pilgrimage sites, but he didn't find the teacher he was seeking until he met a Tibetan master of "crazy wisdom," Chogyam Trungpa, Rinpoche, in 1970 (Fields 310–11). Ginsberg became a fixture at Trungpa's Naropa University, in Boulder, Colorado, and founded there with Anne Waldman the Jack Kerouac School of Disembodied Poetics, which has hosted courses on poetry and spirituality for more than forty years.

Ginsberg's mysticism made the greatest public impact during the 1960s and 1970s, when he crisscrossed the United States and much of the world reading his poetry, chanting mantras, and singing his musical settings of the songs of William Blake to vast audiences in stadiums and at protest marches. In "Wichita Vortex Sutra" (1966), he lambastes the duplicitous language used to justify the Vietnam War ("McNamara made a 'bad guess' / 'Bad Guess?'

chorused the Reporters. / Yes, no more than a Bad Guess, in 1962")[33] and contrasts it to the language of sacred magic. Gathering an eclectic garland of saints and deities as "Powers of imagination," he invokes their authority to work his own magic by creating a new mantra:

> I lift my voice aloud,
> make Mantra of American language now,
> I here declare the end of the War! . . .
> Let the States tremble,
> let the nation weep,
> let Congress legislate its own delight
> let the President execute his own desire
>
> (407)

In Buddhist and Hindu Tantra, a mantra is one or more syllables imbued with the power of the deity or state of mind it summons. In this case, Ginsberg aims his mantra at making the Vietnam War cease and then turns the language of political power ("Congress legislate," "President execute") into a language of ecstasy ("delight," "desire"). Rousing the extensive spiritual traditions of India to participate in his political goal of stopping the war, Ginsberg made mysticism a public force to be reckoned with.

CHRISTIAN MYSTICISM

The third form of mysticism may be the least exotic and therefore the least countercultural, but in the work of American poets, Christian mysticism often mingles with other forms, making for a poetry less orthodox than it might at first appear. T. S. Eliot, for instance, who strove in much of his poetry and prose to present a conservative Christian face, engaged the occult tradition in *The Waste Land*, as mentioned above, and carried on a lifelong dialogue with the Indic traditions of Buddhism and Hinduism that he first encountered as a graduate student in philosophy at Harvard. His most overtly mystical poem, *The Four Quartets*, ends with the following lines:

> And all shall be well and
> All manner of thing shall be well
> When the tongues of flame are in-folded
> Into the crowned knot of fire
> And the fire and the rose are one.
>
> (Eliot 145)

These lines combine words of pious acceptance by the English mystic Julian of Norwich (in the first two lines) and the central symbol of Dante's *Paradiso*, the rose, with the Indic image of fire at the crown of the head, which symbolizes enlightenment, and the tongues of flame that descended at Pentecost on disciples of Jesus. During the course of the poem many other meanings constellate around the fire and the rose, but in each of the poem's central images a conversation is joined between Western and Eastern spiritual traditions.[34]

The most characteristic form of Christian mysticism in Eliot's work is the *via negativa,* which itself has affinities to the Hindu philosophy of Vedanta. In both spiritual disciplines, all the attributes assigned to the divine and to the self are discarded one by one (the watchword of Vedanta is *neti neti,* "not this, not this"), so that what remains finally is the unbounded Absolute. As opposed to occultism, which sees language as magically potent, the *via negativa* regards all words as inadequate and all images as delusory. It is not a path lightly undertaken, for it involves a virtual unmaking of the personality. At a certain stage, mystics speak about a "dark night of the soul" in which everything is thrown into question and the way seems completely lost. The most famous exponent of the *via negativa* is the poet-saint John of the Cross, for whom Eliot had a lifelong affection. In "East Coker," the second of *The Four Quartets,* Eliot writes, "I said to my soul, be still, and let the dark come upon you / Which shall be the darkness of God" (126), and then shortly afterward he paraphrases lines from St. John of the Cross's *Ascent of Mount Carmel:*[35]

> To arrive where you are, to get from where you are not,
>   You must go by a way wherein there is no ecstasy.
> In order to arrive at what you do not know
>   You must go by a way which is the way of ignorance.
> In order to possess what you do not possess
>   You must go by the way of dispossession.
> In order to arrive at what you are not
>   You must go through the way in which you are not.
>
> (127)

This is a classical exposition of the *via negativa,* for which paradox is the most congenial figure of speech. To transcend the individual self, apophatic theology counsels a stripping away of everything that undergirds the limited ego. The process of self-annihilation is frequently painful, as it works to break down barriers between the ego and the divine, seeking a final merging. A more recent poet, Fanny Howe, sees this merging occur most effectively in an interchange with other people. In this way, she joins postmodern and liberation theologians in locating the *via negativa* in the realm of ethics.[36] Like a number of these contemporary theologians, Howe draws inspiration from women thinkers on the cusp between Judaism and Christianity, such as Simone Weil and Edith Stein, and owes a theoretical debt to Jewish philosopher Emmanuel Levinas, who places ethical obligation to others prior to Being itself. For Levinas, the inescapability of the Other (both other people and the otherness of the divine) grows out of the experience of the Holocaust. In Howe's poetry, fiction, and prose meditations, her self-abnegating devotion to otherness also derives from the liberation theology of Gustavo Gutiérrez and from witnessing racism from inside an interracial marriage. A committed Roman Catholic, Howe delves into her own sense of the mystery of the Other as well as into Christianity's relations to its "others," such as Judaism, Islam, and Hinduism. In her poem "The Quietist," for instance, she finds the Indic concept of mantra as sacred sound hiding within the Christian belief that Jesus is the Word of God:

> The holy one called:
> "Just keep that word in your mouth
> Let the sound behind it out."[37]

Denise Levertov locates the exchange between Judaism and Christianity within her own personal heritage. One of her paternal ancestors, Schneur Zalman, founded a still-flourishing sect of Hasidism called Chabad, and one of her maternal ancestors, Angel Jones of Mold, was a Welsh Protestant preacher. Although her father crossed over from Hasidic Judaism to Christianity and became an Anglican priest, he passed on elements of Hasidism to his daughter, translated the most important Kabbalistic text, the *Zohar*, into English, and continued to occupy a prominent role in Jewish-Christian dialogue in the United Kingdom. For Levertov, the Hasidic delight in uncovering sparks of the divine in the ordinary world dovetails with the sacramental disposition that informs incarnational mysticism: "Hasidism has given me since childhood a sense of marvels, of wonder. . . . The Hasidim were a lot like the Franciscans[:] in both movements there was a recognition and joy in the physical world. And a sense of wonder at creation, and I think I've always felt something like that."[38] In "Matins" (1961), she addresses this "Marvelous Truth," asking it to "confront us / at every turn," to

> dwell
> in our crowded hearts
> our steaming bathrooms, kitchens full of
> things to be done, the
> ordinary streets.
>
> Thrust close your smile
> that we know you, terrible joy.[39]

At this early stage in her poetry, Christian faith lies mostly implicit in the title of the poem, "Matins," and in the phrase "terrible joy," which, alongside its reference to the "terrible beauty" commemorated in Yeats's poem "Easter, 1916," could refer to the Incarnation as the source of "Marvelous Truth."

Levertov's wonder at the everyday was inspirational for Robert Duncan, who, alongside his many interests in neo-paganism, retained an affection for Christian mysticism, which resulted in his being invited to speak and read at religious services and conferences. His intense friendship with Levertov (their collected correspondence runs to 479 items) broke apart over their disagreement about the proper relationship of poetry to protest, especially with respect to the Vietnam War. One of the ways they conducted their quarrel was through alternate understandings of Robert Southwell's Metaphysical poem "The Burning Babe." Southwell's Christ, encountered in a vision near the end of his life, brought a message of purification: "Alas (quoth he) but newly borne, in fierie heates I frie, / Yet none approach to warm their hearts or feele my fire, but I." Levertov literalized the "burning babe" in "Advent 1966" (a poem she included in a letter to Duncan):

> Because in Viet Nam the vision of a Burning Babe
> Is multiplied, multiplied,
>   The flesh on fire
> Not Christ's, as Southwell saw it . . .
> But wholly human and repeated, repeated,
> Infant after infant, their names forgotten[40]

Duncan's response, given in "*from* ROBERT SOUTHWELL'S *THE BURNING BABE*," acknowledges that the "burning babe . . . doubled in my sight" (*Collected Later* 510) and it is both Southwell's mystical vision and the children burnt by napalm. What he deplores in Levertov's poem, though, is her raw accusation of American violence, without bearing responsibility for it. Accepting that the fate of the children is likewise "*Our* fate" (512), Duncan challenges himself to imagine this fate and to receive its burden: "All hatred cringes from the sight of it / and would contract into self-loathing . . . I think I could bear it. // I cannot think I could bear it" (513). Where Levertov has converted the mystical into the political, Duncan insists on holding the mystical and the political in irresolvable tension.

Over the course of her career, Levertov became increasingly comfortable as a Catholic, but one for whom politics and a variety of spiritual traditions remained compelling. Like Levertov and Duncan, other American poets who draw on Christian mysticism join poets who explore Buddhism and neo-paganism by crossing cultural boundaries in search of spiritual and ethical nourishment. Finding dominant values of American culture, whether Protestant or secular, too restrictive, they often turn in more than one direction for sustenance. For poets eager to test the full range of human experience, tribal or prehistoric religions also exert a powerful magnetism. This can be felt, for instance, in the ethnopoetics movement that includes Jerome Rothenberg, David Antin, Gary Snyder, Dennis Tedlock, and Nathaniel Tarn or in the archeologically inspired poetry of Charles Olson, Robert Kelly, Armand Schwerner, Clayton Eshleman, Gustaf Sobin, Nathaniel Mackey, and Anne Carson. The paradox of mysticism is that by turning inside to explore spiritual realities poets have been led outside themselves and beyond boundaries of religion, nation, race, and time. Because of this, American poetry informed by mysticism offers striking instances of attentive transactions across cultures and throughout history.

2

Jerome Rothenberg's *Technicians of the Sacred*

Transactions between the Indigenous and the Avant-Garde

I came upon Jerome Rothenberg's literary/spiritual assemblage, *Technicians of the Sacred,* shortly after its release in 1968. Like the *Whole Earth Catalog,* Norman O. Brown's *Love's Body,* and performances of the Living Theater and Peter Brook, the anthology epitomized the 1960s impulse to seek out "ancient wisdom," wherever it might be found, and to bring it into the contemporary world in embodied form. Published again in 2017, in a third, fiftieth-anniversary edition, it not only is a time capsule from a half century back but also remains a compelling argument for the transactions that poetry can produce across the reaches of human time as "indigenous" values (tied to the ecology of specific places) rise from the ashes of postindustrial society. As if by fiat, Rothenberg dramatically expanded the scope of American literature in 1968 by inviting in poetry and other language events from ancient civilizations and more recent anthropological accounts and presenting them in contemporary translations with a lively, vernacular flair. At the same time, he shows by juxtaposition that the avant-garde arts of the modern era have tapped into a main line of poetic making that can be traced back into deep time in the cultures of *Homo sapiens.* Even more than his precursors, such as the Dadaists, the surrealists, and especially the poet and theater innovator Antonin Artaud, Rothenberg inserts shamanistic rites of hunter-gatherers, creation stories from around the world, and ancient divinatory procedures into contemporary performance spaces. His anthology demonstrates that poetry—the imaginative use of language "for experiencing and comprehending the world"—is the shared inheritance of being human (or maybe even of being animal).[1]

Whether in the anthology or in Rothenberg's rendition of it, I have seen this poetry work its magic. When he came to read at Notre Dame, students spoke of how his juicy recitals revealed the joy and toughness condensed in the world's poetry. With or without musical accompaniment, his performances are by turns rhythmic, explosive, and hypnotic. On many occasions, for example, I have heard him chant lustily "Old Man Beaver's Blessing Song" (from the Seneca Nation):

> *all*i*want*'s*a*good*5-c.*seegar*
> *heeheeHOHOheeheeHOHOheeheeHOHO*
>
> (396)

As he repeatedly intones the lines, varying speed, pitch, and accent, he simultaneously employs techniques from Native American chant and Dada sound poetry. Through performances and anthologies, Rothenberg makes available vast poetic resources for conducting the rites of passage at the core of human cultures and for joining the language of here and now to the verbal techniques of there and then. His reverence for the (often irreverent) practices of shamanism makes him a prime exemplar of the antinomian, anti-orthodox tendencies in American poetic transactions with the spiritual. As the pressures of climate change force us to begin thinking of ourselves as a species among other species, *Technicians* deserves renewed attention, for it proposes a poetry and poetics that speak across the millennia of human imagination. Now more than ever, the anthology has much to offer the historians, anthropologists, and sociologists who have begun to take stock of human culture as an evolutionary factor of signal importance.

PRECURSORS

As Rothenberg openly acknowledges, many sources stand behind *Technicians of the Sacred: A Range of Poetries from Africa, America, Asia, Europe & Oceania*: ethnographic accounts of rituals in non-Western, nonurban societies; depictions of shamanism and visionary poetry from psychological, religious, and pharmacological perspectives; scholarly studies of the verbal and written artifacts of particular ancient and modern traditions; translations into English of poetry, song, and mythology from around the world; attempts in movements such as Dada, surrealism, Fluxus, and performance art to bring ritual into everyday life; experiments by New American poets and concrete poets in setting speech patterns and vernacular language into new spatial arrangements on the page; and, in the third edition, "survivals and revivals" by new indigenous poets (xx). As much as this huge variety of artistic, academic, religious, and anthropological source material goes into the composition of Rothenberg's teeming assemblage, one interlocutor, Robert Duncan, provides a special instigation for the anthology and the ensuing intellectual project of ethnopoetics. Often, Rothenberg memorializes the influence by adopting the phrase "symposium of the whole" as a kind of motto. It comes from Duncan's essay

"Rites of Participation," first published in *Caterpillar* 1 and 2 (1967, 1968).[2] Duncan imagines his "symposium" as a new collocation that joins human beings in consanguinity with animals and ultimately with all earthly cells—a coming together in "one fate" brought about by the ecological imperatives of our time. In prophetic tones, he looks toward the emergence of an earthly community that has "gone beyond the reality of the incomparable nation or race, the incomparable Jehovah in the shape of a man, the incomparable Book or Vision, the incomparable species, in which identity might hold & defend its boundaries against an alien territory" ("Rites" 153). If in Plato's *Symposium* Socrates urges his aristocratic interlocutors to undertake an ever more rarified, progressively disembodied sublimation of erotic desire toward ideal Forms, Duncan's notion of community is not hierarchical or discriminatory but grounded in the politics and epistemology of equality and wholeness:

> To compose such a symposium of the whole, such a totality, all the old excluded orders must be included. The female, the proletariat, the foreign; the animal and vegetative; the unconscious and the unknown; the criminal and the failure—all that has been outcast and vagabond must return to be admitted in the creation of what we consider we are. ("Rites" 154)

Accepting Duncan's invitation to inhabit this egalitarian history of species, Rothenberg proposes his own symposium of the whole as "a complex redefinition of cultural and intellectual values: a new reading of the poetic past and present" in which "culture" is thought anthropologically and poetry is defined broadly as the creative verbal address to present circumstances.[3] He coins a new term for this redefinition—"ethnopoetics"—and titles the anthology of essays devoted to it (edited with Diane Rothenberg), *Symposium of the Whole: A Range of Discourse Toward an Ethnopoetics* (1993). Lest the term be confusing, it is important to note that the purpose of ethnopoetics is not to reinforce ethnic boundaries but rather to invite a robust interchange between contemporary poetry and the oldest forms of language art, reincorporating actions consigned to the "non-literary"—such as ritual, shamanism, bodily display, chanting, and dance—into a capacious definition of poetry.

Rothenberg ponders a basic transactional question throughout his work: what can we bring forward from the past that needs to be heard in the present? With respect to this transmission, he develops another signature notion of Duncan's, that of being a "derivative" poet. In an article discussing how the practice of translation relates to his own poetics, Duncan opts for a "poetics in which the poem is thought of as a process of participation in a reality larger than my own—the reality of man's experience in the terms of language and literature—a community of meanings and forms in which my work would be at once derivative and creative." Duncan finds this community of meanings so real and absorbing that he has "at times a feeling that there is no real me, only the process of derivations in which I have my existence."[4] Throughout his career, he refers to his writing as "derivative" rather than "original," highlighting correspondences among words, images, and artifacts from the repertoire of human cultures rather than "expressing" his own thoughts, emotions, or insights.[5] In the introduction to *Bending the Bow* (1968), he situates his poetry within a "*grand collage*," which he defines as "a poetry of all poetries," an assemblage made up of words, images, and passages culled from divergent sources.[6] *Technicians* is just such an assemblage writ large, made up of entire poems and other artifacts, and it sets out to delineate, with salient examples, the outlines of a "poetry of all poetries." As Rothenberg explains,

> Because I don't like to write discursive prose or essays, I find the anthology is a vehicle for saying certain things about poetry that I really can't manage to say otherwise. . . . Through selection, through juxtaposition, through presentation of types of poems, through defining by pointing at something. The presentation of examples is a kind of definition. And it's a fantastic big form sometimes—like collage but on a super scale.[7]

Both Duncan and Rothenberg revere Ezra Pound and Louis Zukofsky as exemplary elders, who summon a vital world culture using translation and collage. The later poets look to Pound's *Cantos* and Zukofsky's "*A*" as works of assemblage composed over decades, where poetry from around the world offers aesthetic, ethical, political, economic, and spiritual tools for the present. Although wary of the sometimes univocal or universal proclamations and judgments of the earlier poets, Rothenberg stages conversations and seeks correspondences among divergent cultures in the implicit belief that such communication is possible and that experiences of people remote from one another in time and place remain commensurate. Eager to enlist Pound's example, Rothenberg includes "*Canto 1*," a translation from the *Odyssey*, in a section of *Technicians* on "Death and Defeat." In the commentary, he makes a case for Pound as ethnopoet:

> Pound opens his master-poem, *The Cantos*, with this translation of Homer (the so-called *Nekuia* or descent-to-the-underworld section), giving it back to us as a poem of beginnings. But it was a poem, even then, calling up the dead in the oldest of poetic traditions, where the journey of the central figure retains a sense, nowhere more than here, of the former ritual. It has thus remained the prototype, in the "West," of the poem of the oral, even shamanic, origins that comes into a fixed (written) form early in the development of writ-

> ing. Pound's brilliance was to connect Homer as a first-poet with the sound of Old English (Anglo-Saxon) verse as another instance of a first-poetry, & to tie both of these to the *new* poetry he shared with other twentieth-century workers. And more than poetry per se, it was a sense of powers & visions that was there to be renewed. (500–501)

By virtue of translation, Pound becomes a kind of shaman, traveling to exotic spirit realms through poetries outside the contemporary, English-speaking world, bringing back, as a shamanic healer would, new songs he hopes will revive a dying civilization. Most important, in Rothenberg's estimation, was that Pound returned from translation journeys with innovative poetry in English that bore the imprint of other times and places: "I think Pound also used translation as a way of expanding the whole historical and cultural range of what we knew about poetry. It wasn't enough to simply say there was a poetry in China. It was really a matter of making the Chinese poetry immediately visible in English. Which is one of the great things Pound did" (*Vort* 107). For Zukofsky, Duncan, and Rothenberg, Pound is the innovator who insists on the necessity of translation and the efficacy of transactions between ancient and contemporary poetry.

In the creative work of editing *Technicians*, Rothenberg follows Pound in two ways. First, he makes visible in English tribal and archaic poetry from around the world—locating, commissioning, or undertaking himself translations that have a currency or audacity like those of Pound. Second, he juxtaposes translations to avant-garde works of poetry and performance art, highlighting similarities. Thus, he accomplishes an interchange similar to the one he praises in *Canto 1*, making ancient and foreign poetry look like "the *new* poetry" and setting the work of his contemporaries within the oldest structures of human feeling and interaction. In the body of the anthology, Rothenberg asserts analogies between the tribal and the modern by selecting translations or retranslations that often display formal characteristics of the New American poetry, which itself grew directly from the innovations of Pound and William Carlos Williams: vernacular and erotic rather than "poetic" diction, avoidance of articles and punctuation, extensive use of abbreviation, and lineation based on breath rhythms, including multiple indentations. This hip, up-to-date style brings translation into the purview of poetic habits in the 1950s and 1960s, which also points to a liability, in that sometimes the translations can sound a bit homogenous. The extensive "Commentaries" section of *Technicians* (nearly two hundred pages) follows Allen's practice in his 1960 anthology, *The New American Poetry*, of appending back matter to create new contexts for the primary work. Rothenberg's commentaries document the original performative circumstances of the translated poetry, as recorded usually by ethnographers, and demonstrate affinities between the translated work and the avant-garde poetry and art of the nineteenth and twentieth centuries.

With Duncan, in particular, Rothenberg shares a fascination with the figure of the shaman, especially as proto-poet. Duncan's interest in shamanism goes back to some of his earliest writing, an ambitious project in prose poetry he called "Toward the Shaman" (1939–1941).[8] Later, he conceived of the shamanic ascent to other worlds as an image for entering the writing of other people to compose his "derivative" poetry. In *Ground Work*, for instance, he mimics Dante, the Metaphysical poets, Rumi, and Baudelaire. In more literal terms, Rothenberg views shamanism as the origin of poetry: "The shaman can be seen as protopoet, for almost always his technique hinges on the creation of special linguistic circumstances, i.e., of song and invocation" (*Technicians* 482). The term "technique" alludes to the title of the anthology, which "itself is a take-off from Eliade's 'specialist of the sacred' who masters the 'techniques of ecstasy'" (*Symposium* 59). Rothenberg found the two phrases in Eliade's *Shamanism: Archaic Techniques of Ecstasy*, which became a primary source text for ethnopoetics.[9] Duncan and Rothenberg both emphasize attributes of shamanism that make it central to a poetry outside religious orthodoxy: the shaman as lone figure who visits other worlds to bring back poetry addressed to social ills; the shaman as healer who unstops the flow of erotic energy and provokes sexual display; the shaman who moves through various life-forms, partaking of the interconnectedness of being; and the shaman as unflinchingly confronting death, darkness, and disease, knowing "negative" forces cannot be shunted aside.

IMPRINTS OF THE 1960S

In New York in the early 1960s, Rothenberg worked alongside several performance artists, especially those in the Fluxus group, whose publisher, Dick Higgins, issued two of the poet's books. *Technicians* originated in part through a conversation with Higgins about Rothenberg's sense of "the closeness of primitive rituals (when stripped-down to the bare line of the activities) to the 'happenings' & 'events' [Higgins] was presenting" (*Technicians* xxxvi). More generally, he drew sustenance from explorations of "primitive" rites and images inspired by Antonin Artaud's groundbreaking book of essays, *The Theater and Its Double* (translated 1958), performances by troupes such as the Living Theater and Richard Schechner's Performance Group, the staging of Allan Kaprow's Happenings, and Carolee Schneemann's mytho-feminist reclamation of the female body as a site for ritual art rather than as an object for the male gaze. Specifically, the anthology "grew directly out of a pair of 1964 readings of 'primitive & archaic poetry' at The Poet's Hardware Theater & the Café Metro in New York. Working with me on those were the poets David Antin, Jackson Mac Low, & Rochelle Owens." In keeping with the emphasis on live performance, Rothenberg chose works for the anthology for their toughness and provocative imagery, not for their "representative" status as determined by academic categories:

> My intention from the start was to find translations that would "translate," i.e., bring-the-work-across or be a living work in English, & that's a very different thing from (in the first place) looking for representative "masterpieces" & including them whatever the nature of the translations. I also have (no question about it) my own sense of what's worth it in poetry, & I've tried to work from that rather than against it. I haven't gone for "pretty" or "innocent" or "noble" poems so much as strong ones. (xxxvi)

In this sense, the anthology follows in the footsteps of another acknowledged precursor, Harry Smith's *Anthology of American Folk Music* (1952), whose songs, rife with bizarre imagery, are voiced in discordant, gravelly, or keening tones.[10] One of the reasons *Technicians* and Smith's anthology have such staying power is precisely because each is a work of art that cannot be easily assimilated to polite taste, made of pieces that are enigmatic, incantatory, often disturbing, and sometimes uncanny. Rothenberg invokes anthropologist Bronisław Malinowski's phrase "the coefficient of weirdness" (xxvii) to characterize the magical language of poems that break through the professional decorum of literature with a rough, unpolished, vernacular style that matches harsh, erotic, or shocking subject matter—works that make something happen rather than reflect on what has already occurred.

In Rothenberg's view, much tribal and archaic poetry operates by collage juxtaposition. One of the first pieces in *Technicians*, "Bantu Combinations," consists of pairs of disparate statements: "1. I am still carving an ironwood stick. / I am still thinking about it. // 2. The lake dries up at the edges. / The elephant is killed by a small arrow. // 3. The little hut falls down. / Tomorrow, debts" (16). In the commentary, he calls these couplets "Examples of plot-thickening in the area of 'image': a conscious placing of image against image as though to see-what-happens." He likens these image transactions to the forms of haiku and the sonnet: "In all these the interest increases as the connection between the images becomes more & more strained, barely definable."[11] Citing an interpretation from the poems' source, *Life of a South African Tribe*—"Sometimes the imagination is so subtle that the result is almost incoherent"—Rothenberg disagrees: "Not subtlety, though, but *energy*:

the power of the word and image." Strong juxtapositions that resist easy understanding release energy and a mysterious "light"—not "the light of logic & simile" but a more penetrating one "to which (for the first time) the word 'vision' might be said to apply" (450). Following this conjunction of image, energy, and vision, Rothenberg quotes William Blake's famous claim to having a multileveled, "fourfold" imaginative vision.[12] Blake's highly creative, nonorthodox spirituality is a constant inspiration to Rothenberg, underlying his conflation of sacredness and spirituality with energy, eroticism, and living beyond nationhood.

Similar to "Bantu Combinations," the "Aztec Definitions" come in short units, which create a whole via unexpected juxtapositions:

> *Ruby-Throated Hummingbird*
> It is ashen, ash colored. At the top of its head and the throat, its feathers are flaming, like fire. They glisten, they glow.
>
> *Amoyotl (a water-strider)*
> It is like a fly, small and round. It has legs, it has wings; it is dry. It goes on the surface of the water; it is a flyer. It buzzes, it sings.
>
> *Bitumen (a shellfish)*
> It falls out on the ocean shore; it falls out like mud.
>
> (21)

Rothenberg notes that these texts were collected only a quarter century after the fall of Tenochtitlan (by Fray Bernardino de Sahagún), so they constitute "a kind of glossary of 'earthly things'—the elders' minds & words are drawn toward definitions of the most ordinary debris of their lives." By drawing attention to small facets of their rapidly changing lives, Fray Bernardino "led them to a reconsideration, to an assemblage of 'things of New Spain.'" Amid the "ordinary debris" of their ruined civilization, "the mind finds release in a strange new encounter; free of ritual & myth [The-System]; it approaches objects as if for the first time testing their existence" (brackets in original). Rothenberg posits an analogy between Aztec "definitions" and contemporary poetry, each taking place within a civilization that has split apart and discharged the debris of its material and verbal life for transactional recombination into striking works of assemblage (457–58). For a contemporary analogue, he cites a portion of Antin's uncanny elegy, "Definitions for Mendy" (1965), which takes definitions for "loss" and "value" from an insurance handbook and a dictionary, improvising a series of discontinuous statements directed at the unfathomable death of a friend:

> Loss is an unintentional decline in or disappearance of a value arising from
>   a contingency
> a value is an efficacy a power a brightness
> it is also a duration
>
> to lose something keys hair someone
> we suffer at the thought
> he has become absent imaginary false
>
> (458)

Alongside valorizing the vernacular flattening of tone evident in Antin's (anti-)elegy, Rothenberg assaults orthodoxy by designating the erotic as central to the sacred. He sees erotic energy as guiding expressions of bodily, ritual (communal), and spiritual states in tribal, archaic, and mystical poetries, operating at each level to intensify experience and break through rigid forms of control. Ultimately, he argues that an erotic poetics constitutes the "*mainstream* of poetry that goes back to the old tribes & has been carried forward by the great subterranean culture."[13] Like Duncan and Gary Snyder, Rothenberg locates a countercultural, shamanistic impulse as arising during the Paleolithic era and surviving in the erotic, visionary, and gnostic strains woven into the great archaic civilizations. It comes forward into the modern era in more or less isolated tribal cultures and in mystical countercultures of the major world religions. This tradition attracts Rothenberg for its ability to break open restrictive societal and mental constructs through provocation and vision, through eruptions of libido, as in the Australian Aboriginal poem discussed below.

For Rothenberg, as for Duncan, ethnographic accounts of Aboriginal mythology and ritual mark an exemplary upsurge of the erotic into human culture. In "Rites of Participation," Duncan discusses Aboriginal mythology based on the works of the Freudian anthropologist Géza Róheim. He cites a lengthy etymological treatment of the word "alcheringa" (ultimately rendered as "dream time" ["Rites" 162–63]), which also becomes the name for a journal Rothenberg edited (with Dennis Tedlock) and a pivotal term in ethnopoetics. According to Róheim, the dream time represents, from a Freudian perspective, the mythical time of the libido, in which parts of and effluents from the human body are cathected upon the landscape. In both Freudian psychology and Aboriginal mythology and ritual, Duncan notes, "the body of man and the body of creation" are brought together (164):

> The "breast, anus, semen, urine, leg, foot" in the Australian song, chant, or enchantment, that are also hill, hole, seed, stream, tree, or rock, where "in the

> Toara ceremony the men dance around the ring shouting the names of male and female genital organs, shady trees, hills, and some of the totems of their tribe," are most familiar to the Freudian convert Roheim. (163)

Duncan claims the erotic, the psychological, the ritual, and the mystical cannot be split apart: "The 'blood' of the Aranda, the 'libido' of the Freudian, may also be the 'light' of our Kabbalistic text" (164). At every level, the erotic underscores and intensifies human experience.

In *Technicians*, Rothenberg extends this erotic poetics by reworking translations of Aboriginal performance poems to emphasize sexual imagery as the basis of a visionary mythology. Near the outset, for instance, in the section "Origins & Namings," he titles a selection from the *Djanggawul Cycle*, "Genesis II." The selection begins:

> [Song 159]
> Go, take that hot stone, and heat it near her clitoris:
> For the severed part is a sacred *djuda rangga*. Covering up the clitoris within the mat, within its transverse fibre, within its mouth, its inner peak . . .
> Go, the people are dancing there, like *djuda* roots, like spray, moving their bodies, shaking their hair!
> Carefully they beat their clapping sticks on the *mauwulan* point . . .
> Go, stand up! See the clansfolk beyond the transverse fibre of the mat!
> They come from the Sister's womb, lifting aside the clitoris, coming out like *djuda* roots.
>
> (9–10; ellipses in original)

In the commentary, Rothenberg emphasizes the sexual nature of the *Djanggawul Cycle*: "A heavy ripeness, the swelling & bursting of a teeming life-source, colors Australian views of the creation." In the Aboriginal songs, he contends, streaming libidinal energy stands revealed as the erotic basis for human culture: "The *Djanggawul Cycle* is the best example the present editor knows, of the celebration of human sexuality & birth in the work of genesis." He contrasts the Aboriginal display of sexuality as the acknowledged basis for culture to its occlusion in normative Western religion: "The body of the sacred sister, heat around the clitoris, the budding tree roots, spray & blood, a swarming sense of life emerging—not two-by-two, in pairs, but *swarming*—was turned-from in the West, reduced to images of evil" (444).

Rothenberg sees the advent of orthodox religion as an imaginative constriction, which brings about a diminution of life energy and thus of "sacredness." In stark contrast, a Baka (Pygmy) song in *Technicians*, "All Lives, All Dances,

& All is Loud," expresses a kinship with all living things through exuberant song, dance, and mimicry:

> The fish does . . . HIP
> The bird does . . . VISS
> The marmot does . . . GNAN
>
> I throw myself to the left,
> I turn myself to the right,
> I act the fish,
> Which darts in the water, which darts
> Which twists about, which leaps—
> All lives, all dances, and all is loud.
>
> (38–39; first third of the song)

Rothenberg's commentary begins with an exclamation: "UNIVERSAL PRIMITIVE & ARCHAIC VISION OF ALL LIFE IN MOTION & SHARING A SINGLE NATURE WHICH IS SACRED" (473). He adduces four analogies for the Baka song: a statement by philosopher Ernst Cassirer that "primitive man" has a "deep conviction of a fundamental and indelible *solidarity of life* that bridges over the multiplicity and variety of its single forms"; "A SONG OF THE BEAR" (Teton Sioux), which runs, "my paw is sacred / all things are sacred"; a statement by the pre-Socratic philosopher Empedocles, "All things possess intelligence & a share of thought"; and a citation from Blake, "For everything that lives is holy" (474). In these examples, the concept of the sacred refers not to objects cordoned off from everyday life but to a celebration of the inherent intelligence of living things and of their vigorous interconnectedness.

BECOMING INDIGENOUS

The avant-garde has been faulted by some as an elitist enterprise, but Rothenberg counters this charge by pointing to its use of vernacular language and embeddedness in everyday life. *Technicians* furthers this argument by staging transactions between innovative and challenging avant-garde works and those of hunter-gatherers. Rothenberg begins his 1967 "Pre-Face" to *Technicians* with the heading, "PRIMITIVE MEANS COMPLEX," enlisting the linguistic truism that there are no primitive languages to support an assertion that there are no primitive poetries, given the imaginative and intellectual sophistication of every culture:

> No people has sat in sloth for the thousands of years of its history. Measure everything by the Titan rocket & the transistor radio, & the world is full of

> primitive peoples. But once change the unit of value to the poem or the dance-event or the dream (all clearly artifactual situations) & it becomes apparent what all those people have been doing all those years with all that time on their hands. (xxx)

He appreciates the intelligence and refinement of nonmodern poets able to infuse the visionary (i.e., the sacred) into the conduct of daily life. In this sense, earlier poets model the kinds of fruitful transactions between art and life desired by the avant-garde.

Technicians enters a tradition of venerating the vernacular in American poetry, which Rothenberg traces to Whitman, Pound, Williams, and Gertrude Stein and which continues, he contends, in Olson, Duncan, Snyder, Antin, Robert Creeley, and Paul Blackburn, among others. *Technicians* also presages a more recent direction in literary studies, opening "American" literature out of the geographical boundaries of the United States and the self-conscious attempt to seek an illusory exceptionalism or essential "Americanness." Rothenberg's contribution to this project can be seen in his persistent posing of American poetry face-to-face with the European avant-garde and with poetries across the world in time and space. If we imagine *Technicians* as convening a "world poetry," then it is characterized not formally or nationally but as a range of imaginative approaches to primary human experiences—such as birth, death, love, war, food, shelter, disease, and cosmology—through a poetics both erotic (in the broadest senses) and vernacular.

Looking back at earlier avant-gardes, Rothenberg notices that not all of them value "the grubbiness of contingency," which "has, in my view of it, kept us more honestly human" (*Pre-Faces* 47). Although Duncan, for example, makes the vernacular a key part of his poetics, his complex notion of it derives from the literary vernaculars of Dante and Whitman. With respect to "grubbiness," Rothenberg finds Duncan's sense of the vernacular too literary, even squeamish. Anecdotally, he tells of attending a poetry reading with Duncan, who denounced in a stage whisper as "pure ugliness" the visceral imagery of a particular poem: "The comment stuck with me, bothered me a great deal in fact." It "came rushing back" to him when he visited Auschwitz and Treblinka. From the perspective of the concentration camp, he argues, ugliness is "poetry's real voice" and cannot be overlooked.[14] Duncan, too, sensed this difference between them. In notes on reading *Technicians*, he is troubled by Rothenberg's avowal that "the great fanged statue of Coatlicue or the multi-breasted Diana of Ephesus" is "more interesting and probably more truthful than the Venus de Milo or Michelangelo's Pietà" (*Technicians* 516). Duncan worries about the extremity of such a view: that "Coatlicue and Diana of Ephesus are more interesting and true, as Auschwitz seems to be the truth of what our world is (or the atom bomb at Hiroshima)—these are the grand, the truly sacred shows of our time that leave the spirit shaking; and all expressions of dignity seem fronts of a lie."[15]

Rothenberg distrusts any impulse to prettify the horrific backdrop of the contemporary world, and in keeping with this he promotes a more inclusive sense of the vernacular, which also coincides with a perspective of radical equality based on the largest range of human experience: "We're now able to draw from predecessors confronted by the same necessities. These include earlier modernists & 'primitives,' along with a range of other human beings, poets of all times & places, who remind us that we're neither the first poets nor will we be the last" (*Pre-Faces* 47). As an ethical imperative, a vernacular approach accounts for the immediate situation (wherever it's found) and the means for confronting it developed by individuals and their neighbors, and it acknowledges that across the world other vernacular solutions also might address it equally well. In recent years, writers in a variety of fields have set forth such a vernacular ethics and aesthetics, which has shaded into an environmental perspective on human flourishing. In poetry, Rothenberg invokes Olson and Snyder as vernacularists who look across many cultures to draw the full dimensions of human experience and expression. In *Symposium*, he includes another ethical vernacularist, the art historian Robert Farris Thompson, a pioneer in tracing the influence of African dance, music, and art on vernacular cultures of the Americas. Rothenberg cites a passage from Thompson's *African Art in Motion* (1974), in which he, like Olson and Snyder, contends that patterns of vernacular interaction between human beings and their surroundings imbue people and their artifacts with dignity and an erotic charge:

> Icon defines itself in act south of the Sahara. Things done, sculpture and dress, combine with things happening, music and dance. A fundamental principle is made manifest: action is a superior mode of thought. Movement serves long-term knowledge with sensuous uprush and spontaneity, answering to the imperatives of life. (*Symposium* 285)[16]

Also cognizant of the many patterns of cross-cultural interchange, the critic Wai Chee Dimock has proposed a new definition of American literature as permeable phenomenon, a definition implicit in *Technicians* and Rothenberg's other anthologies:

> Rather than being a discrete entity, [American literature] is better seen as a crisscrossing set of pathways, open-ended and ever multiplying, weaving in and out of other geographies, other languages and cultures. These are input channels, kinship networks, routes of transit, and forms of attachment—

> connective tissues binding America to the rest of the world. Active on both ends, they thread American texts into the topical events of other cultures, while also threading the long durations of those cultures into the short chronology of the United States. This double threading thickens time, lengthens it, shadowing in its midst the abiding traces of the planet's multitudinous life.[17]

From Dimock's perspective, American literature is embedded within cultures of much longer duration, so that its writing incurs transactions over distances of time and space. *Technicians* is exactly the sort of work Dimock seeks, which opens up "alternate measures—African, Asian, and European" (4)—for an American literature that weaves in the "connective tissues binding America to the rest of the world." For Rothenberg, a sense of deep time allows us to reclaim vernacular energies at the margins of modern culture. He contends, for instance, that where normative science and religion have sought for several thousand years to supersede the past and annihilate the "*old* man," ethnopoetics wants to invite the old man (and old woman) back in—while retaining what Olson calls "the will to change" (*Pre-Faces* 17). Rothenberg promotes a multifarious tradition that "takes vision & conflict as the essential characteristics of poetry," ties them "to the structure of the poem & the dynamics of actual speech," and develops a lineage from the present avant-garde back through earlier innovators all the way to Paleolithic shamans (*Pre-Faces* 33).

In this light, *Technicians* has an essential part to play in current attempts at fathoming the course of human biological and cultural evolution, such as historian Yuval Noah Harari's *Sapiens: A Brief History of Humankind* (2015), sociologist Robert Bellah's *Religion in Human Evolution: From the Paleolithic to the Axial Age* (2011), anthropologist and rock art historian David Lewis-Williams's *The Mind in the Cave: Consciousness and the Origins of Art* (2002), and anthropologist Agustín Fuentes's *The Creative Spark: How Imagination Made Humans Exceptional* (2017).[18] As history pushes back into biology and we begin to see ourselves as part of a much longer human (and animal) continuum, *Technicians* invites a new reckoning of culture based on transactions between contemporary poets, singers, artists, and performers and the biological, anthropological, and historical evidence of who we've been. Lewis-Williams, for instance, uses the examples of cave paintings in Europe and Africa together with cognitive mapping of mental states to argue, like Rothenberg, for the shamanic origins of art. Fuentes contends that human biological evolution has been powered by two forces, imagination and collaboration, placing creativity and community at the heart of physical, mental, and social development and thus reinforcing Rothenberg's contention that poiesis and ritual make us human.

An emblematic example of these new approaches to history and culture,

Bellah's book could be adduced as a commentary on *Technicians*. Bellah was a premier sociologist of religion, who took on the challenge issued by anthropologists and historians to produce an account of religious activity that incorporates prehistory and biological time. Agreeing with biologists that for animal, and even plant, species there is an unbreakable feedback loop between genetics and social behavior, Bellah sets out to show how this feedback loop works with respect to religion. Like Rothenberg and Clifford Geertz, Bellah considers ritual (not beliefs) to be the defining characteristic of religion and that ritual actions create symbolic realities that exist in interchange with the contingencies of daily life (Bellah xvi). He adopts from psychologist Merlin Donald a scheme that accounts for the coevolution of biology and culture over the past one or two million years, in which there are three stages: mimetic, mythic, and theoretic. Mimetic culture, made up primarily of gestures, already involves music and dance. With the introduction of full grammatical languages, probably 250,000 to 100,000 years ago, a new stage arrives with the ability to tell stories. Finally, as social structures begin to stratify and wealth accumulates in the first millennium BCE, an ethical and religious reform emerges that questions old narratives and rituals and strives for spiritual universalism (Bellah xviii–xix). Bellah's book concludes with that latter period, which he calls, following Karl Jaspers, the Axial Age, in four long chapters analyzing the theoretic stage in ancient Israel, ancient Greece, ancient China, and ancient India. Like Rothenberg, his terms for the two earlier periods are tribal and archaic. He cautions, however, against viewing evolution as a progression in which a new stage automatically erases former stages. In fact—and here is where he most acutely reinforces Rothenberg—he insists that all the religious capacities developed (mimetic, mythic, and theoretic) remain crucial as humans move from stage to stage, up to and including the present moment (Bellah xxii–xxiii).

Recent work in applying these insights, such as that of environmental activist David Abram, seeks to follow the arduous, rigorous discipline of becoming indigenous once again. A trained phenomenologist, Abram takes as his guide Maurice Merleau-Ponty's phenomenology of perception, in which perception becomes a fully interactive mode that includes language itself as a gestural dance. In his first book, *The Spell of the Sensuous* (1996), Abram reaches the insight that alphabetic writing has become an all-embracing screen that intermits every act of perception, reducing substantially our ability to engage the natural world. His second book, *Becoming Animal* (2010), chronicles the rending of that screen and the revival of an indigenous spirituality through meditative, attentive perception, which results in actual moments of communication with animals, trees, and even winds, in the manner memorialized by many of the works in *Technicians*.[19] This is a nondeistic mysticism, in which the beings we dwell among offer, as they did to people tens of thousands of years ago, an opportunity to enter the living dance. When I met Abram at a conference, I asked if he knew Rothenberg's anthology. He responded, "Oh yes, it's a favorite!" and began reciting, with suitable hand gestures:

> The fish does . . . HIP
> The bird does . . . VISS
> The marmot does . . . GNAN
>
> All lives, all dances, and all is loud.

Peering through the lens of a social-scientific synthesis such as Bellah's reveals how prescient *Technicians* has been and why it excites admiration from people on the front lines of climate activism, such as those working to prevent species extinction. Right from the start, Rothenberg insisted that tribal and archaic songs and rituals, drawings and dances, give the fullest measure of human spiritual and poetic capacities, incorporating mimetic, mythic, and even theoretic enunciations into ethical transactions with other beings. He also recognized from the beginning a need to account for the explorations of other artists in his own historical moment (initially, the late 1960s), drawing on emergent strands of concrete poetry and sound poetry, minimalism, conceptualism, performance art, multiculturalism, and investigations into the interplay of orality and literacy. In many of these areas, artists were consciously seeking models outside post-Renaissance Western culture, looking to revive spiritual/aesthetic skills that had been deemed "primitive" or "archaic." Likewise, following Duncan's insistence that all beings belong in the "symposium of the whole," Rothenberg released ecological potentials obscured by condescending attitudes toward non-Western cultures, particularly those of hunter-gatherers. The many songs and events that include direct encounters with animals, such as "All Lives, All Dances, & All Is Loud," no longer seem like children's fables when we begin to take seriously interspecies communication and to take stock of what is required to live sustainably in a particular place.

3

Judaism as Loss and the Buddhist Element in Michael Heller's *Eschaton*

"I TOOK SILENCE INTO TIME"

Like Rothenberg, Michael Heller (1937–) is an antinomian poet in the American Jewish secular tradition. Where Rothenberg locates his unorthodox version of the sacred in anthropological and archaic sources, Heller's sense of the sacred involves multiple avowals and refusals. Jon Curley describes one "distinct layer" of Heller's corpus as the "antinomic," which "denotes the embedded logic of opposition . . . between language and silence, doubt and belief, the naming and the withholding of name."[1] The advent of Heller's six-hundred-page volume, *This Constellation Is a Name: Collected Poems 1965–2010* (2012), has prompted sustained scrutiny of a philosophically sophisticated poet whose determination not to align with any specific school of American poetry had slowed recognition of his achievement.[2] At home in the lineages of both Pound and Stevens, Heller also associates with religious and intellectual traditions of Judaism in ways both representative and unique among American Jewish poets. He has staked out his own territory at the intersection of three directions that have beckoned secular Jewish intellectuals—and especially poets—over the past half century: the abiding allure of the urban poetics of objectivism, the haunting strains issuing from the broken monuments of European Jewish culture, and the fascination with Buddhism as a spiritual practice. Responding in adroit and unexpected ways to formal challenges offered by objectivism, Heller likewise maintains a complex poetic engagement with what could be called Judaism as an experience of loss. This essay uses examples from his book *Eschaton* (2009) to probe how Heller's foray into Buddhism adds subtle nuance to his objectivist-influenced treatment of Judaism as loss.[3]

The poetic movement of Objectivism was born out of the Jewish encounter with New York City in the first half of the twentieth century, a time when first and second generation Jewish writers and intellectuals struggled to secure a place in mainstream American culture.[4] In a 1931 issue of *Poetry*, Louis Zukofsky gave the title "objectivist" to a loosely gathered movement of urban poets with leftist leanings. He called for a poetry of witness that resides among the things of the world and regards ideas, social relations, and words themselves as objects for close, unsentimental scrutiny. The three other Jewish poets associated with Objectivism are Charles Reznikoff, Carl Rakosi, and George Oppen. Although largely composed of Jewish poets, Objectivism arose from the larger matrix of imagist poetry and poetics, especially that of William Carlos Williams and Ezra Pound, and poets Basil Bunting and Lorine Niedecker were allied with it in significant ways. Objectivism's influence within the United States has included not only subsequent Jewish poets but also groups such as the Black Mountain poets and the Language poets, and it has spread to France through translation and critical interest.

Among Jewish American poets, it is easy to construct a rough-and-ready list of those for whom Objectivism plays an important role, such as Cid Corman, Milton Kessler, David Ignatow, David Antin, Jerome Rothenberg, Shirley Kaufman, Armand Schwerner, Harvey Shapiro, Hugh Seidman, Rachel Blau DuPlessis, Bob Perelman, Paul Auster, Charles Bernstein, and Joseph Lease. Heller himself inaugurated the critical study of Objectivism with *Conviction's Net of Branches* (1985), clarifying its differences from other movements in modern poetry and declaring it the basis for an ongoing American tradition. He also edited *Carl Rakosi: Man and Poet* (1993), a five-hundred-page collection of essays, interviews, and bibliographies devoted to Rakosi. But it must be said that Heller was closest to George Oppen, both individually and in terms of poetic affinity.[5] Throughout his career, Oppen has remained a touchstone, as Heller's *Speaking the Estranged: Essays on the Work of George Oppen* (2008) makes evident. The volume ends with a memoir chronicling Heller's decisive personal and literary transactions with the older poet.[6]

Another essay in *Speaking the Estranged*, "The Voice of the Impersonal" (106–23), brings Oppen into the company of the Hungarian Jewish poet who wrote in German, Paul Celan, a crucial move for American poets who wish to reclaim some of the legacy of European Jewish culture. In this act of reclamation, Heller joins a wide range of postwar American Jewish poets and thinkers. In *Radical Poetics and Secular Jewish Culture* (a collection to which Heller contributes), several prominent poets confess to writing out of the bottomless loss of European Jewish culture. According to Bernstein, for example, if there is to be a "European poetry and philosophy by the descendants of Benjamin and Heine," then it "must be the task of secular Jewish culture on this side of the Atlantic and of our radical poetry and ambiguating poetics." Bernstein admits to the pitfalls of taking on "this unwanted and perhaps even insufferable task" but affirms fatalistically, "perhaps this is what we were chosen for."[7] He signals his acceptance of the assignment most directly in *Shadowtime*, an opera about the death of Benjamin.[8] Bernstein's assent is echoed by DuPlessis, whose long poem *Drafts* becomes more elegiac as it unfolds: "I feel, increasingly, as the work goes on, that I am being spoken through, almost as if I were single-handedly building into existence some of the work of the lost. That this idea is arrogant, unseemly, astonishing, and shattering does not make it any less palpable, and sorrowful" (Miller and Morris 211).[9] Although lamenting the grievous fates of earlier generations constitutes a through line in the history of Judaism, presented in Scripture and liturgy, the truncation of European Jewish culture has sparked among secular poets in the United States less a religious renewal than a determination to abide within the remnants of loss. Of these poets, Heller perhaps has most consistently made this loss the locus for his poetry.[10]

Heller sometimes figures the condition of loss as a dwelling between irreconcilable positions. It's worth speculating that this double bind may well provide an opening for Buddhist thought to enter his work, since Buddhism unfixes dualisms and other kinds of determinate positions, but more on this later. As a secular Jewish American intellectual, Heller finds himself, as did the Objectivists before him, in the classic Diasporic condition of betweenness: "The 'between' is . . . foundational. It exists in the relational sphere between the law of religious observance and secular life."[11] For many Jewish intellectuals, this Diasporic situation represents a swerve away not only from orthodoxy but also more specifically from the sense of being stuck between Hebraism and Hellenism as the two constitutive strands of Western culture.[12] In *Eschaton*, Heller meditates on this religious and historical dilemma of betweenness in "*Bandelette de Torah*," which commemorates an object—a band and cloak for dressing a Torah scroll, often set over an open scroll in between readings. This fabric was woven in 1761 by "Simhah, daughter of the cantor, Joseph Hay," and is housed in the Musée du Judaïsme in Paris. Looking at the bandelet in a case, Heller reflects, "The hunger was once for textured cloth, brocade / of thread, gold-webbed damask, tessellate fringe, / for sewn-in weight of lead or brass, . . . lost richness." During that time—presumably, the Enlightenment—"The cloth / lay over Europe's open scroll between Athens and Jerusalem" (394). Initially, then, the hunger is for ritual splendor, for celebratory richness amid the austerity of commandments. Behind that yearning, though, resides the desire to bridge the yawning chasm between the two poles of Western civilization, Athens and Jerusalem. Not just in the Enlightenment, when the bandelet was woven, but even up to the twentieth century, there was a "hunger" amid Jewish thinkers to find a language that would somehow stretch across the Diasporic abyss.

During the Holocaust, however, this project came crashing down, and as a consequence Heller finds that the hopeful words of putative reconciliation have instead been burned into the cloth: "Later, terrors / came to be its portion, flames beyond remonstrance, / synagogue and worshipper in ash. / . . . The words were as burls in woven cloth" (395). As though the cloth were a living tree and the words became wounded and rose up as burls (a near homonym for "burns"), the condition of betweenness symbolized by the bandelet is even more painful and fraught after World War II. Now, the woven words exist only "as from an echo / between hope and horror, between sacred sound / and profane air. Between Athens and Jerusalem and America" (395). The migrating senses of Jewish lostness in this poem arise first in the loss of the Enlightenment hope for reconciliation between Hebraism and Hellenism in America. This hope was initially expressed in the nineteenth century by Heinrich Heine, who coined the phrase "Hebraism and Hellenism," and it guided attempts—ultimately unsuccessful—by European Jewish cultural figures to find a language to bridge the gulf at the heart of Diaspora. As a metonym for the disastrous outcome of seeking a language sufficient to betweenness, Heller calls up "Celan in the Seine / with its syllabary" (395), as if the constituent syllables of the language of wished-for connection had been drowned in the 1970 suicide of the Holocaust-survivor poet. Like the other poets in *Radical Poetics and Secular Jewish Culture*, Heller carries over this perilous sense of betweenness from Europe to the United States as an unavoidable Diasporic inheritance.

In *Living Root* (2000), a book-length memoir of growing up in Brooklyn and Miami, Heller personalizes the double bind of betweenness by probing the linked themes of Jewishness and family, especially with regard to experiences of loss.[13] As a meditation on the genesis of poetry, *Living Root* can be placed fruitfully alongside Robert Duncan's two ambitious works of poetic memoir, *The Truth and Life of Myth* and *The H.D. Book*.[14] Like Duncan, Heller searches for the ground of poetry among the incidents of childhood, but what distinguishes their approaches is the family lore adopted by each poet. Duncan's theosophical upbringing instilled a sense that buried meanings were lurking everywhere in myth, folklore, and the literature of fantasy; what he heard from his family was an occult version of the standard parental refrain, "'You won't understand now, but you will later'" (*Essays* 146). Growing up in a Jewish family, mainly in Miami Beach during and after World War II, Heller was shadowed by buried meanings, too, but these vestiges seemed irretrievable as a result of familial experiences of exile—first from the Jewish community of Bialystok, in Poland, and then from New York City. Duncan's life and poetics took place within a horizon of constantly discoverable correlations. Heller's horizon, in contrast, is one of repeatedly revealed losses. Not only does he relive the twofold removal from Bialystok and Brooklyn, but he also finds himself in exile from the comforts of Jewish belief and ritual practice. His multifarious encounters with Diasporic loss tie him closely to Objectivist poets and to modern European poets and thinkers of Jewish exile, such as Benjamin, Celan, Gershom Scholem, Franz Rosenzweig, Martin Buber, Osip Mandelstam, Edmond Jabès, Jacques Derrida, and Primo Levi. In Heller's work, Judaism shoulders an elegiac burden: its intimations of order and redemption are always shadowed by loss—a condition for which his preferred term is "lostness," emphasizing not only incurring a loss but also dwelling within it.

In *Living Root*, Heller inquires how his poetry springs from lostness. To write poetry as a Jew, he explains, aware of a history of violent displacement,

> meant to write amidst ruins, to pipe on the reed of life in a charnel ground. . . . Thus, words, even as they participated in the realm of nostalgia and evoked golden ages, even as they brought glories and prides before the imagination, inscribed lostness. For Jewish practice, which consists of placing layer upon layer of borrowings and accretions, lostness made something cosmic out of dispersal and diaspora. (73)

For all his acute awareness of the centrality of loss to Jewish culture, Heller's poetry inscribes lostness in a unique way. It is not primarily a form of lamentation, deploring destruction and dispersal in all their horror and implacability, nor is it exactly the sort of Kabbalistic exercise in which the physical exigencies of exile infuse affect into a mystical yearning for cosmic reunion. His poetry resides at a slight remove from lament and mysticism while continuing to draw sustenance from them. To maintain this balance of participation and distance, Heller has recourse at critical moments to Buddhist notions of silence and emptiness, notions that do not contradict but rather enlarge his conception of Judaism as loss.

In the first of three sections of *Eschaton*, Heller explores the condition of lostness in a run of six poems treating the triad of Judaism, family, and poetry. In these poems—"The Heresy," "Disaporic Conundrums," "*Bandelette de Torah*," "The Language of the Jews," "East Hampton Meditations," and "The Chronicle Poet"—Jewish concerns emerge explicitly: three poems are grounded in biblical situations and a fourth concerns a ritual cover for a Torah scroll. In terms of family, Heller invokes fathers and mothers several times, as well as distant relatives, "lost with the words // and gathered again only by calling forth / one's family name" (*Collected Poems* 396). Finally, he probes what one poem calls "urgent words" (397), bringing into question the value and capacity of poetry itself. The Jewish lostness of these poems is something different from nostalgia or mourning for irreplaceable states, such as religious certitude, communal solidarity in ghettos and *shtetls*, familial relations in childhood, or an Adamic poetry of confident naming. Instead, the poems figure the state of lostness as a lack of concreteness or fixity, evoking evanescence and uncertainty using primarily images of rain, traceries, and words in air.

The first poem, "The Heresy," speaks of a belief that has melted away in a scientific and demythologizing era. A simple epigraph sets the scene: "*Exodus 20.25*," which reads (in the King James Version), "And if thou wilt make me an altar of stone, thou shalt not build it of hewn stone: for if thou lift up thy tool upon it, thou hast polluted it." The poem takes off from this injunction against craft:

> The god commanded a naked stone be set up
> and with no marks put upon it. But I had
> lost that god or it had become something
>
> like a rain one hears but does not see.
>
> (392)

These lines depict a precipitous decline in religious belief. Right from the outset, "god" is lower-cased, undercutting the force of his commandment to set up an unworked altar. The second sentence falls even further and faster by stating that the divinity who could utter a commandment is himself lost. Not only that, but he has vacated the visual modality and can only be imagined as a sound that is always draining away. Following upon the striking image of divinity dissolving into overheard rainfall, the poet clarifies that the "heresy" invoked by the title is not one of disobeying the Ten Commandments: "I / did not hunger after others, no graven images / to make, no divinities to carpenter out of air." In this seemingly pious avowal of the Second Commandment, Heller positions himself not as worshipper but more assertively as craftsman—as one who might engrave an image or "carpenter" a divinity. We may hear in these words echoes of claims by Blake or Nietzsche for the human invention of divinity, which would certainly be a heresy in traditional religious terms, and yet the poet hints at these possibilities while refraining from fully asserting a craftsman's role in relation to god. It appears from the first half of the poem that the heresy entails not following after "strange gods" but losing or nearly losing touch with divinity.

There is a significant swerve in the final two stanzas of the poem, from which the word "god" has completely disappeared:

I took silence into time, marking the absence
of our late vocabularies in their conspirings,
these new mythologies, as they fell from on high

through our skies and through our roofs
scouring the mind as cosmic rays leave
traceries in the cool white lime of tunnels.

This is a single sentence with one main clause, "I took silence into time," modified by a series of dependent clauses. The dependent clauses should spell out what is involved in the poet's taking silence into time, but at first glance the primary action of these two stanzas seems to occur not in the main clause but in those resting upon it. In the last four lines, what is absent in the main clause, the conspiratorial "new mythologies," becomes another kind of rain, like a shower of cosmic rays that inscribe an intricate pattern within the brain (for which "the cool white lime of tunnels" acts as metaphor). From the evidence of the dependent clauses in these two stanzas, it would appear that the heresy of the title has to do with accepting either scientific evidence or the hermeneutic skepticism of "our late vocabularies" as a reality more primary than the divine. For both kinds of knowledge, the word "traceries" is key, with its primary meaning of Gothic stonework and its connotations of atomic particle patterns, tracer bullets, and deconstructive traces. These would seem to be unavoidable sorts of knowledge in our modern world, "scouring the mind" even beyond one's volition.

Here is where we must return, though, to the main clause of this sentence for another look. Taking silence into time is a radical act of disengagement. It bespeaks the absence of these prestigious "late vocabularies" as much as it does the absence of the divine rain "one hears but does not see." Taking silence into time is a third way, neither theological nor skeptical, much like the Buddhist Third (or Middle) Way. In such a Buddhist approach, binaries dissolve, fixed beliefs and commandments melt, and scientific certainties and skeptical critiques, while recognized, do not become ultimate determinants. If I am right that the phrase "I took silence into time" marks the intrusion of Buddhist thinking into this poem, however, that does not make the thinking less Jewish. Buddhist nondualism functions here as a methodology for loosening the binding effects of grasping after certainty or resting in binaries. Heller is passionately attentive to issues of Jewish thinking and experience, across the entire spectrum from the Torah to the modern efflorescence of Jewish theorists, but he does not find this continuously self-interrogating tradition, no matter how capacious it may be, wholly adequate to his needs. As an approach to betweenness, a discipline of the Middle Way—of both this and that and neither this nor that—Buddhism squares perfectly with Heller's sense of Jewish lostness, in that it prevents him from idolizing any form of thought, no matter how subtle or seductive. From this perspective, even lamentation over what has been lost in Jewish history must ultimately be relinquished. This is Heller's heresy, to bring silence into time.

And in this meditative silence, which rests in a present moment both in and out of history, Heller joins a surprising number of American Jewish poets for whom the practice of Buddhism represents an enlargement, rather than a rejection, of Judaism. The grandfather of this cohort is Allen Ginsberg, who first approached Buddhism during his Beat days with Jack Kerouac and Gary Snyder and then, beginning in 1970, became a lifelong adherent of the Tibetan Buddhism taught by Chogyam Trungpa, Rinpoche. The Jack Kerouac School of Disembodied Poetics, which Ginsberg and Anne Waldman established in 1974 in Boulder, Colorado, at Trungpa's Naropa University, has been a lodestone for poets pursuing Buddhism, including Heller, who has taught and given readings there. Other prominent Jewish poets engaged in Buddhist practice include Armand Schwerner, Michael Brownstein, Norman Fischer (former abbot of the San Francisco Zen Center), Hank Lazer, Leonard Cohen, Stephen Mitchell, and Rodger Kamenetz. In *The Jew in the Lotus* (1994), Kamenetz chronicles an emblematic encounter between Jewish and Tibetan Buddhist communities, which, amid exchanges of mystical doctrines and rituals, was charged with the pragmatic question of how a religious tradition can survive generations of exile. (A hint taken by the Tibetans from the Jews: establish summer camps.) This book popularized the term "JuBu" to refer to Jewish practitioners of Buddhism.[15] As shown above, Heller's incorporation of Buddhism into Judaism, while not unique, is very subtle. Complementing his demonstrated reverence for Jewish texts and Jewish history, albeit from a secular perspective, Buddhism offers him not an alternative religious commitment but rather a kind of mental and spiritual hygiene, a set of practices and understandings that guard against rigid thinking and keep open opportunities for noniconic, antinomian spiritual discovery.

"BARELY UNPACKING THEIR BAGS"

Another poem in this set from *Eschaton*, "East Hampton Meditations," ties Jewish lostness to family and to poetry and also invites a Buddhist incursion. The opening section of the poem returns to the rain of "The Heresy," probing it for revelations not only about dissolving divinity but also about disappearing relatives and vanishing languages:

> It is night now in the world,
> and we are required to wake,
> to think of urgent words,

rain, lightning, fog
lingering past dark
and beading air.

To speak, perforce,
with desire
to form remembrance,

to make our ghosts
as though sense
caught something outside,

as though, in the rain,
one heard strange
muffled tones throughout the night.

(397)

This poem commences with an emphasis neither on divinity nor on modern thought but on words that might be adequate to speak to the "night now in the world," an unspecified darkness that Heller rightly assumes will be familiar to everyone now living. The "urgent words, // *rain, lightning, fog,*" stand for both the physical setting of the poem and the forces at work within the current night of the world. Rain represents the primary atmospheric condition in this section of the poem, but rather than echoing the rumor of a dissolving divinity, its "strange / muffled tones" seem like the lost speech of human beings.

The next section of the poem begins with a reference to Heller's parents and then proceeds to what sounds like a prayer or vow broken off: "*dead parents, / if you are not in my words—.*" It appears that the "urgent words" of this poem must contain not only descriptions of the dark times in which we live but also commemoration of dead parents. And yet words don't seem quite equal to either task because there is a compelling "urgency" during the night, which requires our arrival at "the moment // when we have / shed our words / as artifact" (398)—when we have stopped believing, that is, in the adequacy of the poem. Relinquishing the efficacy of poetry allows us to be "released / out of ourselves // as offshore / lightning rends sky and sea." Recognizing another urgency beyond "urgent words" prepares us for a stroke of light that cuts through the night and the liquid elements—including, in the next section, "the writing / [that] had been this fog / surrounding." If writing is both an urgent requirement of these dark times and an obscuring artifact that must be spurned for light to break through, then what exactly is writing? In section 5, Heller asks,

Why then begin to write,
but to bring back a life,
which, all confused,

is not for *now*
but to remind one
of the dead

or of those yet to come
who might utter
their necessities.

(399)

These lines could almost be a continuation of Rilke's *Duino Elegies*, with their questions about what humans can actually say to one another and to beings such as angels. Heller intimates, though, that writing cannot, no matter its urgency, affect the forces of the present moment. Its tasks might consist of remembering lost loved ones and preparing an opening for what matters to "those yet to come." Interestingly, for a secular poet, Heller also hints at addressing the Jewish afterlife, which is often designated as "the world yet to come."

In the final section of the poem, Buddhist thinking may obtrude again into the remembrance of a family and their Jewish past. The Buddhist mode colors a series of infinitives: "to walk between, / to feel emptiness as freedom, / to remember how one lived // only in silences" (400). In the subsequent line, Heller calls this series of infinitives "freshened astringencies," which is how the arduous yet releasing disciplines of Buddhism have often been characterized. For instance, in the introduction to *Beneath a Single Moon*, an anthology of American Buddhist poets to which Heller contributes, Gary Snyder specifies shared qualities in the poems: "They are unsentimental, not overly abstract, on the way toward selflessness, . . . on the dry side, kindhearted, unembarrassed, free of spiritual rhetoric and pretense of magic, and deeply concerned with questions of knowing."[16] Through the use of such "freshened astringencies," this poem returns to the Buddhist-inspired silence in time found in "The Heresy," walking carefully between alternatives, as a practicing Buddhist might do, and embracing emptiness as a form of freedom. Also, as in the earlier poem, traceries imprint on the mind, but this time they come from memory rather than cosmic rays:

Memory, which burned
in the dark grooves
of beclouded hours,

has left you riven
with traceries,
and having lost your way
you want to honor them.

(400)

In one sense, the traceries here are the sounds of the poetry, with the pattern of *r*s in “memory,” “burned,” “dark,” “grooves,” “hours,” “riven,” “traceries,” “your,” and “honor” interlacing with the long *u* sounds, as in “grooves,” “you,” “your,” and “you,” and the diphthong *ow* in “beclouded hours.” In his beclouded state, the poet chooses to honor memories inscribed upon the mind as images of lost parents, lost ancestors, and a lost Jewish way. Earlier in the poem, just before the truncated prayer to his dead parents, the poet invoked a memory of their visit to East Hampton: “Yes, my parents were here once, / barely unpacking their bags / before they had to leave” (398). Of course, the same could be said of all mortals, who barely have time to unpack our bags, it seems, before we have to leave. Heller's poetry does not endeavor to deny or compensate for inevitable loss—whether of ancestors, of parents, or of Judaism itself as sustaining atmosphere in which to conduct a life. But it does find, with the help of Buddhist thinking, urgent words that light up the lost way with traceries in the long, rainy night.

Heller's extensive attention to Jewish tradition, mysticism, and secular thought is matched by the subtle ways he establishes transactions with Buddhist doctrine and practice. He allows these various strains to rub up against one another to expose remarkable textures. As Heller himself recognizes, Rilke provides a compelling example of a European poet whose ability to dwell in (Christian) religious loss with spiritual ardor and existential candor matches his own. Even though George Oppen has been a consistent touchstone throughout Heller's career, and thus provides a ready model against which to measure his accomplishment, Rilke may well represent, as hinted in the reference above to the *Duino Elegies*, a more telling comparison, especially with respect to gauging the power of spirituality within the context of loss. Heller matches Rilke's simultaneous embrace of belatedness and newness, each one grappling with ways to honor and question both tradition and the new—and achieving a hard-won openness. In Heller's view, “Rilke through the course of his life sensed himself a kind of laborer in beginnings, in unending preparations for work still to come. This attitude was an essential part of his openness and receptivity. . . . And yet, it also brought with it a thirst for great precision.”[17] As Heller contemplates his experiences of Jewish lostness and the sustenance offered by the precision of Buddhist “astringencies,” his apt depiction of the preparatory attitude animating Rilke's work can stand as canny self-description.

POETRY & ITS TIME:
REVISING LITERARY HISTORY

4

"And All Now Is War"

George Oppen, Charles Olson, and Literary Generations

The convenient notion of literary generations has been an essential component of the unavoidably fictional (or at least conjectural) structure of literary history, tending to separate it from history proper. Within the larger notion of periods, named generations have been used as markers in the building of an orderly narrative of innovation, struggle, triumph, and succession. By means of this generational narrative, we have been able to tell ourselves stories about "literature" as a self-enclosed entity that constitutes its own world, ignoring its transactions with the larger world. Historical fact, though, can step in and disturb the recounting of comforting tales of dynastic succession—as, for instance, the fact that Keats and Carlyle were both born in 1795. This fact can stand as synecdoche for the plethora of historical realities that has upset the period narratives of Romanticism and Victorianism and caused a wholesale revision of thinking about nineteenth-century English literature. In addition to their historical overlap, "Romantic" and "Victorian" are not equivalent names, either, for "Romantic" hovers between being a generational and a period term, and it was used traditionally to designate the works of six male poets, while "Victorian" was used in less generational senses to cover a longer period and a much greater diversity of female and male writers of poetry, prose, and fiction. Journals such as *New Literary History* (1970–present) and *American Literary History* (1989–present) have dedicated themselves to working out questions of literary periods and of the relationships of literary works to their historical moments. This essay joins the conversation by looking specifically at how the division of poets into discrete generations can obscure our ability to read the complex interrelations among them across the reified boundaries of generations.

In situating the poetry of the twentieth and twenty-first centuries, poets and critics have been anxious to identify and promote literary movements and to give these movements generational traits. When poets fashion a movement and ascribe certain qualities to it, critics often follow suit by grouping the poets together and by interpreting the poetry solely through lenses ground by the poets. When critics seek to describe and classify poets, they feel an almost magnetic attraction to adopting the generational terms supplied. One way to resist such enclosure is to explore the historical factors behind the invention of specific generational narratives. For example, Lawrence Rainey has demonstrated two pressing personal and social exigencies behind Ezra Pound's promotion of imagism as a movement: the collapse of the means he had worked out to secure a livelihood, and his observation of Marinetti's spectacular success in commodifying futurism while in London from 1912 to 1914.[1] Witnessing the efficacy of generational discourse for obtaining a hearing (and a living) for new writers, Pound then passed along this public relations tip to other poets. A full thirty pages of the Pound/Zukofsky correspondence in 1930, for instance, are taken up with dialogue about how Zukofsky might position the "Objectivists" issue of *Poetry* to market a new generation.[2] Charles Olson inaugurated another Poundian generation in 1950 with his platform essay for *Poetry New York*, "Projective Verse," whose composition occupies much of the first 220 pages of the Olson/Creeley correspondence.[3] Literary historians have been only too happy to follow the lead of these two aggressive forays into public relations, thereby reifying objectivism and projectivism as two distinct and successive generations in American poetry. In this regard, it is instructive to ponder how this received literary history might differ had the critic L. S. Dembo not decided to make the reconstruction of Objectivism a central focus of his 1968 interviews with George Oppen, Carl Rakosi, Charles Reznikoff, and Louis Zukofsky,[4] thus reviving interest in a movement that was largely forgotten, or had editor Donald Allen not put forward Charles Olson, the Black Mountain poets, and "Projective Verse" as headliners for his 1960 anthology *The New American Poetry*.[5] Such editorial decisions often have everything to do with creating literary-historical narratives.

I would like to throw a wrench into the assembly line that moves from an objectivist generation, launched in 1931, to a projectivist one, announced in 1950. The easiest way to begin is to introduce the historical fact that Oppen and Olson were born two years apart, in 1908 and 1910, respectively. Glossing over this potential anomaly by designating Oppen the youngest objectivist and Olson the eldest projectivist has served the generational narrative, but it has done so at the cost of distorting the careers of the poets by framing them solely within the decades in which the generations with which they are associated came to light. In the old view, Oppen is read as a man of the 1930s, for whom the Great Depression, populism, and communism are defining issues, and Olson as a man of the 1950s, enmeshed in the Cold War and the nascent counterculture. Such contexts demonstrably aid understanding of certain facets of the poets' careers, but choosing to read the poetry exclusively through the concerns of one decade proves unnecessarily restrictive, obscuring a number of similarities in the works of Oppen and Olson. As one way to rectify this, I would like to focus on World War II as an intermediary time crucial for both poets. The primary event of the 1940s, the war's huge bulk has not been adequately weighed in the generation-bound history of avant-garde American poetry.

In a century of horrors, World War II holds pride of place for the United States as the most devastating event, both for the number of combatants killed and for the social and psychological strains of total mobilization and of coping afterward with the unthinkable destruction caused by the Holocaust and the atomic bombing of Hiroshima and Nagasaki. This decisive era must be accounted for more fully to render an accurate history not just of the poetry of that time but also of the subsequent poetry produced by those who lived through it. Oppen and Olson participated in the war in different but vital ways—Oppen as soldier, wounded fighting in France, and Olson as propagandist in Washington, DC, working for the Office of War Information. Right off the bat, thinking about the impact of the war on Oppen allows him to escape from the small room labeled as "Objectivism." In some measure, Hugh Kenner can be held responsible for constricting its dimensions with his unfortunately memorable statement: "The Objectivists seem to have been born mature, not to say middle-aged."[6] This image of prematurely wizened poets—who felt, Kenner says, "that the arts ought not to exhilarate, save austerely, and moreover that in a gray time (1931) they had best be gray" (168)—is nothing but a caricature. It contrasts vividly, for example, with Mary Oppen's portrait of George's energetic determination to enter the army in 1944 at age thirty-six: "He was overage for the draft, but he wanted to go. . . . He went in as a responsible Jew, who someone was trying to wipe out and he was not going to stand still."[7]

This hardly sounds like a man who, thirteen years before, had slipped into premature middle age. Nor does the poetry Oppen wrote after the war (which includes all but his short, precocious first book, *Discrete Series* [1934], and a recently discovered book that supplements it) sit comfortably in the imagist tradition of American poetry that Kenner was so instrumental in delineating.[8] In fact, the staggering pressures Oppen exerts upon language, thought, and the verse line bring him much nearer to the younger European poet Paul Celan (1920–1970) than to Pound or Williams (both born in the 1880s). As a Jew whose military unit liberated a concentration camp, Oppen "certainly saw those horrors firsthand" (Young 37), so that the world of "that which happened," as Celan designates the Holocaust, was not at all distant from the threatened facticity of "this in which" Oppen set his writing.[9] Another crucial formative influence for Oppen and Celan—one that the war complicated considerably for each—was the philosophy of Martin Heidegger.[10] Both poets found compelling his probing of the relationship between language, thought, and being, yet each fought off his callousness toward human suffering, striving instead to enunciate an ethics of caring appropriate to a shattered world.[11]

Taking into account Oppen's experience of World War II and his connection to Heidegger, a strong case can be made for thinking him an existentialist rather than an objectivist—or else to expand the definition of objectivism far beyond the pallid epithet "second-generation imagism." One index of the difference it makes when we think of Oppen this way concerns his commitment to "the real" or "the actual." Is it right to assume that these terms rely on an earlier imagist hygiene, prescribing an accurate visual representation of things, or that they draw on the impressionist equation of visual data with emotional states? During an interview with the Oppens that includes discussion of Camus, Sartre, and Heidegger, Kevin Power requests, "talk about 'actualness' and how that enters the poem." George replies, "Well there's that prose section of Pierre Adam in 'Route' when he tells me about his experience. I was conscious, when I wrote that, that any of the existentialists could have written it. I wrote it, nevertheless, because it was actually what he said to me. Existential in the sense that you do what you do and that is the answer. . . . Simply that you are yourself."[12] The story was told to him in Alsace, where he was fighting in the Battle of the Bulge. Many Alsatian men, upon learning they had been drafted into the German army, dug themselves holes in the ground, in which they hid for as long as two or three years. When the Germans learned that men were in hiding, they made reprisals, killing family members and sending wives to the army brothels in Germany. Pierre fed and assisted the men in the holes. "Men would come to Pierre and they would say: I am thinking of making a hole. Pierre would say: yes. They would say then: but if I do they will kill my parents; or: they will take my wife and my children. Then Pierre would say, he told me: if you dig a hole, I will help you" (Oppen, *Collected* 195).

For Oppen, this kind of terrifying existential choice defines the realm of the "actual." This was the actuality faced by French resistance fighters such as Sartre and Camus, and it remained the (usually unstated) background for their existential philosophies. In this sense, the actual encompasses not only the everyday—a realm associated with the objectivists—but also the most extreme experiences imaginable. Turning to Olson, his essay "The Resistance" provides something like a gloss on Pierre Adam's story, asserting that the horrors of World War II have rendered the body the only meaningful instrument of resistance: "When man is reduced to so much fat for soap, superphosphate for soil, fillings and shoes for sale, he has, to begin again, one answer. . . . It is his body that is his answer."[13] Olson claims that bodily acts of resistance, like those of the Alsatians, propel human beings to think concretely through the body rather than through such dangerous abstractions as nation, race, and class. In "Causal Mythology," a talk given at the 1965 Berkeley Poetry Conference, Olson avers, "I don't believe in cultures myself. I think that's a lot of hung up stuff like organized anything. I believe there is simply ourselves, and where we are has a particularity which we'd better use because that's about all we've got. . . . Put an end to nation, put an end to culture, put an end to divisions of all sorts."[14] This notion that large abstractions are specious and that what we think and do must be grounded instead in who and where we actually are jibes perfectly with Oppen's recounting of Pierre Adam's story as existential: "Existential in the sense that you do what you do and that is the answer. . . . Simply that you are yourself."

Although Olson did not fight in the war, he read daily dispatches in Washington, and they directed his thinking along lines that could be called existential. A pivotal example occurs in the aphorism around which he organized his talk, "Causal Mythology": "That which exists through itself is what is called meaning" (*Muthologos* 122). This proposition, that nothing real can be known or done outside one's actual situation, can function as a ready synopsis of existentialist metaphysics and epistemology. When Olson expressed it at the Berkeley Poetry Conference, Oppen received a report from a friend. Writing back, Oppen comments, "Olson's [']that which seems to exist in itself we call meaning['] is a good statement of the thing— . . . That which exists of itself can not be explained it cannot be analyzed, it is the object of contemplative thought, it is known by 'indwelling.' The Given. 'things explain each other / Not themselves.'"[15] The last phrase consists of two lines from Oppen's poem "A Narrative" (*Collected* 151). As he recognizes, these poets share a notion of resistance that extends from the political to the epistemological and is grounded in the inexplicable actuality of people and things. From this perspective, knowledge and action rest solely on individual self-awareness, and yet they bear endless transactional ramifications for society at large. Both poets insist there finally is no substitute for the existential encounter. As Olson jokes ruefully in "Causal Mythology," "You're simply stuck with the original visionary experience of having been you, which is a hell of a thing" (*Muthologos* 122).[16]

In his poetry before *The Maximus Poems*, Olson consistently weighs the effects of the wreckage of World War II on thought and action. There is a recurrent preoccupation with the dead, found in the dream world of "As the Dead Prey Upon Us" or in the opening of "La Préface," an inaugural poem that evokes the concentration camps as the primal backdrop to Olson's setting forth on a new poetry. No matter in what direction the poet turns, the dead cannot be ignored:

The dead in via
          in vita nuova
                    in the way[17]

Not only does he find the way toward a new poetry (and a "new life," alluding to Dante's inaugural poem sequence) blocked, but he must also stop immediately to read what the dead have said—what might be called "the writing on the wall":

"I will die about April 1st . . ." going off
"I weigh, I think, 80 lbs . . ." scratch
"My name is NO RACE" address
Buchenwald new Altamira cave
With a nail they drew the object of the hunt.

(46)

The walls of the concentration camp at Buchenwald provide a palimpsest upon which the new poetry will be inscribed, as though the poet's task were to reenter a Paleolithic cave to begin imagining a new humanity. Changing the image but remaining fixed on the dead of World War II, Olson finds "among the DPs—deathhead / at the apex / of the pyramid" (46). In a sense, everyone after the war is a "DP," a displaced person.[18] This implies that for a culture to emerge from the ashes of war and aspire to a foundational art, such as the cave art of Altamira or the pyramids of Egypt or Mexico, new work must be conceived as a kind of projective funerary art. For, as the Antigone of Sophocles might have said, using Olson's words, "We are born not of the buried but these unburied dead" (47). Likewise, his most famous poem, "The Kingfishers," explores mysterious rites in Greece and Mexico through a Heraclitean acknowledgment of the universal condition of war (for Heraclitus, "war is the father of all"). In the midst of depicting "the priests / (in dark cotton robes, and dirty / their dishevelled hair matted with blood, and flowing wildly / over their shoulders)," who urge the Mexicans to protect their gods against the invading Spaniards, Olson turns aside to utter a general statement:

And all now is war
where so lately there was peace,
and the sweet brotherhood, the use
of tilled fields.

(*Collected Poems* 89)

Based on the shared experience that when "all now is war" everything has changed and that what it means to be human is something new and newly terrifying, Olson and Oppen undertake to write a new poetry. In locating their common ground, I do not mean to suggest that they worked in conjunction. Olson seems to have kept his distance from Oppen, writing to William Bronk in 1962: "I do know Oppen, and though some of my friends thought his review of *The Distances* and *Maximus from Dogtown* . . . was the old business of measuring me by Pound, and I thought myself he raced his motor on *Maximus from Dogtown,* I thought his picking 'The Satyrs' for a voice which was peculiarly my own, true enough. (I haven't yet seen his poems at all . . .)."[19] In the review, Oppen states, "*Maximus from Dogtown* is obviously not part of Olson's best work," but he praises the volume of selected shorter poems, *The Distances*: "What is happening in these poems is that the poet is speaking: they are a discourse, always beautifully modeled and beautifully constructed."[20] According to John Crawford, one of Oppen's most frequent correspondents, he distrusted Olson's egotism. In return, Olson imagined that Oppen's metaphysics precluded a careful attention to history: "I want to open / Mr. Oppen / The full inherited file / of history."[21] Speaking to L. S. Dembo in 1968, Oppen says, "I've read a lot of Olson. I think 'In Cold Hell, In Thicket' is a very fine poem. I don't really like the *Maximus Poems* nor accept them at all" (Dembo and Pondrom 184). It is not surprising that these ambitious poets would seek to circumscribe their points of contact, or that each might find the other deficient politically or philosophically or in historical knowledge.

Despite this, some striking similarities appear when we consider the impact of World War II. For example, although both poets engaged extensively in practical politics stretching back to the 1930s, they left political activism after the war and began to use poetry for espousing a political philosophy shot through with metaphysics and epistemology. This led them to persistently ponder the relationship between the individual and the collective. Oppen's most famous poem, "Of Being Numerous," explores the demands and conflicts and accommodations inherent to the twin human conditions of being "singular" and being "numerous." Olson poses in *The Maximus Poems* an ideal community, which he denominates "the polis" and which achieves collective action only through the responsible endeavors of individuals. In conjunction with the affirmation of resistant individuality noted earlier, there is after World War II a newfound urgency for both poets to speak for the entirety of what Robert Duncan calls "the company of the living."[22] Oppen's use of the first-person plural in "Of Being Numerous" testifies to this desire, as does Olson's project of placing the present at the crosshairs of vast stretches of time and space in *The Maximus Poems.* Ultimately, the poets adopt what might be called a wary prophetic stance, addressing crises of contemporary life in terms not beholden to the old rallying points of religion or nation. I say "wary" to mark the disavowal of received concepts, as though it were necessary not only to save the world but also to reinvent the terms by which it is known. Formally, this stance results in the truncating of syntax and line, creating disruptions that make readers, too, practice vigilance against falling into the easy epistemological grooves the poets roundly condemn. And stylistically, they craft poetry out of notebooks and correspondence, causing an oscillation between lyric and didactic modes of address that keeps form spontaneous and knowledge existential.[23]

Does acknowledging the striking similarities in the poetry and poetics of George Oppen and Charles Olson mean that we should discard completely generational terms like "objectivism" and "projectivism"? I don't think so. I am urging not abolition but rather a more inclusive historicizing. Inevitably, this would involve also exploring the historical exigencies that contribute to coining and maintaining generational terms like "objectivism" and "projectivism," just as much as it would necessitate a more careful historical placement of the works of individual poets and more specific comparisons of poets based upon their responses to particular circumstances. As a practical matter, we need no longer settle for the shopworn clichés that objectivism is concerned solely with the "object" and projectivism is largely a poetry of "process." Instead of unthinking acceptance of the critical value of such generational tags, why not conduct literary history as the more exacting practice that Louis Zukofsky recommended in 1931: "thinking with the things as they exist."[24]

5

"The Lordly and Isolate Satyrs"

Charles Olson's Contemporaries

The centennial of Charles Olson's birth in 2010 provoked a spate of conferences devoted to reassessing his work and its legacy. After his early death in 1970, at age fifty-nine, he was one of the first of the New American poets to receive attention in journal issues and monographs, but then he fell abruptly out of critical fashion and, as for many literary figures, the celebration of his centennial began the process of reconsideration. Of the poets I have written about repeatedly—which would include Olson, Robert Creeley, Robert Duncan, Ed Dorn, Charles Reznikoff, and David Antin—Olson is the only one I neither met nor saw perform, nor had I seen Gloucester, Massachusetts, the site of *The Maximus Poems*, until 2010. As much as the generational narrative promulgated by Donald Allen's *New American Poetry* presented the principle Black Mountain poets, Olson, Creeley, Duncan, and Levertov, as inseparable, Olson himself was inseparable from Gloucester. After delivering a talk in Boston during the flurry of centennial reexaminations, I was able to hop on a train for the hour ride to Cape Ann. Peter Anastas, a Gloucester writer mentored by Olson, met me at the station. Rather than merely point in the direction of the harbor and Olson's apartment, as I had expected, Peter and his partner offered a guided tour of the fishing town, which was larger and more visually compelling than I had imagined. As a port, it has provided subject matter, I learned, for painters from Fitz Hugh Lane and Winslow Homer to Edward Hopper, Stuart Davis, Marsden Hartley, and Mark Rothko. One look at the spectacular horseshoe sweep of the harbor confirms its attraction. I was grateful to be shown the harbor, the beach, and a bit of Dogtown, all of which constitute the intimate geography on which Olson wandered as historian, dreamer, and mythographer. It was on the beach, though in a dream, that he sighted "the lordly and isolate satyrs."

"DRYING OF IT OUT, SHIFTING IT INTO THE REAL"

In 1962, George Oppen ended his review of Charles Olson's *The Distances* and *Maximus from Dogtown* with the pronouncement: "Perhaps we should look to such poems as *The Lordly and Isolate Satyrs*, in which the voice and eye are his alone, for the best prediction of Olson's future work."[1] To which Olson replied in a letter to William Bronk (21 December 1962): "I thought [Oppen's] picking 'The Satyrs' for a voice which was peculiarly my own, true enough."[2] Donald Allen also selected the poem to lead off the fourth issue of *Evergreen Review* (1958) and included it as part of the group of Olson poems to which he gave pride of place in *The New American Poetry* (1960). If the poem appears uniquely or representatively Olson's, its monumental figure of a motorcycle club also locates him at the heart of the transitional moment of the late 1950s and early 1960s, a time in which Cold War anxieties provoked new forms of rebellion such as the Birth of the Cool, the Beat movement, the civil rights movement, and rock and roll.[3] As Joel Dinerstein points out, the emergence of "cool" at this time braids French existentialism and American jazz and film noir into a new style of social rebellion: "In the postwar era, to be cool meant negotiating a resistant mode of being in the world. And the *origins* of cool—as of nearly all art and aesthetics—can be found in the transmutation of pain and loss into something dynamic and uplifting" (5).

In keeping with this style, the poem can be seen as both a deeply personal meditation and a declaration of allegiance to the resistant counterculture beginning to form in the United States. With antecedents in two of Olson's main predecessors, Herman Melville and William Carlos Williams, "The Lordly and Isolate Satyrs" is at once a visionary dream poem and a social document of its moment. Olson's invocation of the motorcycle club moves beyond the aesthetic boundaries we have imagined for the Black Mountain and *Origin* coteries, situating the poem equally within the emerging Beat movement, where it can be compared to Allen Ginsberg's anthem "Howl" (1955–1956), with its "saintly motorcyclists," Robert Frank's demotic photographs in *The Americans* (1958, 1959), Kenneth Anger's gay motorcycle film *Scorpio Rising* (1964), and the social posture of cool rebellion in Hollywood movies and pop songs of the era. Placing Olson within Beat and pop precincts helps to correct the image of him as an ostrich with his head buried in the library and makes evident his desire to join in countercultural breakouts.

Composed in April 1956, "The Lordly and Isolate Satyrs" is based on a dream. A serious reader of Freud and Jung, Olson regarded dreams as imbued with essential psychic information unobtainable by other means.[4] Consequently, the poem's narrative voice bears the hallmarks of dream transcriptions, in which, as though speaking in both third and first persons (brought together at times in the first-person plural), the narrator witnesses and at the same time participates in the events related. As in several striking and mysterious poems Olson wrote during this time, including "As the Dead Prey Upon Us" and "The Librarian," "The Lordly and Isolate Satyrs" goes beyond recounting a dream to register associations and interpretations, both personal and cultural, suggested by contemplating the dream images. It may well be that what drew Oppen to the poem was Olson's expert mining of dream matter in a variety of narrative and lyrical registers, since Oppen himself had recently resumed writing poetry at the urging of a dream.[5] Not enough has been made, though, of Olson's extensive dreamwork. The poet himself was so taken with the three poems mentioned above and a fourth dream poem, "A Newly Discovered 'Homeric' Hymn," that in his correspondence with Donald Allen about a volume of selected poems—which eventually became *The Distances* (1960)—he proposes starting the book with these "fresh" poems and naming it *The Lordly and Isolate Satyrs*.[6] One might argue that Olson's poetry oscillates between the poles of dream and scholarship. The scholarship has been traced expertly by Robert von Hallberg, George Butterick, and Ralph Maud, but Olson's expansive dream meditations have not been accorded similar attention, nor has there been much analysis of how dreams mingle with history, geography, mythology, and philosophy in the complex transactions of his verse. Overemphasis by critics on epic (historical) and didactic (philosophical) styles have obscured Olson's accomplishments as dream explorer and more broadly as lyric poet.

A contemporary report reinforces the importance of dreams for Olson and articulates his difficulty in presenting them convincingly in poetry. In *Black Mountain Days: A Memoir*, Michael Rumaker, a student from 1952 to 1955, offers carefully drawn portraits of his teacher, with whom he remained in close contact after leaving the college. Rumaker confirms, "Charles was deeply fascinated with dreams." In particular, he was "preoccupied with the problem, the puzzle, of how one could dynamically and structurally assimilate dream content into a poem without its 'being boring, like when we simply tell our dreams,' as he put it in class. He later demonstrated how to do this in poems, such as 'As the Dead Prey Upon Us,' which he considered a breakthrough, . . . and 'The Librarian.'"[7] In a letter about one of Rumaker's dream poems, Olson makes explicit his exacting standards for working with dreams in poetry:

> It raises the whole problem of how one gets dream material to avoid its own obviousness. And I take it the rule is the turning of it—drying of it out, shifting it into the real—has to be done by a means of the poem itself, not by exterior devices: such as, in this one of yrs, the coffeee [*sic*] afterwards. That is, you are merely placing it over arbitrarily into the real. Carrying it across. But not changing it, by the act of writing. Thus it too stays description: doesn't get reanimated in another form than the dream-form (the hardest form, I suppose, to force writing to undo, and recreate its own. (175)

Turning from Olson's considered use of dreams to his lyricism, one sees at the outset that the title of "The Lordly and Isolate Satyrs" strikes a lyrical note, employing diction that connotes nobility and classical mythology. In particular, the word "isolate"—rather than "isolated"—stands out. Although it has an antique sound, it is a fairly recent word whose first citation in the *OED* dates from 1819. In Olson's usage, it derives most likely from two of his primary sources, Melville and Williams.[8] Melville famously coined the term "Isolato" to describe the seafaring crew in *Moby-Dick*: "They were nearly all Islanders in the Pequod, *Isolatoes* too, I call such, not acknowledging the common continent of men, but each *Isolato* living on a separate continent of his own."[9] There is nothing surprising in Olson's borrowing this term, since the principles of resistance and self-containment evinced by the dramatis personae of the *Pequod* ultimately make their way to the heart of Olson's poetics and ethics. In *The Grounding of American Poetry: Charles Olson and the Emersonian Tradition*, I argue at length for containment as a primary poetic mode through which, paradoxically, Olson endeavors to engage the world.[10] He echoes Melville's equation of "*Isolatoes*" with "Islanders" when he declares *The Maximus Poems* addressed to the self-contained individuals he finds in his own community: "Isolated person in Gloucester, Massachusetts, I Maximus, address you / you islands / of men and girls."[11] In addition to cribbing Melville's extravagant lyrical diction in "The Lordly and Isolate Satyrs," Olson mimics him and other predecessors such as Hart Crane and Edward Dahlberg by employing this diction subversively to at once amplify and ironically deflate figures from vernacular culture—including the motorcycle club in the present poem.

Likewise concerned with resistant isolation, Williams employs high diction much more sparingly than Melville. In one of his most complex meditations on social worlds, "To Elsie" (1923), Williams uses the term "isolate" twice. At the outset, he locates "The pure products of America" who "go crazy" in remote and in-grown communities:

> mountain folk from Kentucky
>
> or the ribbed north end of
> Jersey
> with its isolate lakes and
>
> valleys[.][12]

In this instance, the "isolate lakes and // valleys" separate people who live among them from society at large. By the end of the poem, the term "isolate" no longer refers to social confinement or containment but rather to the discreteness and rarity of a precious object:

> It is only in isolate flecks that
> something
> is given off[.] (219)

The salvific "something"—an indefinable and uncontrollable vividness that shines "in isolate flecks"—takes refuge in a rural folk culture that repels cosmopolitan influence. With neither high culture nor any "peasant traditions to give them / character" (217), these "pure products of America" are left to populate their imaginations solely with images from commercial culture. The ominous and enigmatic final stanza of the poem, "No one / to witness / and adjust, no one to drive the car" (219), can be read as lamenting the certainty that isolate flecks of beauty, though exuberant and bearing the nation's precarious aesthetic hopes, inevitably must go astray within a popular culture dominated, in the 1920s, by the automobile.

If "To Elsie" recognizes that one social response to the Machine Age can be found in the "devil-may-care men who have taken / to railroading / out of sheer lust of adventure" (217), "The Lordly and Isolate Satyrs" pinpoints a similar response to the furious industrialization that occurred during and after World War II. Olson memorializes the motorcycle club as a resistant social nexus newly emergent in popular culture, dressing his satyrs in the cool guise of Marlon Brando in *The Wild One* (1953) or James Dean in *Rebel Without a Cause* (1955).[13] The poem begins:

> The lordly and isolate satyrs—look at them come in
> on the left side of the beach
> like a motorcycle-club! And the handsomest of them,
> the one who has a woman, driving that snazzy
> convertible
>   Wow, did you ever see even in a museum
> such a collection of boddisatvahs [*sic*], the way
> they come up to their stop, each of them
> as though it was a rudder
> the way they have to sit above it
> and come to a stop on it, the monumental solidity
> of themselves, the Easter Island
> they make of the beach, the Red-headed Men
>
>   These are the Androgynes,
> the Fathers behind the father, the Great Halves
>
> (CP 384)

Olson portrays a set of male cyclists (with only one woman, who accompanies the leader with the "snazzy" convertible) in awe-inspiring terms, comparing them not only to ithyphallic satyrs but also to monumental Asian bodhisattva sculptures, to the massive stone statues of Easter Island, to the androgynes of Aristophanes's myth recounted in Plato's *Symposium* (whose splitting in half accounts for the human need to reunite with a perfect mate), to the Fathers in Freud's theory of culture as dependent on fratricide, and (further on in the poem) to angels. As the poem continues, Olson bestows on these mysterious, singular figures a garland of hypostasizing epithets: "Red-headed Men," "Great Halves," "Themselves," "the lonely ones," "Source," "The Visitors," "Resters," and most tellingly, "the Contemporaries" (CP 384–87). As much as the epithets point to ontological qualities, they also resonate with names for mid-1950s musical groups, such as The Clovers, The Four Lads, The Drifters, The Del-Vikings, and The Coasters. Finally, Olson equates the dream motorcyclists who show up on Gloucester beach with sailors, comparing the choreography of their swiveling to a stop to the way a sailboat comes about to dock.

The tone of this opening section is characteristic of Olson's style at its most exuberant: humorous overstatement, sexual provocation, and the blending of diction (high: "lordly," "handsomest"; and vernacular: "Wow," "snazzy"). All these qualities meet in the service of an edgy yet tenacious pursuit of mythical powers lying within the purview of modern life. Depicting his satyrs as members of a motorcycle club presents a ripe opportunity for such agitated mythologizing. They could be characters, for instance, in a new Homeric Hymn, on the order of the Homeric Hymn to Dionysus—in which the god looks like a human boy to a gang of pirates, but once carried aboard a ship lets loose a murderous flow of wine, an uncontrollable growth of ivy, and a ferocious lion and bear. And indeed, Olson prized the early Greek poetry of Hesiod and the Homeric Hymns as models for the encounter of humans with elemental, untamed forces, using the title "A Newly Discovered 'Homeric' Hymn" (CP 363–64) for the dream poem that directly precedes "The Lordly and Isolate Satyrs" in *The New American Poetry*. In each instance, he adopts a lyrical posture of greeting and supplication with respect to the dangerous, more-than-mortal beings encountered. At the opening of "A Newly Discovered 'Homeric' Hymn" he proclaims, "Hail and beware the dead who will talk life until you are blue / in the face" (363). In "The Lordly and Isolate Satyrs," he begins one stanza with "Hail the ambiguous Fathers" (CP 385) and the next stanza with "Hail them, and watch out." In each poem, he salutes entities both familiar and threatening, harbingers of emergent powers (the dead, the Fathers) that Olson must account for both personally and as a watchman for society at large.

In an extensive and compelling discussion of this poem, Rachel Blau DuPlessis echoes Michael Davidson's more general accusation that Olson attends too exclusively to the Fathers and thus removes women from the possibility of poetic action.[14] "The word 'hail,'" DuPlessis contends, "now theoretically marked by its status in an Althusserian understanding of subjectivity, is precisely germane" to a reading of the poem as a rite of masculine initiation: "As the speaker pays ritualized homage to the figures of the motorcycle gang that he has conjured from his own dream, these figures from his own subconscious are 'hailing' him—calling him into an enriched maleness. The poem offers a narrative in which this onlooker, at first awestruck and fearful of the 'monumental solidity' and phallic totality of these invaders, ends by an identification with them."[15] DuPlessis's forceful interpretation of the poem as a drama of wish-fulfillment, in which Olson identifies with the patriarchal power displayed on the beach in his dream, can be deepened and extended by looking closely at the contexts of the poem's publication and by listening carefully to the varieties of tone within it. Although Olson may be "hailed" in an Althusserian sense by masculine dream figures, he also issues cautionary commands to himself: "beware" and "watch out." Likewise, his evocation of a motorcycle club can be interpreted not only as a desire to take on the mantle of the father but also as a plea to enter the brotherhood of the newly emergent counterculture.

"ANOTHER MAN WHO HAS COVERED YOU LIKE YOUR OWN SKIN"

In its first publication, "The Lordly and Isolate Satyrs" led off the fourth issue of *Evergreen Review*. By virtue of the journal's fame and wide circulation and the prominence of the poem in this issue, it was, in Ralph Maud's estimation, "Olson's most conspicuous publication to that date."[16] A pioneering literary quarterly issued in print runs of 100,000, *Evergreen Review* was launched in 1957, the year of the trial of *Howl and Other Poems* and of the publication of *On the Road*. It presented translations of mid-century French literature and existentialist philosophy, in company with the outsider American verse that its coeditor Donald Allen would soon christen the "New American Poetry." In the early issues of the journal, Allen highlighted the emerging avant-garde poets and locales he would feature in his epoch-making anthology. The second issue, for instance, titled "San Francisco Scene," garnered notoriety for its depiction of the city as a new cultural capital and home to the San Francisco Renaissance and to what Kenneth Rexroth in the opening essay calls, somewhat facetiously, "the New Generation of Revolt and Our Underground Literature and Cultural Disaffiliation"—shortly to be dubbed the Beat movement.[17] The most influential editor of avant-garde poets during this period, Allen was so taken with the force and authority of Olson's writing that he made a long-term commitment to publishing it, beginning with the 1958 Grove Press reprint of Olson's first book, *Call Me Ishmael*, and continuing with a generous selection of his poems and "Projective Verse," which led off, respectively, the poetry and the poetics sections of *The New American Poetry* (1960).[18]

Olson's prominence in the anthology as spokesperson for the coterie to which he is assigned has been remarked often enough, but confining him to the scope of Black Mountain College and the associated journals, *Black Mountain Review* and *Origin*, blinds us to the wider milieu in which he acted. When seen in the historical context of *Evergreen Review*'s first four issues, "The Lordly and Isolate Satyrs" appears simply as part of the emerging American counterculture that would first coalesce in the 1950s and then burgeon dramatically in the 1960s. Initially, the heuristic labels that Allen enshrined to designate communities in his anthology (formed in conversation, and sometimes disagreement, with Olson, Duncan, and others [Golding 185–96]) were necessary for situating forty-four nearly unpublished poets. The provisional groupings—"Black Mountain," "San Francisco Renaissance," "Beat Generation," and "New York School"—have since reified as badges worn to proclaim affiliation. Compartmentalizing poets so strictly obscures how often those from supposedly distinct groups met and conversed with, corresponded with, gave readings with, published with, learned from, disagreed with, and defended one another. As Olson himself remarks in his 1965 "Reading at Berkeley":

> You know, it never was true that San Francisco was the source of the revolution or the *Evergreen Review*. And I think it's only been made accurate, as, in fact (if I may criticize my own editor and publisher), the divisions of *The New American Poetry* weren't accurate either. That, as Mr Dorn carefully said to me (and I urged Mr Allen, in a sense, not to divide his book that way, not by places) has been divisive.[19]

In fact, at the time Olson met Allen in Gloucester, Massachusetts, in 1957, Black Mountain College had closed and the *Black Mountain Review* had ceased publication. Olson made a momentous visit that year to San Francisco, and his letters to Allen in the late 1950s show how strongly he identified there not only with Duncan but also with Ginsberg, Kerouac, Philip Whalen, Gary Snyder, and Michael McClure. Duncan, who had already begun to affiliate with Black Mountain poetics, had been instrumental for a decade in convening the San Francisco Renaissance, an important background for the Beat movement—with which the other poets mentioned were aligned. At this time, too, Olson met with Robin Blaser, who was living in Boston and introduced Olson to Allen. He encountered New Yorkers, such as LeRoi Jones (Amiri Baraka), who also published Olson extensively, and Frank O'Hara, whom Allen valued as highly as Olson and to whom he likewise made a long-term publishing commitment. From the broader, more sociological perspective evident in the mix of American poets and artists in early issues of *Evergreen Review*, it would make sense to apply a single capacious label to the poets in the Allen anthology:

Beat, or Cool. No matter how vociferously Olson or Duncan or O'Hara might seek at times to distance themselves from avowed Beats such as Ginsberg or Kerouac or Gregory Corso, all of them contributed to what Rexroth calls the "revolt" against and "disaffiliation" with dominant social, political, and sexual mores. And, as Allen points out, they all adhere to "the practices and precepts of Ezra Pound and William Carlos Williams" (xi)—although the list of common precursors should also include Hart Crane, D. H. Lawrence, objectivism, and surrealism. In this larger sense, Olson might be viewed within the New American poets as another member of a loosely interwoven collective of countercultural practitioners.

At the same time that the first issues of *Evergreen Review* were publishing a panoply of poets who would appear in *The New American Poetry*—Olson, Duncan, Ginsberg, O'Hara, Corso, Kerouac, Snyder, McClure, Whalen, Blaser, Barbara Guest, Brother Antoninus (William Everson), Lawrence Ferlinghetti, Jack Spicer, and Paul Blackburn—the quarterly also drew attention to jazz and postwar American art, paying heed especially to photography. Most early issues contain a portfolio of photographs, and images by accomplished photographers grace the covers—including one by Fred Lyon of the San Francisco skyline as described in the "Moloch" section of "Howl" (second issue) and one by Hans Namuth of Jackson Pollock sitting on the running board of a disintegrating automobile (third issue). The fourth issue's cover image (fig. 1), a candid shot of three motorcyclists by Swiss photographer Robert Frank, is clearly meant by the editor to illustrate Olson's poem. The photo was titled *Newburgh, New York, 1955*, when it was published shortly thereafter in Frank's landmark book, *The Americans* (1958, 1959).[20] Olson writes with gratitude to Allen about how well it fits his poem: "Did anyone tell you how it is to be put out there by another man who has covered you like your own skin?"[21]

Frank drove ten thousand miles around the United States for a year on a Guggenheim fellowship, shooting over a thousand spontaneous negatives that document a new postwar America to itself and to the world—covering the country like its own skin. Like Olson, Frank seeks to create a balance between spontaneously captured features of the external world and the idiosyncratic quality of individual perception. In the introduction to *The Americans*, his friend Kerouac says of Frank: "With that little camera that he raises and snaps with one hand he sucked a sad poem right out of America onto film, taking rank among the tragic poets of the world" (9). Frank's raw images—of racial conflict; of small-town desperation and big-city political venality; of isolated misfits, lonely jukeboxes, and endless blacktop—enact a transformation of private, unposed moments into icons of the social dissolution and rebellious transience of postwar culture. The emphasis on transience and rebellion can be seen in *Newburgh, New York, 1955* as well as in another

Figure 1. *Newburgh, New York, 1955*, by Robert Frank, on the cover of *Evergreen Review*, no. 4 (1958).

photograph in *The Americans* of black motorcyclists, male and female, called *Indianapolis, 1956* (fig. 2).

In the first image, the central figure, wolfing down a hotdog, turns menacingly, as if disturbed or provoked by the photographer. In the second the couple, molded almost into a single creature, like the reunited androgyne, stares down pensively at something outside the frame. Here, Frank captures two beautiful, ineffably cool subjects in loose embrace in a segregated setting, drawing power, as Kerouac observes, from the American tragedy of race. "Look closely / at them," Olson begs the viewer of his own cyclists, in a differently segregated setting,

> they are the unadmitted, the club of Themselves,
> weary riders, but who sit upon the landscape as the Great

Figure 2. *Indianapolis, 1956*, by Robert Frank, from Frank's *The Americans* (1958, 1959).

> Stones. And only have fun among themselves. They are
> the lonely ones
>
> (CP 385)

In contrast to his more enthusiastic, sometimes even bombastic, poetic pronouncements, Olson devotes this passage to poignant depiction of a resistant and defiant but nonetheless isolated group of outsiders. The last sentence, "They are the lonely ones," sounds again like a pop song lyric, anticipating perhaps the chorus to Paul Anka's "Lonely Boy" (1959): "I'm just a lonely boy, lonely and blue / I'm all alone with nothin' to do." Often supported acoustically by the Wagnerian "Wall of Sound" first constructed by producer Phil Spector, such pop songs of the late 1950s and early 1960s attempt to raise adolescent isolation to a monumental and mythical state. In that sense, they have a similar goal to Olson's equation of motorcyclists and satyrs, for this is the moment when adolescent insurrection first embodies the anxieties of an entire culture. Although Frank's photos and Olson's poems take a more worldly and grownup perspective than Anka's song, the poem and photos nevertheless share with Ginsberg's "Howl," Kerouac's *On the Road*, the Brando and Dean films, and pop songs addressed to anguished teenagers the nascent project of grounding a countercultural ethos in the restless posture of youthful rebellion.

"THESE ARE OUR COUNTERPARTS, THE UNKNOWN ONES."

Like the subjects of Frank's photos, Olson's lonely cyclists initially separate themselves from the dreamer. They are cool, isolated, and self-contained. This is true both of "the club of Themselves" (385) and of the blond who "was as distant as the others. She sat in her flesh too" (386). Olson also situates the cyclists as primitive beings who display a "monumental solidity" and a phallic potency in their role of "the Fathers behind the father" (384) and "the Sources" (384). In addition to their atavistic appearance, their origin is distant in space: having migrated, "they came riding in from the sea" (385)—as the newly born goddess does in the Homeric Hymn to Aphrodite. Ultimately, though, for all their isolation, distance, and phallic potency, these beings have a direct, material effect upon the dreamer, bringing unimagined benefits: "They are between us / and the ocean. And they have given us a whole new half of the beach" (386). Not only do they add geographical, and presumably psychic, territory, but they also effect a change in perception: owing to their presence, Olson marvels, "we saw twice as much" (385). With respect to both the new portion of beach and the new mode of perception, the lordly and isolate satyrs have caused a signal transformation:

> The difference is
> we are more on it. The beauty of the white of the sun's light, the
> blue the water is, and the sky, the movement on the painted lands-
> cape, the boy-town the scene was, is now pierced with angels and
> with fire. And winter's ice shall be as brilliant in its time as
> life truly is, as Nature is only the offerer, and it is we
> who look to see what the beauty is.
>
> (387)

As in Blake's *Jerusalem*, the mundane world is suffused by divine presences, beings that also owe their existence to the heightened perception of the dreamer. Like Blake, Nietzsche, and Lawrence, Olson believes that, in the words of *The Marriage of Heaven and Hell*, "All deities reside in the human breast."[22] His identification with the seemingly alien and fleshly solidity of the satyrs in this lyrical passage causes a conversion in awareness of self and world. The ordinary landscape "is now pierced with angels / and with fire," conjuring up the brilliance of life at its most vivid—a state of heightened meaning and intensity in which he yearns to reside constantly. Ultimately, as Emerson does, Olson sees nature as the "offerer" of such radiant moments of beauty. The rebels on wheels who bear this gift from nature are the true "Contemporaries," and they belong, he recognizes, to a vibrantly erotic experience of the present historical moment. In a climactic stanza halfway through the poem (the only one that is double-spaced) he proclaims:

> These are our counterparts, the unknown ones.
>
> They are here. We do not look upon them as invaders. Dimensionally
>
> they are larger than we—all but the woman. But we are not suddenly
>
> small. We are as we are. We don't even move, on the beach.
>
> (386)

Seeing "the unknown ones" as "our counterparts" transfixes the ecstatic dreamer in an intransitive state ("We are as we are") and seems to bring the poem to an awestruck equilibrium. After noting, "We don't even move," as though his breath is suspended, Olson comments, "It is a stasis," and then, a few lines later, "As of this moment, there is nothing else to report."

This moment of stasis becomes an inflection point. The panting cyclists who have ferried in a sense of timeliness and erotic magnification suddenly forfeit their exalted status by breaching silence and chatting among themselves, thus losing composure. The poet notices with disappointment "the way their face breaks when they call across to each other," so that "the face / loses all containment," and without containment, Olson contends, force dissipates. As a result, "They are not gods. They are not even stone." Instead, they descend into adolescence: "They are fifteen year old boys at the moment / they speak to each other." Olson sums up this troubling alteration by claiming, "When they act like us / they go to pieces." Earlier in the poem he had outlined what it means to "act like us." After hailing the satyrs and the increase in vision they bring ("we saw twice as much" [385]), he steps back for the first time to describe the normal people on the beach, in marked contrast to the motorcycle club: "We were as usual, the children were being fed pop / and potato chips, and everyone was sprawled as people are / on a beach."

Pointing out that "the lordly and isolate satyrs" lose the power of containment when they lapse into the state of mere mortals "sprawled . . . on a beach," Olson expresses a major tenet of his philosophy. He states it most succinctly in the second half of "Projective Verse," which is devoted to "the degree to which the projective involves a stance toward reality outside a poem."[23] Speaking of the benefits of having the correct attitude toward objects—that is, the humility to regard oneself as no more than an object—Olson insists:

> It comes to this: the use of a man, by himself and thus by others, lies in how he conceives his relation to nature, that force by which he owes his somewhat

> small existence. If he sprawl, he shall find little to sing but himself. . . . But if he stays inside himself, if he is contained within his nature as he is participant in the larger force, he will be able to listen, and his hearing through himself will give him secrets objects share. (247)

From Olson's perspective, the venal expansion of ego that bedevils human self-conception and intercourse with others and with nature condemns us to the flabby, pathetic posture of sprawling on a beach indulging the children in "pop / and potato chips." Mimicking the silent, self-contained demeanor of the motorcyclists ("our counterparts"), on the other hand, would align human beings in a proper "relation to nature" and allow us, thus, to perceive "secrets objects share."

Throughout the poem, Olson endeavors to gauge how the "lordly and isolate satyrs" both resemble and exceed the human beings on the beach. At times they appear to him like divine emanations or monumental avatars of a titanic prehumanity. At other times, they appear as restless rebels who have in their adolescent awkwardness joined a motorcycle club. Across this spectrum, which includes the divine, the primitive, and the adolescent, a powerful erotic charge remains constant. At several points during the poem, Olson's erotic gaze fastens on the woman who accompanies the leader. To some extent, his avid interest reduces her to a human scale that doesn't admit the added dimension of the satyrs, but she still partakes of the cool self-containment that marks the cyclists.[24] As a figure of beauty, she is "a dazzling blond, the new dye making her hair a delicious / streaked ash," and yet, "She was as distant as the others" (386), without quite taking on their larger-than-life status. Olson's interest in the leader's woman could mark the phallicism in the poem as emphatically heterosexual, but the burgeoning eroticism in his treatment of the motorcyclists also spills over into homosocial and homosexual channels.[25] Looking to one of the fountainheads of Western erotic philosophy, Plato's *Symposium*, Olson invokes Aristophanes's myth of the original humans, who had twice the limbs and organs of present humans and represented three sexes (double-male, double-female, and male-female). In this way, he opens the poem explicitly to homosexuality and androgyny.

Near the beginning, after he calls the motorcyclists "the Androgynes" and "the Great Halves" (384), he turns to speak in homosocial terms of three poets: the one he "loved most," who confessed to Olson his pain "the night he got drunk, / and I put him to bed" (Robert Creeley?); another, whose "Sources" were snarled "all in his mouth" (John Wieners?); and a third who was a "Yiddish poet / a vegetarian" with something conspicuous "inside his pants" (Allen Ginsberg?). Offsetting his regard for these poets and their erotic dilemmas,

Olson remains fascinated by the group of phallic motorcyclists, who "sit there, up a little, on their thing" (386), which is a "huge third leg like carborundum" (387).[26] Although carborundum (silicon carbide) compound is most commonly found in abrasives, Olson must be referring to its extreme hardness, which led to its use in armored vests and automobile parts. As in Greek depictions of ithyphallic satyrs, Olson's portrayal of hypermasculine cyclists is inherently comic and, at least to a certain extent, queer. In this way, he anticipates another trailblazing artwork focused on a motorcycle club, Kenneth Anger's 1964 film *Scorpio Rising*, in which Anger converts the fetishism and masculine high jinks of a Brooklyn motorcycle club into a homoerotic *Walpurgisnacht*, timing the scenes to coincide with twelve pop songs of 1963.[27] Straying into queerness, Olson does not embrace it wholeheartedly like Anger (whose cyclists were reportedly ignorant of being cast as homoerotic satyrs) or like Ginsberg in "Howl"—which was written the year before "The Lordly and Isolate Satyrs." Ginsberg's "angelheaded hipsters . . . let themselves be fucked in the ass by saintly motorcyclists, and screamed with joy," but Olson, while recognizing the cyclists in his poem as libidinous forces, resists merging with them physically and mentally, for they "are our counterparts, the unknown ones. / They are here. We do not look upon them as invaders" (386).[28]

In its polymorphic eroticism, "The Lordly and Isolate Satyrs" provides Olson with a canvas on which to imagine the enhanced beach at Gloucester as a site where elemental powers emerge from the sea. Oppen is right when he declares it a poem of Olson's "in which the voice and eye are his alone." The eye perceives a remarkable theophany and the voice adroitly combines expressions of awe with a late 1950s demotic speech. Counter to Olson's reputation for exclamatory didacticism, this poem shows a striking, and by no means uncharacteristic, ability to mix tones and levels of diction to create a lyric poetry that feels at once temporally specific and open in time. Part of its openness can be traced to Olson's use of the first-person plural. Although the poem recounts a dream of his own, he narrates it from the standpoint of a shared experience, which the reader is invited to enter—and thus to refresh in time. In the last stanza, he subtly disengages from the suspended time of the satyrs and returns to quotidian life, marking how extraordinary their appearance has been:

> We stay. And watch them
> gather themselves up. We have no feeling except love. They are not
> ours. They are of another name. These are what the gods are. They
> look like us. They are only in all parts larger. But the size is
> only different. The difference is, they are not here, they are not

on this beach in this sun, which, tomorrow, when we come to swim,
will be another summer day. They can't talk to us.

(387)

These oneiric-mythic-prehistoric divinities reveal the splendor of life and thus inspire devotion while maintaining a distance and monumentality and lacking the ability to communicate directly with humans. Choreographing a dance of intimacy and separation with larger-than-life beings, Olson joins artists of the postwar era in invoking motorcyclists as embodiments of irrepressible and overflowing sexual energy. Unlike Beat artists such as Brando, Frank, Kerouac, and Ginsberg, though, Olson infuses an elemental (if sometimes mock-heroic) power into his bikers. In this ambitious poem, he strives to paint an appreciative portrait of the iconic motorcycle club of the late 1950s and, at the same time, to incorporate self-contained erotic energies from a dream into his own expanded perception of the world. Through a lyric engagement with the full range of internal and external realities, he means to become himself one of "the Contemporaries."

6

Laurie Anderson in the Reagan Era

Laurie Anderson is an heir to John Cage, Merce Cunningham, and other pioneers of what has loosely been called "performance art." For many years I taught a course called "Poetry and Performance," which looked at commonalities between contemporary poetry and a wide range of performance art. Anderson was usually the culminating figure of the course, drawing together many of the vocal, musical, bodily, and electronic performing styles and the major themes of "storytelling," "tuning," and "cross-cultural conversation." Along with her work as composer, musician, storyteller, visual artist, electronic inventor, choreographer, video artist, and filmmaker, her poetic investigations of language—often using recycled phrases and clichés—show her to be a deft practitioner of (mediated) oral poetry. Her signature deadpan delivery, hesitant speaking rhythms, unexpected syllabic accents, and electronic vocal modulations make for an instantly recognizable, cyborgian verbal style. This style, with its emphasis on defamiliarizing everyday speech, permeates the epic or operatic works she stages, which often include other musicians and dancers and animations projected on huge screens.

In 2003, I taught "Poetry and Performance" in London, with a final assignment of attending an Anderson performance at the Barbican Centre. Not long before she arrived, she appeared on a webcast from the Kelly Writers House at the University of Pennsylvania, in conversation with Alan Filreis. I phoned in to pose a question: "Given your poetic soundings of contemporary language, do you feel an affinity to particular poets?" She mentioned her love for Anne Carson's poetry and translations, how much she missed Allen Ginsberg—whose "ecstatic voice" made him "our Rumi"—and that she had recently learned to appreciate Gertrude Stein through a German performance mashing *The Making of Americans* with *Pet Sounds* by the Beach Boys. But the underlying answer was no, she didn't see her work as responding to prior poetry or as part of a poetic lineage.[1]

I was disappointed she didn't recognize how her own linguistic inventiveness made a place for her among the innovative poetry included in my course, such as Ginsberg's *Howl*, the talk poems of David Antin, Jerome Rothenberg's *Technicians of the Sacred*, Claudia Rankine's *Don't Let Me Be Lonely*, Laura Mullen's *Murmur*, and Nathaniel Mackey's *Whatsaid Serif*.[2] That she belonged there was certainly apparent to the students. In 2017, she published a book-length reflection on her career, *All the Things I Lost in the Flood,* which finally acknowledges the centrality of words to her work. In the introduction she recalls Hurricane Sandy in 2012 flooding her basement in New York City, destroying everything stored there:

> Nothing was left. The seawater had shredded and pulped everything. Even the electronic equipment was now a lumpy gray sludge. At first I was devastated. . . . The day after that I looked at the thick binder with lists of things that had been lost in the flood; I realized that . . . having these long lists was just as good as having the real things. Maybe even better.[3]

This prompted her to contemplate the relationship of language to grief: "Language is about loss and in a way words are memorials to things and to states. The word 'yellow' is a memorial to the color yellow." The loss of the physical props for performances stripped her art down to its core, revealing it as essentially a language art. Although she has been classified as a multimedia artist, she came to realize, "At the root of all of these works are stories. They are the engines. Stories and words are what I love most."

The essay that follows developed out of teaching Anderson's videos and CDs as American literature. Rather than look at her borrowings from the Bible, Shakespeare, and Melville, or examine the pervasive influence of William Burroughs's dictum, "Language is a virus from outer space," I have chosen to investigate songs from her CD *Strange Angels* (1989) as intertextual performances that portray the United States cross-culturally and cross-temporally.[4] Through the lens of Anderson's poetic understanding of the Reagan Era, as articulated in this album, her larger endeavor comes into focus: mounting an alternative, self-critical reading of American history that implicates both her country and herself.

HIAWATHA

In the 1980s, following on stylistic breakthroughs of the previous decade in pop art, minimalism (both visual and musical), performance art, and conceptualism, figures like Laurie Anderson, Robert Wilson, Jim Jarmusch, Spalding Gray, and David Byrne of the Talking Heads developed a carefully calibrated, deadpan verbal delivery to mix the avant-garde and the everyday. This resulted in making strange simultaneously the high theory of the intellectual elite and the slogans and clichés of popular culture. The artists often combine biting political irony with studied naivete, searching for personal pathways through the monumental landscape created by media-delivered language and images. It's almost like a gambit in chess, where a piece is offered for capture to achieve a larger strategic end: by ceding commercial imagery a certain standing, artists can reveal the essential weirdness of contemporary life as viewed from the perspective of an insider, rather than standing outside and wielding the cold blade of ideological critique. A multimedia performance artist, Anderson landed a contract with Warner Brothers Records in 1981 on the strength of the unexpected success of her song "O Superman"—thus bringing the Downtown New York avant-garde directly into mainstream culture. Like the figures mentioned above, she began performing in the 1970s, and she shared their delight in the Dada and neo-Dada experiments of earlier precursors such as Duchamp, Schwitters, Cage, and Warhol. And like many artists of her time, she culls from a variety of disparate sources—not primarily through allusion (as with modernists such as Joyce, Eliot, or Pound)—but through postmodern appropriation. Combining music, dance, video, and storytelling, her multimedia assemblages evince a dense verbal texture, interweaving phrases from *Moby-Dick* and *The Tempest*, for example, with lines from the "Star-Spangled Banner" and the jingle for Hamm's beer.

The unexpected juxtapositions, delivered in her deadpan verbal style, contribute to weird performances of sometimes epic scale, offering a gimlet-eyed perspective on an imperial civilization whose mounting bizarreness her work reveals. Like Charles Olson, Anderson can skew her perspective on reality by incorporating dreams into her songs, as one mode of distorting the everyday. Narrated matter-of-factly, the dreams uncannily resituate banal tag ends of contemporary life, as though American culture were under scrutiny by the proverbial "anthropologist from Mars." Speaking of her four-part epic, *United States* (1984), Henry Sayre claims, "It is perhaps not too much to suggest that Anderson manages to 'deterritorialize' the United States, to give her audience a sense that they are in some measure *outside*—or wanderers within—the very place they live."[5] Her two monumental multimedia works, *United States* and *Home of the Brave* (1986), offer political statements indirectly by deconstructing clichéd ways of thinking and speaking, making them appear stranger and stranger. Telling stories and dreams in a quizzical and jerky verbal style and often employing the "Voice of Authority," an electronically modulated microphone that creates a "male" vocal style, she accomplishes an intimate alienation that is as much about gender and technology as it is about nation. Ruminating on her computer-generated male voice, she says, "It's also the voice of a shoe salesman or of a guy who's trying to sell you an insurance policy you don't want or need. He's a bit insecure but cheerful, not very bright but quite pompous anyway. It's only recently that I realized that this guy is based on my first ideas of who men were."[6]

"Hiawatha," a song from her 1989 album *Strange Angels*, incorporates voices of authority from the Reagan Era not through an electronic filter but by collaging together appropriated language, thus probing the mythic underpinnings of American exceptionalism as invoked by the Reagan presidency. "Hiawatha" is a verbal mash-up of phrases with a "Western" flavor, taken from song lyrics and other artifacts of popular culture, framed at the beginning and end by lines from Longfellow's *The Song of Hiawatha*:

By the shores of Gitche Gumee
By the shining Big-Sea-Water
Downward through the evening twilight
In the days that are forgotten
From the land of sky blue waters

And I said: Hello Operator
Get me Memphis Tennessee
And she said: I know who you're tryin to call darling
And he's not home
He's been away
But you can hear him on the airwaves
He's howlin at the moon
Yeah this is your country station
And honey this next one's for you.

And all along the highways
And under the big western sky
They're singing Ooo oooooo
They're singing Wild Blue.
And way out on the prairie
And up in the high chaparral
They hear a voice it says: Good evening
This is Captain Midnight speaking
And I've got a song for you
Goes somethin like this:

Starlight Starbright
We're gonna hang some new stars
In the heavens tonight.
They're gonna circle by day
They're gonna fly by night
We're goin sky high. Yoo Hooooo hooo.
Yeah yoo hooo Ooo Hooooooooo

So good night ladies
And good night gentlemen
Keep those cards and letters coming
And please don't call again.

Geronimo and little Nancy
Marilyn and John F. dancing
Uncle took the message
And it's written on the wall.
These are pictures of the houses
Shining in the midnight moonlight
While the King sings Love Me Tender.

And all along the watchtowers
And under the big western sky
They're singing Yoo hooooo
They're singing Wild Blue.
And way way up there, bursting in air
Red rockets, bright red glare
From the land of sky blue waters
Sent by freedom's sons and daughters.
We're singing Ooo hoooooo
We're singing Wild Blue.
We're singing Ooo hoooooo
Ooo Hooooooooo

And dark behind it rose the forest
Rose the black and gloomy pine trees
Rose the firs with Cones upon them
And bright before it beat the water
Beat the clear and sunny water
Beat the shining Big-Sea-Water

The first four lines of the song come directly from Longfellow, but the fifth line ("From the land of sky blue waters"), which synchs seamlessly with the previous four, derives from a long-running commercial jingle:

From the Land of Sky Blue Waters [(Echo) Waters]
Comes the water best for brewing,
Hamm's the beer refreshing,
Hamm's the beer refreshing,
Hamm's!

Anderson's artful collage equates the high-culture-cum-children's-rhyme of Longfellow's nineteenth-century poem with a jingle that markets beer to working-class consumers. The commonality resides in the nostalgic use of Native Americans by both sources to sell mythical American self-satisfaction. In fact, the rhythm of the beer advertisement is carried by "Indian" tom-toms. Anderson uses an achingly nostalgic singing style for this first stanza, luring listeners into complacent appreciation of the mythology of the American imperium.

In the next stanza, her voice shifts into the mode of chanted speech first made famous in her unlikely hit song, "O Superman." The text quotes from and paraphrases Chuck Berry's "Memphis, Tennessee" (1959), which begins:

> Long distance information, give me Memphis, Tennessee
> Help me find the party trying to get in touch with me
> She could not leave her number, but I know who placed the call
> 'Cause my uncle took the message and he wrote it on the wall

("And I said: Hello Operator / Get me Memphis Tennessee / And she said: I know who you're tryin to call darling / And he's not home / He's been away.") After the high culture of Longfellow and the low culture of beer, Anderson's drawing from one of the originators of rock and roll, Chuck Berry, might be seen as a gesture toward the middle. So already by this point in the song, she has bound together three levels of American society, all focused on "Western" imagery, while employing almost none of her own words.

In the rest of the stanza, she stays in the register of popular music by including other references to the radio and to disc jockeys. "Howlin at the moon" invokes Chicago rhythm and blues singer Howlin' Wolf, and "Yeah this is your country station / And honey this next one's for you" alludes to Joni Mitchell's song "You Turn Me On, I'm a Radio" (1972):

> Oh honey you turn me on
> I'm a radio
> I'm a country station
> I'm a little bit corny

In the following stanza, Anderson wraps rock and roll back into the larger themes of nostalgia-fueled American imperialism. It begins with "All along the highways," which morphs later into "All along the watchtowers," evoking Bob Dylan's 1967 song (made even more famous by Jimi Hendrix in 1968). The first mention combines the song with the title of Dylan's earlier album, *Highway 61 Revisited*. Then, Anderson turns to the opening of the "Air Force

Song" ("Off we go into the wild blue yonder") with "Wild Blue" and revisits the mythical Western context by naming a television show, *High Chaparral* (1967–1971). The stanza ends with the radio character, Captain Midnight, who then utters the ultimate nursery rhyme of wish fulfillment, "Star light, star bright."

As the song progresses, Anderson appropriates and reprises appropriations, constructing a nostalgic kitsch of Western Americana perfectly suited to the Reagan Era—whose sentimental motto, "Morning in America," was first enunciated in a 1984 campaign commercial touting the success of his first term as president. Anderson slyly introduces Reagan himself in the lines "Geronimo and little Nancy / Marilyn and John F. dancing," where President Kennedy is paired with Marilyn Monroe and "little Nancy" (Reagan) is dancing with "Geronimo"—a wonderfully ironic epithet for her husband, aka "The Great Communicator," who played a Confederate general fighting the Apache chief Geronimo in Lewis R. Foster's film *The Last Outpost* (1951). This same stanza reprises "Memphis, Tennessee" and *The Song of Hiawatha* and then finishes with a reference to Elvis Presley's tearjerker "Love Me Tender" (1956).

The following stanza contains one of Anderson's constant targets of defamiliarization, "The Star-Spangled Banner":

> And way way up there, bursting in air
> Red rockets, bright red glare
> From the land of sky blue waters
> Sent by freedom's sons and daughters.

In the current age, the "gifts" of "freedom's sons and daughters" are delivered to the world by lethal rockets—as though the national anthem, penned during the War of 1812, a song of desperate hope, were instead a prophecy of the many American military conquests to come. By deftly weaving together a panoply of nostalgic sources, Anderson seduces the listener into celebrating American exceptionalism in ways she undercuts not by ideological critique but by the queasy feeling evoked through the very acts of juxtaposition. By paying attention to the seams so carefully disguised by Anderson's seductive vocal style, one watches the knowingly constructed facsimile of American mythology—the fabled "Morning in America"—begin to crumble, leaving behind a portentous hollowness.

STRANGE ANGELS

In performances at the end of the 1980s, especially in her CD *Strange Angels*, Anderson began to add explicitly spiritual themes to her subversively seductive political and cultural forays. Traditionally, angels function as bearers of spiritual gifts, but making sense of such offerings or learning to live alongside angels in the present is not without complications in a secular, cosmopolitan world. The opening stanza of the title song, "Strange Angels," portrays the abode of the angels, heaven, not as reward for a well-spent life on earth but as something like a self-contained simulacrum that paradoxically holds open an experience of temporality:

> They say that heaven is like tv
> A perfect little world
> That doesn't really need you
> And everything there
> Is made of light
> And the days keep going by
> Here they come here they come
> Here they come.

The question implicit in this verse is whether the light emanates from heaven or from a cathode-ray tube, and thus whether the medium (TV) exists within the spiritual or vice versa. The one thing we know for certain is that, like televisual images, daily life rolls by in unending incipience: "Here they come here they come / Here they come."

Or does it? The album was released at the triumphant climax of the Reagan Era—the epoch of the Eastern European revolutions, the destruction of the Berlin Wall (Reagan: "Mr. Gorbachev, tear down this wall!"), and the ensuing dissolution of the Soviet Union. This was the moment widely hailed as "The End of History," an apocalyptic culmination that lent credence to the perennial evangelical warning that the Kingdom of Heaven is at hand. If any moment during the past half-century felt like a break in time—contrary to the uninterrupted dailiness of heaven that Anderson posits—this was it. To commemorate this heady period, Leonard Bernstein conducted Beethoven's *Ninth Symphony* in Berlin with an international orchestra, a Christmas 1989 performance broadcast around the globe. Rather than offering an "Ode to Joy" (or as Bernstein had it, an "Ode to Freedom"), Anderson's song invokes an oddly monotonous paradise, as unencumbered by life's exigencies as television is—and yet as ubiquitous as TV too. At this heightened juncture of history, she notices, people do not so much live their lives as watch them go by as though backlit on a television screen. This is not so surprising considering that Americans had grown accustomed to watching history unfold on television, beginning with the assassination of John F. Kennedy and continuing with the assassinations and riots of 1968 and the long-running Vietnam War. In the late 1980s, though, it seemed as if the spectators had climbed directly into the televisual spectacle of history or as if gnostic forces on the loose were capable of intruding into daily life through the video screen. The chorus of the song captures this intimation that celestial beings are infiltrating time, ostensibly to fulfill biblical prophecy but not in ways anticipated by conventional religion:

> Strange angels—singing just for me
> Old stories—they're haunting me
> This is nothing
> Like I thought it would be.

At this historical juncture, angels descend to serenade the individual soul, seeming to complete the "old stories" but in ways utterly unfamiliar and unexpected. So, who are these "strange angels," and why are they here? These questions can best be addressed by tracing three lineages for Anderson's heavenly hosts. One goes back through director Wim Wenders's (and screenwriter Peter Handke's) 1987 film *Wings of Desire* (*Der Himmel [Heaven] über Berlin*) to an earlier source in Rilke's *Duino Elegies*. The angels in the film and in Rilke's poetry have wonderful powers, such as clairaudience and eternal life, but they yearn to experience human sensations, especially love, and to participate in the embodied history made by people interacting with objects. The second lineage can be anchored in two sculptures by postwar German artist Anselm Kiefer, *Angel of History* (1989) and *Book with Wings* (1994), and then traced back through Walter Benjamin's famous invocation in "Theses on the Philosophy of History" of an angel of history, which in turn was inspired by *Angelus Novus* (1920), a Paul Klee painting he owned.[7] A third direction takes cognizance of the devastation of AIDS. It points forward from Robert Mapplethorpe's 1987 photographic portraits of Anderson on the album covers of *Strange Angels* to Tony Kushner's epoch-defining play, *Angels in America* (set in 1985–1990, premiered in 1991).[8]

To begin exploring these lineages, it might be helpful to gloss Anderson's use of angels by invoking Harold Bloom's *Omens of Millennium: The Gnosis of Angels, Dreams, and Resurrection* (1996).[9] Tracing angels to their first appearance in Iranian Zoroastrianism around 1500 BCE, Bloom argues they have been crucial figures in the gnostic religions of the West, which themselves sprang from Zoroastrian dualism. He also contends that the reappearance of angels in the millennial religions of America, obsessed as they are with literalizing a personal relationship to God for each believer, is no coincidence, given that angels have taken starring roles as messengers and revealers of divine knowledge in the long histories of Zoroastrianism, Hermeticism, Christian Gnosticism, Sufism, and Jewish Kabbalah.

Anderson was initiated into angelology by her maternal grandmother, a Southern Baptist missionary, who "practically had the Bible memorized" and took her as a girl to Billy Graham meetings in Chicago—about which she remarks, "*that* was real theater."[10] As a result of her grandmother's influence, biblical imagery—often made strange by her deadpan, hesitant delivery—pervades Anderson's work. The proximate cause, though, of her turn to angels was most likely an encounter with Wenders in 1986. Anderson tells of meeting him by chance in the Berlin airport and striking up a friendship: "He was working on his script for 'Wings of Desire' at the time and so a lot of the conversations were along the lines of Do angels wear black raincoats and follow you to the library, or not?" (*Nerve Bible* 203). The strange angels in Wenders's film do wear black raincoats and alight on steeples and other architectural high points of Berlin, listening in on the thoughts of its human inhabitants (most strikingly in the beehive hum of a public library), to proffer solace to the emotionally wounded. The angels evince a laser-like telepathic ability and seemingly infinite compassion, but as immortal, non-fleshly beings, they cannot feel human sensations. One of them, Damiel (Bruno Ganz), falls in love with a trapeze artist (Solveig Dommartin) and resolves to descend into mortality to experience not only human love but all the attendant sensations of embodied life: tasting coffee, smoking cigarettes, feeling the pain of a wound, and so on. He tumbles down near the Berlin Wall, which manages to captivate the camera nearly as fully as the human actors, and the wall and Wenders's angels provide a cinematic backdrop to Anderson's *Strange Angels*.

What is remarkable about the song "Strange Angels" is the ease with which Anderson embeds herself in cultural history while remaining firmly planted in the present moment. Nested within her song's reliance on the rumpled angels of *Wings of Desire* is the ur-text of Rilke's *Duino Elegies* (1923), whose "Ninth Elegy" commands human beings, "Praise this world to the angel, not the unsayable" world, naming for the angel the things formed by the transient hands of mortals, such as "house, / bridge, fountain, gate, pitcher, fruit-tree, window."[11] It is this world of built things and the human sensations that accompany them—animated, as Rilke claims, by love—that provides the spiritual and emotional drive to the screenplay by Wenders and cowriter Handke. For Rilke, it seems almost inconceivable that angels will be seduced by the humble pursuits of humans, but in *Wings of Desire* Damiel cannot resist the temptation to fall into human life—goaded on by Peter Falk (playing himself) as an angel who earlier made the plunge. The dramatic setting for Damiel's fall is the divided city of Berlin at the last moment of its scission. Alongside the terrifying beauty of Rilke's post-religious angels and the pathos and poignancy of the compassionate but desirous angels in *Wings of Desire*, Anderson posits her strange angels as harbingers in 1989 of world-historical change:

> Strange angels—singing just for me
> Their spare change falls on top of me

Rain falling falling all over me
Strange angels—singing just for me
Old stories—they're haunting me
Big changes are coming
Here they come
Here they come

In this final double chorus, Anderson emphasizes a revolutionary incipience by using the word "change" twice, in two different senses. First, she imagines raindrops as being the "spare change" of the angels, as though their message of change were pouring off as pure excess into the hands of beggars. Then, she affirms the angels' transformational capacity with more urgent anticipation: "Big changes are coming / Here they come / Here they come."

From the perspective of the present, Anderson's angels represent change not only by looking forward but also by looking backward. This becomes apparent in "The Dream Before," another song on the *Strange Angels* CD. Once again, the setting is Berlin, but a different filmmaker, Rainer Werner Fassbinder (1945–1982), acts as interlocutor in the first stanza:

Hansel and Gretel are alive and well
And they're living in Berlin
She is a cocktail waitress
He had a part in a Fassbinder film
And they sit around at night now
Drinking schnapps and gin
And she says: Hansel, you're really bringing me down
And he says: Gretel, you can really be a bitch
He says: I've wasted my life on our stupid legend
When my one and only love
Was the wicked witch.

In this stanza, Anderson partakes of a trend in contemporary fiction of rewriting classic fairy tales by projecting them into the present. Locating her update of "Hansel and Gretel" in the emotionally claustrophobic world of Fassbinder's Berlin, Anderson provides a 1989 context for the second and concluding stanza of the song, which is a piece of pure appropriation from the intellectual life of an earlier Berlin:

She said: What is history?
And he said: History is an angel
Being blown backwards into the future

He said: History is a pile of debris
And the angel wants to go back and fix things
To repair the things that have been broken
But there is a storm blowing from paradise
And the storm keeps blowing the angel
Backwards into the future.
And this storm, this storm
Is called
Progress

This condensation of Walter Benjamin's ninth thesis on the philosophy of history (Benjamin 259–60) into the language of fable or fairy tale evokes the "angel of history," which for Benjamin had both Marxist and mystical implications. The original of this angel he imagined he saw in *Angelus Novus,* a painting by Paul Klee that he worked very hard to acquire and that now resides in the Israel Museum in Jerusalem (fig. 3). In Anderson's hands, the angel of history becomes another strange angel in the pantheon of messengers announcing the end of history in 1989. Like the angels in *Wings of Desire,* this compassionate angel would like "to go back and fix things," but the winds of "progress" make repairing history impossible. Just as Anderson's Hansel cannot go back into the legend and repair his relationship with the wicked witch, Benjamin's angel is incapable of *tikkun olam,* of rectifying what has been broken.

Another artist fascinated with Benjamin's angel of history, who belongs in this constellation with Anderson, Wenders, and Rilke, is Anselm Kiefer. In 1989 Kiefer built a lead bomber weighing a ton, which he titled *The Angel of History* and sold to the National Gallery of Art in Washington, DC (fig. 4). With his title, Kiefer explicitly ties Benjamin to the death-dealing instruments of World War II, during which Benjamin himself lost his life. Kiefer's angel of history seems at first shorn of compassion, as if its only job were dealing death. Strangely, though, atop the wings of the leaden bomber are lead books, stuffed with dried poppies, as though the impossibly heavy bomber were carrying magical books filled with sleep-inducing opium. The artist evokes apocalyptic angel imagery again with an astonishing lead sculpture from 1994 called *Book with Wings* (fig. 5). The lead for this piece was acquired from the roof of the Cologne cathedral (then being remodeled) and was molded by Kiefer into an image that could also have the title *The Angel of History.* If history is a book, then it records the pile of debris that Benjamin's angel wants to lift up and redeem. The immense leaden weight of the sculpture makes palpable the impossibility of this task. How could wings of such mass ever fly?

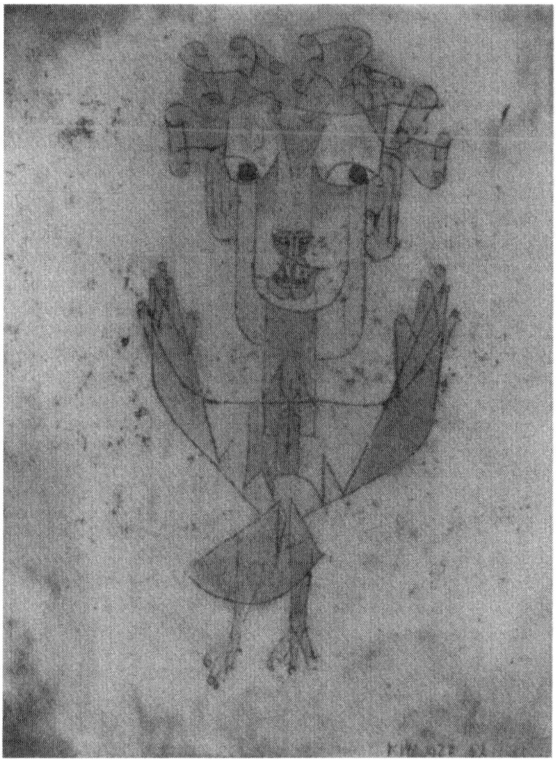

Figure 3. *Angelus Novus*, 1920, by Paul Klee. Israel Museum, Jerusalem.

Moving on to the third lineage in which Anderson's work is embedded, we can see in the cover images for the album *Strange Angels* one more facet of the End of History in the Age of Reagan. On both the front and back are portraits of Anderson by the controversial photographer Robert Mapplethorpe. The one on the front cover presents Anderson with eyes closed and index finger behind her ear, as though listening to unseen intimations (fig. 6). On the last page of the album's liner notes, there is a letter to the recently deceased Mapplethorpe from someone named "Ingrid." Ingrid informs him that he continues to occupy public awareness through the good offices of Senator Jesse Helms, who denounced an exhibition of Mapplethorpe's sexually explicit work as part of his justification for proposing a ban on government funding of obscene art. She also tells him, "The first time I listened to Laurie singing Strange Angels it felt like the song was going through the air to find you." Mapplethorpe, whose recent death from AIDS had followed that of his lover, Sam Wagstaff, made gay sex a central focus of his photography and became a prominent symbol of the ravages of the AIDS epidemic and of

Figure 4. *The Angel of History*, 1989, by Anselm Kiefer. National Gallery, Washington, DC.

homophobic persecution. This letter affirms that in some measure *Strange Angels* is addressed to Mapplethorpe and the scourge of AIDS—as is much of Anderson's work. More recently, Patti Smith's memoir, *Just Kids* (2010), relives this time, narrating in a voice of remarkable innocence her complex, heartbreaking relationship with Mapplethorpe.[12] Anderson's "strange angels" also descend from earlier gay figures, the "angelheaded hipsters" (Ginsberg 9) addressed in Allen Ginsberg's "Howl," those who "wound up with a sob behind a partition in a Turkish Bath when the blond & naked angel came to pierce them with a sword" (12). In this sense, Anderson's angels are the men who perished at the onset of a modern plague, and the album thus anticipates one of the culminating artworks of its era, Tony Kushner's epic play, *Angels in America*, which weaves themes about homophobia and gay self-hatred into a political indictment of betrayals of American values during the Age of AIDS.

In her performance piece *Voices from the Beyond* (1991), Anderson delivers a monologue about Mapplethorpe and the Helms controversy called "Large Black Dick." She contends that Mapplethorpe "was after the big taboos, things like: What do sex and religion have in common?" (*Nerve Bible* 244). Another song on the *Strange Angels* album, "Ramon," implores its audience to extend the compassion called for by an age of plagues, a compassion that might dissolve the homophobic (self-)hatred practiced by Senator Helms—or by Roy Cohn, fixer for Joseph McCarthy and mentor to Donald Trump, who receives a reckoning in *Angels in America*. The song begins,

Figure 5. *Book with Wings*, 1994, by Anselm Kiefer. Modern Art Museum of Fort Worth.

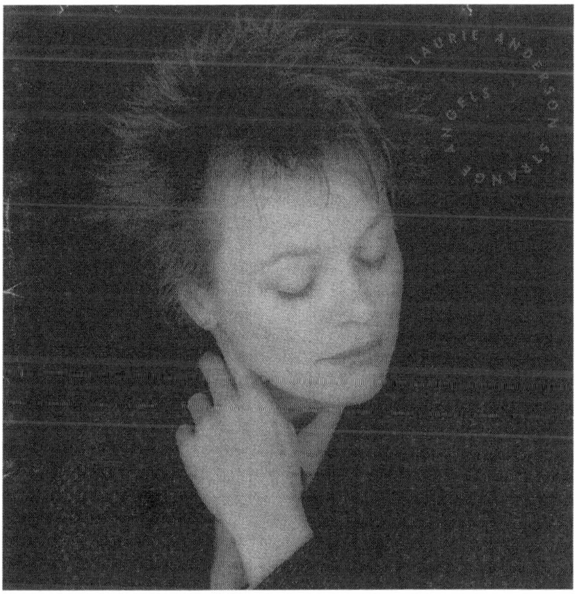

Figure 6. *Laurie Anderson*, 1987, by Robert Mapplethorpe, on the cover of Anderson's *Strange Angels* (1989).

Last night I saw a host of angels
And they were all singing different songs
And it sounded like a lot of lawnmowers
Mowing down my lawn
And up above kerjillians of stars
Spangled all over the sky
And they were spirals turning
Turning in the deep blue night.

This particular host of angels takes off in a vortex "traveling at the speed of sound," but it seems to collide with another of Anderson's sly references to the "Star-Spangled Banner," which injects politics into this ostensibly visionary moment. In a covert allusion to Genesis, the angels leave behind "a man who'd fallen"—presumably, in this case, Ramon—who "was lying on his back in the snow" (making snow angels?). Ramon becomes the focus of the rest of the song, which urges a desperate benevolence as spiritual value:

So when you see a man who's broken
Pick him up and carry him
And when you see a woman who's broken
Put her all into your arms
Cause we don't know where we come from
We don't know where we are.

After the angels retreat from the Garden of Eden or the Apocalypse, we are left with broken human beings. And the burning question is how to respond to this fact. Have the strange angels entered into this moment of history for cosmic reasons beyond our ken, and have they left a legacy? After the visionary ecstasy of singing hosts of angels and the spiraling patterns of stars, however, existential enigmas remain. Even though we don't understand the present in its utter complexity, nor do we know whence we come, we do face ethical challenges that demand response. Is this compassion something we have learned from the angels or is it something that in the wake of their retreat we find has been ours all along?

Is this the end of history or its beginning?

Over a long and rich career, Laurie Anderson has brought poetry to performance art in order to pose such questions. Her ability to assemble materials from vastly disparate realms into songs that probe individual reactions to national dilemmas makes her one of our most valuable poetic thinkers. It might not be stretching the point too far to label her a kind of prophet. This is true not only of the songs from *Strange Angels* but also of the way pieces she had written in the 1980s and 1990s seemed to forecast the reactions of the nation to September 11, 2001. Listening to a recording of the concert she gave one week after the attacks, at Town Hall in New York City, elicits a chilling recognition, as uncanny for the listener as for the one delivering the lines. As Anderson recalls,

> Lines from "O Superman" like "Here come the planes. They're American planes. Made in America." felt like I had written [them] yesterday. In fact, I wrote that song in 1980 during the Iran-Contra affair, which now seemed like part of a longer conflict that continues to rage between the worlds of Islam and the West.[13]

The works she wrote in the 1980s have retained their purchase on present conditions in a way few pieces composed during that era have. It may be that strange angels have been speaking to Anderson all along, giving her keys to understanding a climactic time in American history, one she saw taking shape in the Age of Reagan. At any rate, her careful acts of appropriation and defamiliarization have retained the capacity to speak to the American conflict with Islam, which began in the Iran Hostage crisis of the Carter/Reagan transition, flared up in George H. W. Bush's Gulf War, intensified after 9/11 in the wars in Afghanistan and Iraq instigated by George W. Bush, was perpetuated by Barack Obama despite an attempt to make peace with Islam, and rises now in furor with the combined demonization of Islam, embrace of dictators, and retreat into isolationism as Roy Cohn's acolyte, Donald Trump, dismantles the American imperium.

POETRY & THE ARTS: MULTIMEDIA EXCHANGE

7

Robert Creeley, Marisol, and *Presences* as Transaction Network

I first encountered Robert Creeley's *Presences: A Text for Marisol* (1976) on a remainder table at Moe's Books in Berkeley shortly after it was published. It figured as one of the primary texts for my first critical book, *Poet's Prose*, and I always hoped it would be reprinted. Finally, the University of New Mexico Press has done so, in the Recencies series edited by Matthew Hofer. The new edition includes an appendix of items from Notre Dame's Robert Creeley Collection. One of the great joys of having Creeley's own library housed in Special Collections at Notre Dame's Hesburgh Library is being able to bring students, friends, and visiting writers to view it. The poet filed in many of his books a wealth of items associated with the particular volume. In addition, the collection includes Creeley's own copies of his sumptuous collaborations with major artists. These museum-quality books were published in very limited editions, so even poets and critics with a deep interest in Creeley may never have seen these gorgeous works.

Two of the largest and most visually arresting books are *Numbers* (1968), Creeley's collaboration with Robert Indiana, and *A Day Book*, with R. B. Kitaj (1972). *Numbers*, printed by Domberger Editions in Stuttgart, Germany, contains silk-screen versions of Indiana's paintings of the integers from 0 to 9, accompanied by poems (in English and German) for each number by Creeley.[1] The vibrant colors of the silkscreens literally dazzle, and their hues and shapes and the negative spaces they generate differ dramatically from page to page. *A Day Book*, also printed in Germany, by Graphis, is another jaw-dropping work of book art, though quite unlike *Numbers*. *A Day Book* consists of thirty pages of prose, illustrated by Kitaj with etchings, screen prints, and lithographs. Also striking is the variety of the pages, with every leaf made of different material (many kinds of handmade paper and also plastic and oilcloth) and a unique typeface for each page of prose.

My viewing of *A Day Book* began in 1972, at Robert Duncan's house in San Francisco, where a copy had just arrived. Because the two poets could not afford to purchase limited editions of each other's work, they agreed to trade author's copies. I remember a magical afternoon sitting with Duncan on the couch in the front bay window, lifting heavy leaves out of the Plexiglas box and marveling at this new kind of book. The collaborations with Indiana and Kitaj are direct precursors to *Presences,* Creeley's book with Marisol, which followed in 1976. Planned as a coffee table art book, *Presences* was eventually printed by Scribner's in the smaller trim size of Creeley's poetry books. It is immensely gratifying that one of Creeley's most revelatory collaborations is now, in a somewhat larger format, finally back in print.

CREELEY'S COPY OF *PRESENCES*

The Hesburgh Library at the University of Notre Dame purchased nearly the entire personal library of Robert Creeley (1926–2005) from his widow, Penelope Creeley.[2] Normally, libraries acquire the papers of a famous writer, rather than the books owned, but Creeley's books are special. Whether they are volumes of his own work or of one among his vast circle of friends, acquaintances, and students, many of the more than six thousand books are stuffed with material he deemed pertinent to it or to people associated with it.[3] Like most writers, he prized books highly and lavished care on them, and he was religious about not marking or dog-earing pages. More distinctively, though, he employed books as filing cabinets, inserting items such as letters, postcards, reviews, interviews, photographs, and hotel bills. As Penelope remembers,

> For him the books had become a beloved record of his life. They contained the ideas, the thoughts, the speaking breath of his friends. He did not write in books, but he kept things in them. Letters, announcements, tickets, brochures, mementos of contact in the world with increasingly scattered, always dear friends. These were his bookmarks. These were the books wherein he had found his life.[4]

In particular, copies of his own books testify to his vital transactions with editors, publishers, designers, printers, and illustrators. These various partners planned and executed with him unique and beautiful objects, which were much more than transparent containers for text. One example of a lovingly designed object filled with such "bookmarks" is Creeley's copy of *Presences: A Text for Marisol.*[5] It contains a title-page drawing and inscription by his principle collaborator, the Venezuelan pop artist Marisol Escobar (1930–2016); postcards and letters from Marisol and from the book's designer, William Katz; a photograph of Katz; and letters from Mexican poet Octavio Paz and professors Sherman Paul (University of Iowa) and Albert Cook (University at Buffalo). Many of the postcards display images or graphics by Marisol, some enhanced with drawings by the senders, Marisol or Katz. In this instance, as in countless others, a book in Creeley's library opens onto a network of transactions that extends through the design, the publication, and the subsequent life of the book. For Penelope, whose partnership with Robert was just beginning in 1976, the volume provided a first glimpse into the intertwining relationships that sustain the creation of such a beautiful object:

> Those very early first days brought another education for me, regarding books. This time it was about the book as a physical object, and about Robert's friendships and loyalty. Before I left New Zealand, Robert had sent me a beautiful, newly-minted copy of *Presences*, his book with Marisol. Everything about it delighted him. He told me in detail all about its production, from its elegant design by Bill Katz to negotiations as to who the publishers would be. It had been a harrowing process, but the end-product was entirely satisfying. Bill's mock-up for the book's front page was one of the first things we ever framed. I still enjoy its tender presaging of the book-to-be. ("Robert and Books" 3)

Creeley considered creative alliances integral to the making of art. As he proclaimed in a lecture near the end of his life, "Poetry is a team sport: you can't play it all by yourself."[6] The shared quality of creation is on display in his extensive, often daily correspondence with Charles Olson (published in ten volumes), in his lifelong habit of collaboration with visual artists and designers, and in his live and recorded performances of poetry with jazz musicians. I would wager that no poet of his generation was as keen as Creeley to work with visual artists, in particular. In fact, his collaborations were the subject of a museum exhibition, "In Company: Robert Creeley's Collaborations," organized in 1999 by the Castellani Art Museum of Niagara University, that traveled to the University of North Carolina at Greensboro, the University of South Florida, Stanford University, and the New York Public Library. His collaborative practice, especially with European artists, was also the inspiration for a 2011 symposium at the University of Caen, France, "Collaboration and the Artist's Book: A Transatlantic Perspective." In addition to his work with Marisol and Katz, he cooperated on books, posters, and sculptures with major artists of his generation (John Altoon, John Chamberlain, Jim Dine, Robert Indiana, Alex Katz, R. B. Kitaj, René Laubiès, Sol LeWitt) and of the succeeding generation (Georg Baselitz, Joe Brainard, Francesco Clemente, Cletus Johnson, Archie Rand, Susan Rothenberg, Donald Sultan, James Surls, Robert Therrien).

Regardless of whether the project began with text or artwork or was a simultaneous effort, artists have testified gratefully to the ease of working with Creeley and to the sense that he "got" what their art was about. As Clemente puts it, "Part of my fascination with these particular collaborations is how every time he seems to perceive what the form of the work is. He invents his own corresponding form that somehow has the same structure" (*In Company*

26). Echoing this affirmation of Creeley's uncanny ability to mimic the form and retrieve the experience underlying a work of visual art, Marisol wrote him, after receiving the text for *Presences*, "It is really amazing how you could do something so close to me from seeing me so few times."[7] Clemente highlights the satisfaction that accrues from such mutuality: "I think that is the most gratifying experience that any painter or poet can have—to be understood. . . . You know that you're not crazy and you're not alone" (*In Company* 26).

The collective artwork that became *Presences* owed its genesis to an earlier team effort, the sumptuous edition of *Numbers* by Creeley and Indiana (1968). As the poet recalls, "'Presences' began with the publication of 'Numbers' insofar as the sculptor Marisol had seen that collaboration with Robert Indiana and myself, and considered I might be the appropriate writer of a text to accompany photographs of her work, which a New York publisher had then in mind to bring out as a book."[8] Katz was instrumental in both publications, inviting Creeley to compose *Numbers* with Indiana and later drawing Marisol's attention to that gorgeous, large-format volume, with Indiana's brilliant silkscreened numbers and Creeley's poems in bold, sans serif type, printed to the highest standards by Domberger Editions in Stuttgart, Germany.[9] Katz was Indiana's studio assistant for more than a decade, initiating and overseeing print projects including *Numbers*, which came about in the following way:

> I met Poldi Domberger of Domberger Editions on a plane. He wanted to publish something of Bob Indiana's because it lent itself to silkscreen. The idea grew. . . . The first thing that was suggested was *Numbers* because the *Numbers* paintings had been shown in Europe [in 1965] and were in museums. I thought a text would give it added dimensions. I asked Bob [Creeley] and he wrote me back and said he would love to. (*In Company* 22–23)

The 1971 plan for a Marisol project was to produce not a limited edition like *Numbers* but an impressive coffee table book with reproductions of Marisol's sculptures, to be published by Harry Abrams. Says Creeley, "It began as a book for Abrams. There was a great moment when I was given a thousand dollars as an advance, and I sent the text and nothing happened. Then I got a letter saying they really couldn't do it. Their editor had advised them that it was just random stuff taken from the writer's wastebasket."[10] Katz confirmed for me that the editor had uttered this judgment and that he, Katz, had hurried over to see Abrams, whom he knew, and to insist the text was a powerful work of art in its own right. When the publisher refused to budge, Katz finally asked him, "Have you read it?"

"No. I don't have time to read all the books I publish. I just publish them."

Katz then suggested he have someone read the text to him, possibly while being driven to his country home, but it proved a dead issue.[11]

At this point, it fell to Creeley to take the next step. He issued portions of the prose text in magazines—*Big Sky, Fiction, Spring Creek,* and *This*—and the entire text was printed in Richard Grossinger's magazine *Io.*[12] His trade publisher at the time, Scribner's, ultimately undertook to print it with black-and-white images of Marisol's sculptures, in the trim size they used for his poetry (approximately 5.5 × 8.5 inches). *Presences: A Text for Marisol* saw the light of day, finally, in 1976. As a book, it has several remarkable features: it lacks pagination; every page, of both image and text, is bled to the edges (including the gutter); and a photograph faces every page of text—but staggered, so that recto and verso pages of text follow recto and verso images. The book is broken up into five numbered sections, each consisting of six pages in Creeley's original typescript. A day's writing would be planned in advance to consist of either one, two, or three of these large, typed pages, ordered in the five sections as 1,2,3; 2,3,1; 3,1,2; 1,2,3; 2,3,1. As he had earlier in the poem "Numbers," written for his Indiana collaboration, Creeley ascribed quasi-magical or phenomenological qualities to the numbers. In the introduction to the British publication of *Presences,* he explains its structure:

> I wanted a focus, or frame, with which to work, and *one, two, three* seemed an interesting periodicity or phasing. That is, using a base of one-page, two-page, three-page units (again single-spaced in their initial composition on the typewriter), each section of the text was then six pages, and that times five was thirty—returning me to a *three.* I then hit upon a simple way of avoiding intensive repetition of units in the sequence, simply by taking the last number of 123 and putting it first, making it 312, etc. (*Mabel* 6)

He also adhered to the regimen of thirty typed pages for *A Day Book* and *Mabel: A Story,* the contemporaneous prose works included with *Presences* in the British edition of *Mabel: A Story and Other Prose.* Separately, *A Day Book* and *Mabel: A Story* were also published in Europe as limited-edition collaborations with artists, the former with R. B. Kitaj and the latter with Jim Dine.[13]

Presences stands out from the other two collaborations in several ways. In the first place, Kitaj and Dine created images to accompany a text that Creeley had already composed, whereas for *Presences* Creeley wrote a work to respond to Marisol's sculptures. Second, the texture of Creeley's prose is different in each of the three texts. *A Day Book* consists literally of the jottings of thirty separate (not always consecutive) days and reads like a diary. In *Mabel,* Creeley meditates on women and his relations to them, often in the form of fantasies and anecdotes. *Presences* is a direct attempt to mirror in writing Marisol's activity in sculpture. As he explains to an inquisitive art historian, "What we both wanted, then, was an active complement, rather than a descriptive prose text and/or a sense of illustration in the images themselves."[14] Of the three texts, the prose of *Presences* has the most varied textures, through which Creeley seeks to explore "a diversity of senses of human 'presence,' in a diversity of modes, e.g., everything from tape 'cut ups' to almost nostalgically familiar 'narrative.'" In one section, he finds himself "using a postcard of a reproduction of Poussin, plus the German well-wisher's message at the back, plus the random 'voice' of a radio playing in my shed, etc." As the examples of "cut ups" and of found text and overheard speech might suggest, one way to consider this prose would be as assemblage, and in this sense its method mimics closely the assemblage technique of Marisol. Such avant-garde methods, Creeley claims, should not be seen as ends in themselves but rather as means to investigate personal and interpersonal situations: "At the root, however, is insistently Marisol's own preoccupation with terms of being human, and its various possible 'representations'" (Letter to Kinsey).

The photographs in *Presences*, arranged by Marisol and Katz, give evidence of a further turn in the feedback loop. Two of the sculptures, *Baby Girl* (1963) and *The Generals* (1961–1962), were known directly to Creeley because he saw them in the Albright-Knox Art Gallery, in Buffalo, New York, where he lived while teaching at the University at Buffalo (1966–2003).[15] Other encounters with Marisol's art took place mainly through *Marisol*, a 1968 Venezuelan volume she sent him and whose double title page she illuminated and signed.[16] The photographs in *Presences* were selected by Marisol and Katz when they received typeset pages of text to lay out: "Finally, when the book was in proof, Bill Katz told me that one evening in company with Marisol they put all the page proofs and photographs on the floor, and decided on the appropriate juxtapositions. She also is responsible for the decision to 'bleed' the prose pages, so as to keep some textural balance with the 'bled' photographs. It was my decision to have an image always facing a page of text" (Letter to Kinsey). Thus, the monumental frontality of Marisol's sculptures matches pages of text that have a similar visual effect, as if the blocks of Creeley's prose poetry were things that fill space like the assemblages Marisol built up from blocks of wood. Including the covers of the book, there are photographs of thirty-seven of Marisol's sculptures, with from one to four views of each piece. In these photographs, as in a technique from independent film, the viewer is often brought in close for a detailed perspective but never allowed to pan out to get an installation view of larger bodies of work. John Yau notes, "This lack of an overriding perspective parallels Creeley's writing, its accumulation of details and palpable perceptions" (*In Company* 71). Every aspect of the making of the book promotes *immersion* in Marisol's art and in Creeley's language.

AUTOBIOGRAPHICAL ASSEMBLAGE

In the early 1960s, Marisol became an internationally celebrated pop artist. Born in Paris in 1930 to a wealthy Venezuelan family, María Sol Escobar grew up there and in Caracas. Her mother committed suicide when she was eleven, after which she refused to speak; for the rest of her life her voice was whispery and reticent. She studied art at the Jepson Art Institute in Los Angeles, the École des Beaux-Arts in Paris, and, most importantly, with Yasuo Kuniyoshi at the Art Students League of New York and with Hans Hoffman in New York and Provincetown. In 1957, she was included in a group show with Jasper Johns and Robert Rauschenberg, artists with whom she shared commitments to folk art and to assemblage, and she was exhibited at the Museum of Modern Art in "The Art of Assemblage" in 1961 and "Americans, 1963."[17] At first, pop art was reviewed derisively by critics loyal to abstract expressionism, but as it gained acceptance in the 1960s Marisol was considered a primary figure. Her gallery and museum exhibitions drew huge crowds, and she and her work were featured in art, fashion, and general circulation magazines. As one critic notes, "probably more reviews, in fact, were published on her contemporaneously than on any of the male Pop artists."[18] Her early reputation even eclipsed that of her close friend Andy Warhol. Like Warhol she devoted works to public icons—in her case the Kennedy Family, the British royal family, Lyndon Johnson, John Wayne, and Bob Hope—all of whom she portrayed in a deceptively naive though sometimes clearly satirical style. Interestingly, Creeley does not seem to engage this side of her work in his writing of *Presences*, and she responds by including only a few of them in the book.[19]

Balancing her interest in public figures and their representation, Marisol concentrates on intimate personal details—especially those of her own body. She obsessively casts her face and body parts for inclusion in many of her sculptures, even those not ostensibly autobiographical. In a discussion of this aspect of her work, she suggests self-portraiture is a mere expedient: "I'm always there (in my studio) when I'm working. I work very often late at night. I can't call up a friend at one in the morning to make a cast of his face."[20] She goes on to admit, however, that incorporating herself is actually essential to her art: "Whatever the artist makes is always a kind of self-portrait. Even if he paints a picture of an apple or makes an abstraction. When I do a well-known person like John Wayne, I am really doing myself." This act of measuring herself against or as part of everything she portrays has great resonance for Creeley. It bespeaks an existential commitment he values so highly that in an essay, "Inside Out: Notes on the Autobiographical Mode," he quotes Marisol as an authority on autobiography: "The sculptor Marisol speaks of using herself, over and over, in her work. 'When I show myself as I am I return to reality.'"[21] In the final section of *Presences* (V.1), Creeley rings a series of changes on phrases by Marisol that reflect her belief that self-placement is necessary to representing the world accurately. A brief example from this section displays how Creeley collages together words from Marisol, which he employs again and again as something like mantric phrases: "I return to reality. I had no other model. I used myself over and over. I put things where they belong. I show myself as I am."

In addition to plaster casts of her face and body parts, Marisol utilizes other media, such as photography and drawing, to affix her own likeness onto sculptural figures in group or family scenes. In these works the crudeness of the carved wooden blocks that represent torsos or entire bodies contrasts with photographs of faces or with real objects, such as hats, dresses, sunglasses, or jewelry. By emphasizing materiality through features such as the blockiness of wood, the evidence of the hand in painted surfaces, the plaster of cast body parts, and the chemically printed surface of photographs, Marisol's sculptures activate a variety of media to produce "presence." The diversity of representational means helps to denaturalize the self-portraiture. Speaking of the images of women in Marisol's sculptures, for instance—most of which bear representations of her own anatomy—Cécile Whiting notes how the various means employed relativize one another:

> A photograph is but a flat picture next to the cast of a breast; a cast of a breast is but plaster next to an actual necklace; a necklace is but paste next to a photograph of real gemstones. Marisol's sculptures thus present the femininity they have come to represent not as a stable entity known transparently but as something cobbled together from representational parts. . . . The juxtaposition of various elements and the radical discontinuities between them draw attention to the processes of representation through which woman is known. (Whiting 226)

Thus, at the most basic level, Marisol is an artist of assemblage. No matter how familiar or self-referential her subjects, the juxtaposition of sculptural materials enables her autobiographical art to reveal something new about herself and others. In its greater insistence on materiality, assemblage can accomplish a different kind of presence than that of traditional sculpture, which often seeks to embody timeless and placeless illusion. Unlike traditional sculpture, assemblage does not pretend to self-sufficiency but asks the viewer to jump in, to complete the artwork, to actually exist within it. Likewise, if perspective can move the viewer through a scene, sometimes leading the eye toward a vanishing point, Marisol's works, in contrast, possess a complex "thereness"—attributable to shifts in scale, to the blockiness of figures, and to the variety of materials—that keeps inviting the viewer to begin seeing it over and over, constantly calling attention to points of irresolvable contrast rather than urging a synoptic view. In an interview with Creeley, Kevin Power makes explicit the connection between the variety of materials employed by Marisol and the variety of verbal modes in Creeley's prose. He asks, "In the Marisol text are the presences, like the Marisol figures, facets of your various concerns e.g. language per se, the imagination made actual, autobiography, the role of pronouns, etc?"[22] Creeley agrees, affirming that senses of presence he shares with Marisol result from combining disparate materials to create an experiential assemblage: "Yes, presences, just dimensions of human presence, occasions of human presence, modes of human presence. I was trying to get hold of different kinds of experience of presence. It's a situation that lets you ring the changes!"[23]

He rings the changes right from the beginning of *Presences*: "Big things. And little things. The weight, the lightness of it. The place it takes. Walking around, it comes forward, or to the side, or sides, or backward, on a foot, on feet, on several feet" (I.1). Here the "dimensions of human presence" invoked by a Marisol sculpture provoke a meditation on conflicts of scale and how to orient oneself with respect to an object. In constructing the book, Marisol makes the right identification of images to match with this section of prose: two views of the gigantic *Baby Girl* (1963), 74 × 35 × 47 inches. This is one of the pieces Creeley saw in the Albright-Knox Art Gallery in Buffalo, New York, and it made a powerful impression. The reversals in Creeley's prose seem to represent his coming to terms with stark reversals in the sculpture, where a huge, seated baby (more than six feet tall) dwarfs her mother, a diminutive doll adorned with Marisol's face.[24] Creeley takes at "face-value" this topsy-turvy world, registering the overwhelming, contradictory feelings it provokes. As the reader mentally "comes forward, or to the side, or sides, or backward" to assess the prose, one sees that on the page it too has an outsize and block-like quality, echoing the baby's blockish head and boxy body. In the work of both artists, an improbable combination of horror and humor lends a disorienting, confrontational quality to their approaches to everyday life, requiring that the reader or viewer come to terms with unanticipated shifts in scale and materials.

In *Baby Girl*, the assemblage is made of a perplexing array of materials and modes of representation: a carved wooden head, with a painted face, and a satin ribbon tied to a wooden topknot; a body made from a wooden box, with a painted dress skirted at the bottom with real fabric; carved blocks for legs; and a tiny, opposable wooden doll, bearing on its face a photograph of Marisol's face, standing on one of the baby's huge legs. Throughout *Presences*, Creeley, too, joins many kinds of verbal material and compositional layers in his prose assemblage. At the level of the sentence, he cobbles together and works variations on phrases not only by Marisol but by William Blake ("Fire delights in its form" [I.2]), Federico García Lorca ("Vestida con mantos negros / piensa que el mundo es chiquito / y el corazón es inmenso" [V.1]), Evelyn Waugh ("He bore a preternatural resemblance to his caricatures in the evening newspapers" [I.1]), François Villon ("Où sont les neiges d'antan?" [I.2]), John Lennon ("As soon as you're born, they make you feel small" [III.2]), W. B. Yeats ("hid his face amid a crowd of stars" [IV.3]), and Ezra Pound ("The rat has teeth" [V.2]). At the level of the individual section of *Presences*, Creeley collages together discourse from a variety of media, as in the example above of the postcard with an image of Poussin's painting *L'Inspiration du poète*, whose handwritten greeting he also includes, along with a voice overheard from the radio (IV.1); or in section III.1, a cut-up version of a tape-recorded conversation about music among friends. At the level of the volume as a whole, the fifteen sections and the postscript include writing from an array of modes, which range from improvising on sayings and clichés to excavating memories to recounting fables to scrutinizing the dimensions of present occasions. Most of these modes themselves are shot through with collage elements, making assemblage the most prominent transactional technique throughout the writing.

Another type of transaction involves cutting between Spanish and English. For instance, the Spanish words quoted above from the first stanza of Lorca's "La Soleá" appear in the last section of *Presences* (V.1). A literal translation would read, "Dressed in black veils / she thinks the world is tiny / and the heart is immense."[25] Creeley set this stanza, with its phenomenological reversal of scale, as epigraph to an early story, "A Death," where it carries over an ominous quality from its original context: as Lorca's poem continues, fluttering black veils suggest that a woman has leapt from a balcony. Creeley inserts phrases from this stanza into a section of *Presences* that also contains quotes from Marisol. It begins,

> Voices from the silence. Silencio immenso [*sic*]. Darkness falls from the air. When I show myself as I am, I return to reality. Vestida con mantos negros. Somewhere else, sometime. Walking in the rain.
>
> When I show myself as I am, I return to reality. Piensa que el mundo es chiquito. Goes green, goes white. Weather falls out, raining. Applause at the edges. Seeing wind. When I show myself as I am, I return to reality. People should think of themselves when they live alone. Goes white.

This assemblage interweaves two sentence openings from Marisol ("When I show myself" and "People should think of themselves") and a reversal of a line about the dire fates suffered by famous women, from Thomas Nashe's "Summer's Last Will and Testament," which reads, in context, "Brightness falls from the air, / Queens have died young and fair, / Dust hath closed Helen's eye." To return to reality is not necessarily a happy prospect, especially for powerful women, but it does allow the autobiographer to strip away pretense and to "show myself as I am."

Other Spanish phrases, in translation, also enter *Presences*, contributing to an interlingual assemblage. From the Venezuelan catalog given him by Marisol, Creeley has translated and incorporated suggestive phrases, each occupying a separate page in the original. For example:

> [1] *¿Románticas historias . . .*
> [2] *¿Frágiles símbolos de una lumbre incierta?*
> [3] *Acaso el sol terrible de los trópicos iluminó un instante la noche profunda de sus ojos.*

In section IV.2, he works through these materials:

> [1] Romantic histories? Or [2] fragile symbols of an uncertain light. It is not clear to them why the car has stopped so far from the town to ask directions, or why it should be of them, so faintly apparent from the roadside where the car has been pulled over. . . . There is no sound from the car as the people in it, not quite possible to see clearly, wait for further explanations. [3] In case the terrible sun of the tropics shines for an instant, she wears sun glasses, a profound night of the eyes. This is the woman to the left of the driver, hooded figure, they now discern, with long talonlike fingers holding the wheel.

The two images accompanying this passage are details from *Women Sitting on a Mirror* (1965), showing two of the three women in the sculpture—each with plaster features cast from Marisol's face—wearing actual sunglasses beneath parasol-like plastic hats. In the Venezuelan book, a detail of the same sculpture accompanies the Spanish phrase about the tropical sun and the night of the eyes (into which Creeley wedges "she wears sun glasses"). Having lived for significant amounts of time in Mallorca and Guatemala, Creeley crafts a prose that brings the reader into a multilingual world, where Spanish and English speak to one another analogously to how poetry and art converse within *Presences*. In acknowledgment of this interlingual conversation, the Mexican poet Octavio Paz wrote Creeley in 1973 requesting permission to publish two or three sections of *Presences* (accompanied by reproductions

Figure 7. Buzz Spector, *Creeley's Creeleys* (2007). Interior dye diffusion print (Polaroid), 34 × 22 inches (Edition of 10). Reprinted with permission of the artist.

of Marisol's work) in his magazine *Plural* (1972–1976). In his self-appointed role of keeping alive dialogue between cultural figures in the United States and Latin America, Paz recognizes the beauty of Creeley's encounter with Marisol and offers to translate it into Spanish.

The letter from Paz was found in Creeley's copy of *Presences*. Before his library was purchased, Creeley's books were mainly in the care of publisher and book dealer Steve Clay, who wrote descriptions of them and their contents (available in the finding aids of the Hesburgh Libraries) before selling them. During this time, the artist Buzz Spector made two large-scale Polaroid photographs of arrangements he constructed of Creeley's books. One is of a stack of books by Charles Olson, with a few volumes and photographs open in front of it, titled *Creeley's Olson* (2008, 43 × 22 inches). The other is of a large array of Creeley's own books, titled *Creeley's Creeleys* (2007, 43 × 22 inches; fig. 7). An artist whose work consists mainly of arrangements and alterations of books and elements from books, Spector sees Creeley's volumes not only as evidence of collaborations with artists, writers, designers, photographers, editors, and publishers but also as primary artistic materials. Spector's portrait of Creeley's own copies of his books, laid out on a well-worn wooden floor, draws attention to how they inhabit space, as though this were a display whose sculptural and architectural qualities might resemble those of a Marisol installation. *Presences* can be seen about halfway back, a little to the left of center. Through its photographic magic, *Creeley's Creeleys* raises Robert Creeley's network of transactions to the status of a work of art in its own right.

8

The Language Art of David Antin's Talk Poems

He was an eminently philosophical poet, but David Antin (1932–2016) could never be called psychological, for he eschewed introspection and the search for motives and believed in thought as action. The talk poems were designed to demonstrate how a person might think about a difficult problem in the presence of other people, for whom this problem might also matter. Antin was assiduous about taping each of his performances, and the cassette recorder left its mark as did the people in the room. The beginnings of pieces are often concerned with placing the microphone and starting up the machine, and there might well be a pause halfway through when he ejected the cassette tape and turned it over to continue recording. As philosophical inquiries, his talk poems are filled with a surprising number of stories about his friends and family, which serve to illustrate points or provoke new perspectives on knotty issues. The main collection of recorded talk poems, now housed at the Getty Research Institute, holds 285 audiotapes and 4 videotapes. Antin made certain that many of the tapes were transcribed, but he published relatively few of the talk poems. Looking into his working process to discern different layers of intention could yield fascinating results. The layers might include the intention to talk about something in front of a particular group of people at a specific time; the intention to record the performance; the intention to transcribe the recording; the intention to edit the transcription; the intention to publish the talk poem (often first in a magazine); and the intention to organize talk poems into a book. Delaminating the layers would reveal some of the complexity of Antin's methods and goals.

The three books of talk poems he issued with New Directions—*talking at the boundaries* (1976), *tuning* (1984), and *what it means to be avant-garde* (1993)—were allowed by the press to go out of print, and copyright reverted to the author.[1] When I learned that the University of New Mexico Press was planning to launch "Recencies," a series of new editions of significant out-of-print postwar poetry and prose, I proposed a selection from those three volumes. The book, *How Long Is the Present*, came out in 2014, two years before Antin died, and was launched with new talk poems in New York City at the Poetry Project and in San Diego at D. G. Wills Bookstore.[2] The following essay is a revision of the book's introduction.

HOW TO READ A TALK POEM

in fact everybody has some
notion as to what is an experience and what is not an experience
and a lot of it has to do with what you think is either beneficial
or real   it doesn't have to be beneficial   it might just simply
be real   and your definition of the real has a lot to do with your
notion of what an experience should be   because your definition
of the real is more like a hope about things that should prove to be
real   the real is like a construction   something that you
build   piece by piece   and then it falls on you   or you
move into it

(David Antin, "is this the right place?")

When first encountering a talk poem by David Antin, a reader is apt to be puzzled. What to make of this strange mass of language, with no capitalization or punctuation, broken into strings of phrases by open spaces, with neither left nor right margins justified? It doesn't look like poetry and it doesn't look like prose.[3] It has none of the markings of either—line breaks, stanzas, paragraphs, section titles, epigraphs, and so on—that would help the reader gain an overview of the structure of the piece and discriminate between primary and secondary ideas and images. The only way to find your bearings is to plunge into the verbal flux—to imagine yourself listening to a speaker addressing an audience on a specific occasion, offering no signposts along the way but pausing between utterances to catch his breath and recalibrate. Distinct from either verse or prose, an Antin talk poem is a transcription of the actual flow of thinking and of telling stories, spoken by someone probing a question in the presence of others listening closely. In this case, the question has to do with the nature of experience, which Antin, following John Dewey's definition of "*an* experience" in *Art as Experience* (1934), regards as a sequence of events that coheres or takes a shape, rather than as a single, immediate impression.[4] Equally, though, he is inquiring into the nature of reality, which he regards as socially constructed rather than as a given condition. Associating these seemingly ordinary terms, experience and the real, he points out how each depends upon the other philosophically and that neither is wholly isolatable as a concept. From another perspective, this slice from a talk poem sounds like the verbal play of someone else in the pragmatist lineage, Gertrude Stein. Like Antin, Stein probes the conditions of experience by making ordinary language both its vehicle and its subject matter, such that the more she repeats words the less familiar they become. And just as listening to a recording of Stein reading her writing aids tremendously in following her thought, so hearing Antin deliver a talk poem on the PennSound website accustoms one to his rich Brooklyn accent and wry, ironic vocal inflections—and to how the written transcriptions imitate the rhythm of his thinking aloud.[5]

In the course of a talk poem, Antin occupies several roles usually conceived of as discrete and even antagonistic: avant-garde poet, philosopher, critic, comic, and performance artist. His unique versatility derives from the breadth of his training and the variety of his occupations: educated in engineering and linguistics, he worked as a technical translator, an art critic, and a museum curator before spending many years as professor in the Visual Arts Department at the University of California, San Diego. As a critic, he published a selection of his classic essays on literature and art, *Radical Coherency* (2011), with the University of Chicago Press.[6] As a poet, he associated first with the poetic and artistic movements of Deep Image and Fluxus and then with the merger of poetry and anthropology called ethnopoetics, made up of poets, performance artists, translators, and ethnographers, whose convener, Jerome Rothenberg, was a lifelong friend.

Antin was born in 1932 and grew up in Brooklyn during the Depression and World War II, moving from New York City to San Diego County with his wife, the mixed media artist Eleanor Antin, in 1968. His early books of poetry, *Definitions* (1967), *Autobiography* (1967), *Code of Flag Behavior* (1968), *Meditations* (1971), and *Talking* (1972; 2001), are literally "experimental": each one involves conceptual experiments with language (usually someone else's—seldom his own) in a range of social situations.[7] Gradually, he became disappointed with the poetry reading as a mode for making public these experiments. The works collected in *Talking* show him searching for more satisfying ways to perform poetry in public as a primary activity rather than a reenactment, and he achieved a breakthrough in the last piece, "talking at pomona," a discourse improvised on the spot and recorded on tape, listening to which convinced him he had stumbled on a new kind of poem.

This performance overcame what he had begun to see as the Achilles heel of the poetry reading: its creative inertness. By thinking aloud, with nothing to back him up but his own intelligence and a rapport with the audience—as if walking a tightrope without a net—Antin risks creating something new. He considers the poetry reading, by contrast, merely an exercise in portentous recitation, one in which the poet impersonates "the poet."[8] Impatient with this artificial reenactment, he turns his dissatisfaction, in one of his talk poems, into a philosophical inquiry into "the present":

> when i look into my book and
> take my words   go back to them and recover them   i lose
> track of anything i would call the present   and i have a taste

for the present which i imagine you can forgive me
if you dont forgive me im sorry its a strong and peculiar
taste and the present is a difficult thing to have a taste
for its very difficult because in satisfying it the question
i always have to ask myself is what is the present and
how long is it? how long is the present?

(*Present* 158)

In this extract from the talk poem "how long is the present," Antin probes both conceptions of the present moment and the language for describing it. Although in this passage the string of five words at the end poses a question, the same string appears as the title of the piece without a question mark, which causes its meaning to oscillate between "how long *is* the present?" and "how *long* is the present!" If we collate these two senses, the result is an understanding of the present as both a specific interval for examination and a matter of duration. Thus, the present appears as a time span anywhere from incomprehensibly short to unimaginably expansive, and locating it could be either the most obvious thing or an uncertain and arduous undertaking. Further questioning of the length of the present can lead to awareness of how difficult it is to discern and inhabit a particular moment. Shifting gears, an invocation of "the present" in a published talk poem can refer to the historical moment of delivering the improvised discourse (whose circumstances and audience Antin is at pains to describe), or it can refer to something broader, to an interpretation of the cultural era in which the talk poem first appeared, for instance. Alternatively, readers can think of the present as the time in which they encounter a talk poem, for it speaks to minds attuned differently (in 2020, say) than were minds in the 1970s and 1980s.

Antin's acerbic view of the poetry reading as a pointless exercise is a specimen of his iconoclastic stance and his desire to expose what he sees as shoddy thinking. Speaking at times with the cocky assurance of a scientist, he searches for underlying principles or axioms that have general application, removing obfuscation where possible while still respecting what cannot be fully comprehended. Not surprisingly, when he first began delivering and publishing talk poems they caused a furor in the poetry world. He was denounced as an anti-poet for sacrificing features that distinguish poetry, such as meter, verse, condensation, and the pursuit of beauty. Responding with a calm and relentlessly rational provocation, he asserted that the techniques of poetry have outlived their relevance, that they can be seen, sociologically speaking, as residues of an arcane practice with no application to the present. Writing poetry this way, he claims, amounts to turning one's back on the world and going into a closet to address an imaginary audience of connoisseurs. He urged poets to abandon the "craft" of poetry and return to the poet's time-honored role of considering matters of real consequence to a company of actual people.

This radical revaluation of the means and purpose of poetry became so scandalous that Harold Bloom walked out of a symposium on contemporary poetry in Washington, DC, when Marjorie Perloff endeavored to speak of Antin and John Cage as poets (an incident Antin treats with great humor in "what it means to be avant-garde" [*Present* 322–28]).[9] Bloom was not alone in his rebuke, for even many of the more "experimental" poets of the 1970s were caught off guard by Antin's pointed challenge to poetry as an exalted vocation. To clear the ground of competing formal claims for poetry (labeled by some critics as the "raw" and the "cooked" camps), he proposed an axiom that radically expands its boundaries, in which poetry is simply "the language art." This definition regards any artful use of language as poetic. Drawing on his extensive studies in world poetry and in linguistics, Antin maintains that the vernacular, the language of living discourse, is wholly adequate to making as much sense as can be made of the complex situations in which we find ourselves.

PLACING ANTIN AS POET AND PHILOSOPHER

Posing subtle questions in everyday language about fundamental concepts such as experience or the present or the real, Antin attempts to slip free of hidebound forms and preconceptions that constrain thinking to inquire freshly about how we see our lives and therefore how we live them. This method places him in a lineage of maverick sages in American culture that goes back at least as far as Ralph Waldo Emerson, whose essays, like Antin's talk poems, can be seen as limit cases for the definition of poetry. Both Emerson and Antin rethink fundamental issues by relying on their own intellects and their own words while paradoxically foraging across a spectacular range of human knowledge for examples of pragmatic and expansive approaches to life. For his part, Antin draws on expertise in art history, philosophy, linguistics, chess, baseball, science, mathematics, and engineering for the analogies he pursues. Where Emerson preserves a balance between affirmative and skeptical outlooks, though, Antin leans more heavily on the skeptical, declaring with a biting wit that most of our mental mistakes come from assuming certainty in situations replete with unknowns.

Like his greatly admired predecessor, Ludwig Wittgenstein (much of whose work comes down to us as notes taken by others during his oral performances), Antin catches language in the act of reassuring us that we know what we're doing—when in many ways we haven't a clue.[10] The talk poems proceed from a stance favored by Emerson and Wittgenstein and also by Socrates—a profoundly attentive state that could be called not-understanding—in which the greatest gains for thinking are made by assuming we know very little and so posing questions acutely. Ever the pragmatist, Antin takes no one's word for the truth of a proposition or judgment but insists on testing everything by the yardstick of experience. Refusing to cover experience with a tissue of clichés that passes for understanding, he embodies Emerson's ideal of "Man Thinking," whose office is "to guide men by showing them facts amidst appearances."[11]

If the poet's job is also, as Russian formalist critic Viktor Shklovsky contends, to take ordinary appearances and make them strange, then Antin enacts this role assiduously, defamiliarizing common nostrums and summoning individual experience to challenge automatic assumptions. To invoke experience as a proving ground, he recounts quizzical stories from his own life and those of family members and friends as examples of the sorts of questions he is asking. We might even think of the stories as signaling an epic dimension to the talk poem—for Antin frequently compares it to the oral mode of the Homeric epics and other nonliterate poetries. But we might just as easily pause before applying the term "epic" to Antin's narratives, which dwell on the strangeness of the everyday rather than summoning the glories and battles of gods and heroes.[12] If we characterize epic less by subject or diction than by a paratactic syntax that sets phrases in unexpected relationships—as critics have described Ezra Pound's *Cantos* and other modern long poems that claim an epic ancestry—then the term may account partially for Antin's project. From an Emersonian perspective, though, Antin's paratactic dialogues would be regarded most properly as a form of oratory, which Emerson celebrates as a freewheeling collagist enterprise, akin to verbally throwing in the kitchen sink. Comparing oratory to a panharmonicon, an early-nineteenth-century music synthesizer, Emerson lauds it as an efficacious democratic form: "here everything is admissible, philosophy, ethics, divinity, criticism, poetry, humor, fun, mimicry, anecdotes, jokes, ventriloquism. . . . It is a panharmonicon. . . . Here he may lay himself out utterly, large, enormous, prodigal, on the subject of the hour."[13]

Like Emerson the master lecturer, Antin first offers his thinking to audiences on the road, using the occasion of speaking aloud to strangers as a creative goad. He moves through many registers of discourse searching for elusive truths, "lay[ing] himself out utterly, large, enormous, prodigal, on the subject of the hour"—a description that could apply as well to the poetry of Walt Whitman or Charles Olson. For Antin, the live audience convened at a specific time and place becomes an integral part of the composition of the talk poem, in that it brings pressures of an actual situation to bear on his thought process. The talk poems are thus not only oratorical but improvisatory. Just as a jazz musician works tirelessly at exploring musical sequences and combinations in preparation for reacting spontaneously onstage, so Antin carries his ongoing thinking about fundamental issues into a room with a group of people and begins to improvise. To some extent, then, individual talk poems form episodes in an open-ended philosophical project. Certain large questions—such as what is the nature of experience, or how do we define narrative and what is its relationship to story, or what do we mean by understanding—tend to occupy his thinking for many years. Each of these vital enigmas rears up like a mountain in the landscape of his thought, with individual talk poems as bids to forge a path up the mountain, during which they encounter obstacles, hidden passageways, and unexpected views. As with jazz improvisation, the audience for a talk poem plays a vital part, eliciting, as Antin imagines or notices their reactions, unanticipated conjunctions that might otherwise not occur.

In his dedication to improvisation, Antin acknowledges following in the footsteps of Jack Kerouac's "spontaneous bop prosody," where a prohibition on revision increases dramatically the element of risk (although the prohibition is not observed to the nth degree in either case). As an improviser, he joins Kerouac and a range of twentieth-century American poets influenced by jazz spontaneity, including William Carlos Williams, Olson, Robert Creeley, Amiri Baraka, David Meltzer, Clark Coolidge, and Nathaniel Mackey, among others. From another musical perspective, Antin's conversion of oratory to poetry draws on the precedent of John Cage. Although Cage composed lectures using chance procedures that do not include verbal improvisation, the unexpected combinations of text, silence, and gesture that make up his lectures introduce elements of spontaneity and surprise. Cage's persistence in attuning himself and his audience to the infinite potential for both discovery and absurdity in the present moment remained an inspiration for Antin, as can be seen in his book of talk poems, *john cage uncaged is still cagey* (2005).[14] In the 1960s, Antin joined with Fluxus writers and artists influenced by Cage, such as Jackson Mac Low, Allan Kaprow, George Brecht, and Dick Higgins, to explore the improvised rituals of everyday life. The invocation of ritual was part of a turn toward anthropology as a source for poetry, which resulted in a series of enactments in New York City of archaic and tribal poems in translation. These performances led to Rothenberg's groundbreaking anthology *Technicians of the Sacred* (1968), a compilation of rediscovered and retranslated poetry from around the world and across the ages that Rothenberg juxtaposes to avant-garde poetry and performance art.[15]

Alongside Rothenberg, Diane Rothenberg, Dennis Tedlock, Gary Snyder, and Nathaniel Tarn, Antin was a principal participant in the resulting movement of ethnopoetics, which sought to radically expand the options for contemporary poetry by placing it in conversation with the most far-flung verbal inventions. Antin shied away from the more religious aspects of ethnopoetics —especially the high valuation of myth and the sacred—in favor of a secular and vernacular exploration of timeliness and inventiveness as hallmarks of serious poetry. His faith in the vernacular stems from doctoral studies in linguistics, which convinced him of the sterility of technical and professional jargons for making sense of the exigencies of actual situations. One of the hallmarks of the talk poems is the surprising extent to which Antin strips the jargon from scientific and technical ideas by translating them into vernacular language and making them analogies in the service of everyday dilemmas. Most plainly, his respect for the vernacular informs Antin's abstention from capitalization (pioneered by Williams and e. e. cummings), which subtly reinforces his refusal of hierarchies of thought.

As an aspect of his ethnopoetics, Antin has seized on the poetry and philosophy of classical Greece as a primary model. Taking seriously arguments by Eric Havelock, Walter Ong, and Marshall McLuhan that a different mode of thinking held sway before the extensive use of writing, Antin often compares what he does in a talk poem to oral performances in ancient Greece. In a sense, he also literalizes the "secondary orality" that McLuhan and Ong attribute to the electronic age—not by adopting a technological determinism but by arguing for the primacy of the dialogic encounter in a world dominated by electronic mediation. By demythologizing, deinstitutionalizing, and dehierarchizing, he endeavors to create conditions for an ethos like that of Heraclitus, Parmenides, or Socrates, where poetry, philosophy, and storytelling remain interwoven and where, as historian of philosophy Pierre Hadot contends about the ancient world, philosophy's main purpose is not to defend propositions but to train the individual for attentive living amid the hazards of the present moment.

Although he opposes the propensity of technology to flatten thinking and to discourage face-to-face encounters, he is by no means a technophobe. When he invented the talk poem in the 1970s, Antin employed the latest media (magnetic cassette tapes, electric typewriters) to enlist in the medial experiments of conceptual art and performance art. In fact, he was almost alone among poets in joining both artistic movements, which themselves share much in common. Recoiling from the triumph of formalism in the art world, conceptual art held that testing ideas is paramount in a work of art. The godfathers of conceptual art are Duchamp and Cage, both of whom persistently attract Antin's commentary, and among its other practitioners those he values include Robert Morris, the Fluxus movement, Jackson Mac Low, Andy Warhol, and Vito Acconci. Likewise owing a debt to Cage, performance art arose originally from legendary Dada and surrealist theatrical manifestations. It also leans on conceptual art by refusing the fourth-wall illusions of theater in favor of assessing ideas in a milieu often saturated with autobiography. Within the wide spectrum of theatrical, choreographic, musical, and video-based performance art, Antin joins artists devoted particularly to storytelling, such as Laurie Anderson, Spalding Gray, and Eleanor Antin, to open up pointed questions about identity, sexuality, politics, and social behavior. As a performer with a remarkably stripped-down, antiformal demeanor, he stands in front of an audience garbed in casual clothing, fussing with his tape recorder, beginning without any obvious verbal markers, and then speaking uninterruptedly in an ironic Brooklyn accent for anywhere from a half hour to an hour or more. Rather than try to persuade by mounting consecutive arguments, as a lecturer might do, he aims instead to provide a model of how the mind works in a social situation, and so he professes comfort with people arriving late or leaving early. Those who remained often found him a spellbinding storyteller and a paragon for the contemporary era of Emerson's ideal of "Man Thinking."

THREE BOOKS PUBLISHED BY NEW DIRECTIONS

Antin's first three books devoted entirely to talk poems were issued by one of the premier US publishers of avant-garde writing, New Directions Press. *talking at the boundaries* (1976) sets out the rules for the talk poem: it must be spoken and created at a specific time and place in front of a live audience. In this book, Antin also offers his famous, facetious definition of a myth—"a terrible lie told by a smelly little brown person to a man in a white suit with a pair of binoculars"—which accomplishes in one fell swoop a sociological critique of the racist, condescending attitudes of anthropology and a deflation of the heightened claims made by poets for myth as a special form of knowledge. In line with this sociological attack on the pretensions of anthropology and poetry, he also initiates a persistent critique of the "professional" as one whose knowledge does not serve human needs but is a tool for gain, prestige, or control. Stepping beyond disciplinary boundaries in his approach to thorny dilemmas of life, he uses phenomenology, storytelling, and humor to break open reified notions of truth, fact, representation, history, and literature. In "the sociology of art," for example, he turns the tables on customary thinking about the advantages of literacy. As a heuristic device, he offers a contrast between "oral" and "literal" cultures, using "oral" to refer to a culture for which writing is not a primary means for doing things and "literal" as shorthand for rigid practices and orthodox attitudes derived from literacy. The oral (formerly called "primitive") endeavor to follow the right process, Antin finds, has distinct advantages over the literal (which used to be called "civilized") obsession with forms and their replication. Disputing the importance of the literalist striving for certainty and formal correctness, he poses art as an inherently risky undertaking and defines an artist as someone who is willing and ready to act in a situation for which he or she is unprepared.

The centerpiece of *tuning* (1984) is a new theory of communication. Deconstructing "understanding" as an inadequate metaphor for how people reach mental alignment with one another, Antin advances "tuning" as a better model than conceptual agreement. Tuning suggests a dynamic theory of interaction, in which continual mental and verbal adjustments are made to proceed more or less in step with others for a relative period of time. Variable attunement also enters into his discussion of the notion of value, which he ponders by exposing currency, real estate, and the art market as flawed systems of valuation. Advocating a vernacular approach to the arts that favors actions addressed to real people in specific occasions, he rails against the "lust to produce the unassailable object" or the desire for greatness or timelessness. This desire is so corrosive because it directs energy away from present circumstances toward an imaginary, illusory future. In "dialogue," Antin mounts his most sustained critique of professionalism through telling a series of cautionary stories: of a seminarian too zealous in pursuit of religious knowledge to survive as a professional minister, of a gangster who uses professional lawyers to keep the criminal case against him from coming to trial until he dies, of a brilliant ballplayer who plays so intensely he injures himself and ruins his career, and of his own comic attempts as a young man to become a "professional" smoker. The final story in "dialogue" concerns the hazards of his participation in an "art and technology" exhibition as a conceptual poet. Betrayed by professionals, Antin resorts to repairing his invention, a Rube Goldberg machine for recording stories, by borrowing tools from the Yiddish-speaking goldsmith who works in the museum basement. The goldsmith records for the story machine a heartbreaking narrative about the unlikely survival of his love for the violin across decades of not playing it. This love makes him a true "amateur."

In *what it means to be avant-garde* (1993), Antin overhauls a tired term from art history. He contends that shock and newness, which used to define the avant-garde, now pertain mostly to commercial marketing strategies. Conversely, artists who wish to assert an avant-garde pedigree find themselves trapped in the paradox of upholding the tenets of a fairly long tradition of innovation and therefore of appearing as anything but new. He steps away from the rhetoric of shock, newness, and tradition to demonstrate, mainly through entertaining and enigmatic stories, how an ability to respond with full humanity to unexpected circumstances is truly avant-garde. This brings him to a theoretical crux, in which he looks at the concept of story itself and must differentiate it from narrative. Antin views a story as a series of events that lead to a transformation, while a narrative is a more complex and motivated activity that submits the possibility of transformation to the pressure of desire. In other words, narrative goes beyond story by placing a previously adequate sense of self at risk to an impending change. In "the price," he tells stories that when looked at carefully can be seen to approach the condition of narrative, for the protagonists—his family members—confront the promise of a transformation with trepidation, knowing that every change comes at a price. Pondering the prices paid to maintain or surrender a particular sense of identity, Antin also brings the concept of narrative into the vicinity of the interrogation of value that dominates *tuning*. The volume *what it means to be avant-garde* ends with a novella-length talk poem, "the structuralist," concerning the hazards of a structuralist, dedicated to generality, who undertakes the irreducibly singular task of autobiography. Having supplied many of the most influential theories of narrative, structuralism has, Antin feels, a fatal tendency to elide the desiring subject in favor of a general pattern. Thus, it offers the clearest interlocutor for his own opposing theory.

ANTIN'S IMPACT

Antin continued to perform and publish new talk poems into his eighties. In addition to printing them in journals, he issued two collections after the New Directions books, *john cage uncaged is still cagey* (2005) and *i never knew what time it was* (2005), and he includes some talk poems in *Radical Coherency* (2011), his selected essays on art and literature.[16] As a title, *i never knew what time it was* hints at an affinity with the philosopher Stanley Cavell, the title of whose autobiography, *Little Did I Know* (2010), also gestures at a methodology of not-knowing or not-understanding that sets itself apart from "professional" philosophy.[17] A telling comparison can be made between these two dissident figures—one who presents his work as a quarrel with poetry, the other as a quarrel with philosophy. As secular Jewish thinkers, they find the ordinary uncanny and look to Wittgenstein as an essential precursor. Each carries a commitment to ordinary language into an investigation of everyday experience within the Emersonian, or broadly pragmatist, tradition of American philosophy and poetry. Curiously, the conjunction of Antin and Cavell has a physical embodiment in the poet Charles Bernstein, who was a student of Cavell's at Harvard and later conducted an illuminating *Conversation with David Antin* (2002).[18] As the most public spokesperson for Language poetry, Bernstein offers in the *Conversation* irrefutable evidence of Antin's importance for this major avant-garde movement. In fact, the talk poems were already in the 1970s a decisive though not uncontested example for Language poets, some of whom fought with Antin for the mantle of premier avant-garde exponent. A famous instance of this combat occurred in San Francisco in 1978, at the Talk Series curated by Bob Perelman, where several poets interrupted Antin's talk and tried to engage him in a debate about the form of the talk poem.[19]

Antin's talk poems, especially those concerned with story and narrative, have also influenced innovative fiction, as an issue devoted to him by the *Review of Contemporary Fiction* (2001) testifies.[20] One of the fiction writers most profoundly under his spell was Kathy Acker, known for her delirious, punk-inflected appropriation of prior works. Acker credits Antin with introducing her to conceptual art and with setting her free to create the voice of her fiction, a voice that bears the imprint of ferocious intention: "What David really taught me is . . . just think what do you want to do and do it. Form is determined not by arbitrary rules, but by intention. And intentionality is all."[21] Her writing style draws on Antin's use of the vernacular, extending his conceptual poetic project into a wide range of fiction, autobiography, pornography, and poetry, which she translates through a female voice by turns abject and outraged. Like Antin, she both appropriates and undermines, revoicing texts in a colloquial style and keying them to the vicissitudes of human desire.

Antin's talk poems have played a role, too, in new forms of writing in the twenty-first century. Among poets in the wake of Language poetry, the international movement of conceptual poetry, including Craig Dworkin, Kenneth Goldsmith, Caroline Bergvall, and Vanessa Place, owes some of its impetus to Antin's example. A Norwegian performance poet based in the United Kingdom, Bergvall works between languages—English, French, and Norwegian—seeking to locate hybrid subjectivities emerging in a time of accelerated migration. Her long, appreciative review of the Antin/Bernstein *Conversation* usefully questions Antin's distinction between the oral and the literal in an internet age of distributed sociality.[22] Bergvall's own performance work takes electronic, textual, and embodied forms, bringing to the fore the wide variety of social worlds in which poet and audience now interact. On the prose side of contemporary writing, Antin's work speaks to a heated debate about the relationship of "the real" to fiction and memoir. In *Reality Hunger: A Manifesto*, for instance, David Shields contends that the novel is fundamentally a lie because it pretends not to draw on stories from real life, while the memoir pointedly ignores the compromises it makes with truth by employing fictional techniques.[23] What we require, he argues, is a mode of writing that regards reality as both experienced and constructed, which the writer and editor John D'Agata calls the "lyric essay." Not surprisingly, *The Next American Essay*, D'Agata's influential anthology of lyric essays, includes a talk poem by the man who spent forty years investigating how to represent the relationship of reality to experience.[24]

Beyond his influence on these developments in creative writing, Antin's talk poems have much to contribute to a major intellectual crux of our time, the bid to cross barriers erected over the past two centuries between the sciences and the humanities. Antin has expressed sympathy for a new era of Enlightenment, affiliating with earlier thinkers such as Bacon and Diderot to whom the notion of "two cultures" had not yet presented itself. For today's audiences, the talk poems offer salutary examples of work that refuses to recognize distinctions between modes of knowledge. With training in engineering and linguistics, Antin's easy familiarity with scientific and technical discourses becomes apparent not only in the ways they enter his stories and examples but also in his use of the incisive tone of voice of a mathematician or logician impatient with conceptions deemed "trivial" and favoring ones that look "interesting." But just as he uproots unquestioned assumptions about poetry, he also critiques science for its rigid protocols and enchantment with its own jargon. Erasing divisions between the humanities and the hard and social sciences, the talk poems cover the entire intellectual gamut, disregarding mental obstructions that litter the field of human knowledge and experience. Assuming a matter-of-fact, iconoclastic tone, Antin deploys various methods from the arts and sciences—often through startling modal shifts—redefining the grounds for conceiving of intricate social phenomena, such as an artistic movement or a political event or a form of media.

Above all, the talk poems evince a vaunting ambition for the language art while minimizing poetry's most telltale quality: form. In its place, Antin emphasizes other efficacious features: the role of language in probing understanding, including the exploration of language itself; the instigation of original thinking; the use of narrative for heuristic purposes; and the spare but telling application of rhetorical devices (metaphor, analogy, allegory). None of these can be assigned exclusively to poetry (unless we adopt Antin's totalizing definition of it), but he exploits them to inquire relentlessly into what poetry can do. Notwithstanding his dismissive definition of prose as a mere printing convention, as "concrete poetry with justified margins," his talk poems have been claimed also as essays or fiction by writers wishing to expand the repertoire of prose. The talk poems occupy a most consequential position, however, within the purview of poetry as a contemporary art form, issuing challenges to cherished conceptions of the art and opening new avenues for discovery. Like the conceptual pioneers who downplayed technique but redefined the medium and contexts for visual art, such as Duchamp, Kaprow, and Warhol, Antin was an adventurous pioneer assessing and transgressing the limits of poetry. Giving up the attractive coloration of meter, rhyme, alliteration, assonance, and stanza form, his talk poems proffer instead brilliant bursts of intellectual light provoked by radical demythologizing, linguistic playfulness, conceptual enigmas, new theoretical discoveries, and uncanny narrative collisions among a company of memorable characters.

9

Audio File Audiophile

Listening for Ambient Poetry

When poetry is placed in relation to other arts, people often assume it is somehow more "pure" and therefore distanced to a degree from other practices, as though its job were to observe and comment on great sculpture or ravishing dance but not exactly to get down on the ground with them. I see poetry participating in much more robust transactions with other arts, borrowing and contributing to modes of composition that take place across the entire artistic spectrum. I want a literary criticism sensitive to these transactions, one that sees poetry not only heeding other arts but also partnering in and sometimes leading the artistic scene of a particular time and place. During the postwar period, it was still common for poets to write not only path-breaking works of poetics (which continues) but also important art, film, dance, theater, and music criticism (which is less the case these days). Likewise, practitioners of these other arts wrote cutting-edge theory and criticism for their own art forms and for work with which they identified across mediums. This was especially true during the time that many in the arts embarked on an accelerated fusion, launched in postwar movements like Semina Culture and Fluxus and continuing in conceptualism, minimalism, punk, performance art, video art, hip-hop, and digital sampling.

One of the impediments to these kinds of aesthetic cross-fertilization has been an academic criticism that prefers nomenclature and procedural rigor over the more generous transactional thinking favored by artists—which is open-ended, boundary-crossing, assemblage-generating. In visual art thinking, for example, artists themselves and, to a lesser extent, poets wrote the exciting pieces in the first fifteen or twenty years of *Artforum*. With the rise of a journal such as *October*, the art historians take over—with an interest primarily in legitimating new movements within the norms of art history, rather than in nurturing the cross-fertilization craved by practitioners. The same academic control occurred in writing about poetry, with the conversion from an emphasis on poetics in poetry magazines of the 1970s, such as *Caterpillar*, *Io*, *The World*, *L=A=N=G=U=A=G=E*, *Montemora*, and *This*, to the instant hegemony of poststructuralism in academic journals. Like other shifts in intellectual fashion, this new mode of inquiry was a mixed blessing, beneficial for some kinds of thinking and not for others. One negative consequence arrived with the new guidance to appraise poetry solely with reference to language and discourse, which unintentionally eclipsed recognition of its life-sustaining relationships to sister arts.

The following piece uncovers buried connections between poetry and music. It was written for a seminar at the 2011 Modernist Studies Conference in Buffalo, New York, "Modernist Soundscapes," led by Steve Evans and Kaplan Harris. We were guided by the question of how to understand the bewildering fact that millions of sound files of poetry readings are downloaded annually from PennSound (hosted by the University of Pennsylvania).[1] One of the founders of PennSound, Charles Bernstein, has been a staunch advocate for the significance of the audiotext. Speaking to one of his classes at the University at Buffalo Poetics Program in the 1990s, I was awestruck by the large shelf of audiotapes along one wall of his combined office/classroom, an archive that allowed him to easily incorporate examples of audio performances into discussions of poems. Besides PennSound, other great archives of taped poetry readings have been assembled by Paul Blackburn (whose collection resides at the Archive for New Poetry at University of California, San Diego) and at the Poetry Center of San Francisco State University (the locus classicus for poetry readings recorded on audio- and videotape since the 1950s).

The scholarly assumption is that one listens to audiotapes of readings to hear new things: early versions of poems that vary from the published form, contextual discussions of the origins of poems, emphases placed on words or phrases that bestow unexpected prominence, or verbal changes made on the spot that alter meanings of an already published poem. Listening for these reasons may account for a relatively small number of the files downloaded from a site like PennSound or the arts site UbuWeb (curated by Kenneth Goldsmith), but I would warrant the vast majority of listening situations occur in less critical or less attentive circumstances—with one or more other things going on at the same time.[2] Rather than lament this fact, why not take it as an opportunity to think about the poetry reading audio file as a form of ambient music, in which the sonic saturation of spoken language creates a habitable environment akin to that constructed by the richness of musical sound? Listening to the audio file of a poetry reading is as distinct from witnessing the event as it is from reading a poem silently to oneself. While attending a reading, one may be mesmerized by the person of the poet interacting with the words, watching how she works her way into the language enunciated and projects this inhabitation out toward an audience, or observing how the audience engages with or turns aside from the performance. With an audio file of a poetry reading, though, there is no actual poet, no audience, and no possibility of locating oneself within the physical space of the reading. Listening to an audio file is a situational activity, in which a steady flow of words takes place for a period of time, often in the presence of other files and applications on a computer (or other device) and alongside events within the present location of listening. In essence, an audio file is most often encountered as a form of ambient music. It creates an allover sonic environment that shuttles back and forth between foreground and background of awareness.

As chronicled by Mark Prendergast in *The Ambient Century* (2001), ambient music's history begins with experiments in aural texture by Mahler, Satie, Debussy, and Ravel; continues with the generation of noise and electronic sounds in Varèse, Cage, and rock and roll; and comes into its own with minimalism, techno, electronica, sampling, and remixing. Its main components are timbre and texture, repetition and rhythm, and the electronic generation of sound. Brian Eno, one of its most articulate practitioners, calls it "a drift away from narrative and towards landscape, from performed event to sonic space."[3] When it settles to the background, ambient music provides a programmed sonic environment in which other events can also take place. When it moves to the foreground, ambient music's textures become more prominent, so that particular sounds dominate the experience of the moment. Whether as background or foreground, ambient music creates a space to inhabit, a space less subject to rational thought than to the phenomenology of sensory and proprioceptive experience. As Eno claims, the music should "accommodate many levels of attention without enforcing one in particular."[4]

From a putatively archeological stance, a listener can tune out the ambient quality of an audio file and listen to it forensically in search of clues that divulge a writer's thoughts about a poem or add to the genetic or textual history of its composition or dissemination. Although a historian or literary critic might assume this is the correct mode of encounter, I believe that most of the millions of files downloaded annually from PennSound and other sites are listened to ambiently, entering an unplanned electronic *mix*, blending with other sources of sound streaming in electronically or taking place live in the room. Having noticed the unique timbral properties of poetry audio files, DJs have begun to mix them with sampled electronic music and programmable beats. In contemporary music, the appropriation of digitized material is known as sampling, and the inter-animation of language art with sounds, still and moving images, and theory and commentary is called mixing. DJ Spooky (Paul D. Miller), for instance, has taken many of the classic audio files of modernist poetry, such as Gertrude Stein's "If I told Him" and "A Valentine for Sherwood Anderson," Kurt Schwitters's "Anna Blume" and *Ursonate*, James Joyce's "Anna Livia Plurabelle," and vocal texts by Antonin Artaud, Marcel Duchamp, Hans Arp, and Jean Cocteau and mixed them with contemporary forms of electronic music.[5] The verbal audio files he selects to remix have distinctive vocal qualities that lend them an aural presence beyond that of a run-of-the-mill poetry reading, their sonic timbres and rhythms adding to the multilayered ambient space. Spooky calls sampling and mixing "Rhythm science" and speaks of a different kind of forensics than that practiced by the scholar: "Rhythm science is not about 'transparency' of intent. Rhythm science is a forensic investigation of sound as a vector of a coded language that goes from the physical to the informational and back again. Rhythm science. Rhyme time. Rough trade. Sound" (*Rhythm Science* 4–5).[6]

Stein in particular has emerged as a key progenitor of poetry audio files and of ambient poetry itself. Her famous Caedmon recordings, made originally in New York City (January 30, 1935) during her lecture tour of America, have a firm precision and an unfaltering rhythm. For today's listener, these audio files cry out for mixing with electronic beats, since her stylistic hallmark of repetition with slight variation is the primary formal trait of much ambient music. Listening to an audio file of her reading is an inherently immersive activity, in which both the rich vocal timbres of her delivery and the repetitive verbal rhythms of her style create an allover, highly textured environment. As what Eno calls a "landscape" or "sonic space," her writing refuses to yield to distanced contemplation. It demands inhabitation. In her "completed portrait" of Picasso, "If I Told Him" (1924), for instance, she constructs a sound and rhythm environment by rhyming the phrase "if I told him" with the word "Napoleon":

> If Napoleon if I told him if I told him if Napoleon. Would he like it if I told him if I told him if Napoleon. Would he like it if Napoleon if Napoleon if I told him. If I told him if Napoleon if Napoleon if I told him. If I told him would he like it would he like it if I told him.[7]

After taking in the satiric intent of Stein's comparing the physical stature and ambition of Picasso to that of Napoleon, and her sly speculation about how he might react to such an appraisal, the listener settles into the primary activity of the portrait as audiotext, which is to evoke the sensuousness of ambient listening. Stein's portraits of people have been called "cubist," but from the sonic perspective they are anything but angular, jagged, or juxtapositional. They are saturated with the pleasures of repeated and slightly modified sound in rhythmic divisions of durational length. In this sense, Stein can be seen as a progenitor of minimalist music, as influential as her contemporaries Satie and Ravel. It is hard to imagine the groundbreaking minimalist opera *Einstein on the Beach* (1976), by Philip Glass and Robert Wilson, for instance, without the ambient verbal music of Stein, amplified by the symphonic textures of Virgil Thompson. As Glass recalls, he and Wilson were glad to meet Thompson while working on *Einstein on the Beach* because Thompson "had made a wonderful piece, *Four Saints in Three Acts,* with the texts of Gertrude Stein," and he was "the only American composer of opera whom Bob and I took seriously."[8] The influence of the Stein-Thompson opera can be felt in *Einstein* in the many "Knee Play" sequences, with their reiterated numbers, solfège, and repetition of Steinesque poetry by autistic teenager Christopher Knowles, such as:

> Will it get some wind for the sailboat. And it could get for it is.
> It could get railroad for these workers. And it could be were it is.
> It could Franky it could be Franky it could be very fresh and clean.
> It could be a balloon.
> Oh these are the days my friends and these are the days my friends.[9]

Another poet who uses repetition with variation to create poetry as ambient music is John Taggart. In poem sequences such as "Marvin Gaye Suite" and "Rothko Chapel Poem," he uses rhythmic repetition to structure blocks of poetry that partake of the immersive ambience of the audio file. "Marvin Gaye Suite" (1991) begins with an evocation of one of the signature ambient moments in popular music, the opening to Gaye's "What's Going On" (1971), where we are dropped in the middle of a buzzing crowd at a party, with no particular sounds or vocables on which to focus until a saxophone finally arrives to provide a platform for Gaye's first words, "Mother, Mother":

> 17 seconds of party formulaics by professional football players
> intro of 17 seconds of hey man what's happening and right on
> party of those gathered to be laid by the voice that lays
> don't have to be a jock to be gathered brought together for the lay
> Marvin mixed over the party Marvin calls out twice to mother
> surely mother must be the answer forget about the father's tongue
> if not one then the other not father unexpected relief of the other
> . . .
> and in the mean time it's right on baby it's right on right on
> I'm a witness I'll talk to him so I can see what's going on
> what's going on party of those gathered brought together for the lay
> party of those gathered to be laid by the voice that lays[10]

Taggart weaves together the crowd sounds and the words of Gaye's song with his own experience of an erotic/spiritual listening, setting the poem within the song as part of its extended ambient condition. That is, the poem unfolds not as a distinct aesthetic event but from *inside* the space of the song. It is a listening to and meditation on and reception of and response (as in call-and-response) to the song and as such cannot exist without it. If you do not hear this song or call it up in memory, the poem gives you very little room in which to move. As a work of art participating in the ambient environment of Gaye's discography, especially the nine songs that make up his classic album *What's Going On*, the nine poems of "Marvin Gaye Suite" imitate sounds and voices and open Gaye's songs out to myriad biographical, spiritual, and musical contexts in which they continue to reverberate.

Although you must hear Gaye singing (at least in memory) for Taggart's poem to attain its full ambient resonance, poet Nathaniel Mackey has managed in his ongoing serial novel, *From a Broken Bottle Traces of Perfume Still Emanate* (1986–), to create in language the phenomenological condition of living inside an imaginary improvisatory jazz band, The Mystic Horn Society (earlier named the Deconstructive Woodwind Chorus and the East Bay Dread Ensemble, later Molimo m'Atet).[11] Within the novel, every thought expressed can be matched by instrumental articulations by the band, and every sound produced by the band can be heard as a thought entering into dialogue with earlier thoughts. Initially, we are taught by Mackey how to encounter the ambient space of thought-as-sound and sound-as-thought through a device similar to Taggart's habitation within the songs of Marvin Gaye: the epistolary narrator N. can be heard describing in exquisite detail the thoughts, motives, and effects of specific moments in classic jazz recordings. N. lives so deeply into these recordings that he is able to portray the qualities of their sounds and relate a sound or a song to others within a huge interactive web composed of jazz, soul, and world music. This ability may be a defining quality of the jazz buff, but Mackey transcends that designation by creating verbally new, non-existent jazz audio files that the reader can experience and move around in. In the novel, N. presents his band as writing, rehearsing, and delivering actual songs, complete with names and dates of composition, that have never been heard. His descriptions of the mental, physical, imaginal, responsive, erotic, allusive aspects of making music in the complex society of a jazz band are so finely drawn and so linguistically labile (full of puns and sound slippage) that the reader enters into an ambient condition that is tantamount to hearing the non-existent audio file of the "song" Mackey has composed in language.

As in Mackey's novel, Pamela Lu's *Ambient Parking Lot* (2011) creates an ambient audio space inhabited by a group of "musicians." With a title referring to Brian Eno's groundbreaking 1978 album, *Ambient 1: Music for Airports*, Lu's poetically resonant satirical novel exposes the milieu of the audio file audiophile.[12] She creates a group of characters who go to extraordinary lengths to document the ambient sounds of parking garages, which they present as a new musical and political manifestation.[13] The novel begins with the description of a recording session in a California garage:

> The recording of "Ambient Parking Lot #25" went off without a hitch. Production efforts approached the sublime. We watched in rapture as the parking lot cooperated with our long-arm mike and seemed to relax into the session. The seven-inch vinyl single was released two and a half weeks later on an indie label underwritten by the University of Krakow, with liner notes cribbed from an anonymous dissertation on Hugo Boss. (3)

Following this send-up of obsessively nerdish sensibilities, Lu quotes from the imaginary dissertation on fashion designer Boss: "The moment is in the line. The line is in the secret. The secret is in the crease. The crease is in the power. The power is in the moment." Lu wants us to hear the mock-profundity of these words in several registers: as a secret formula for creating fashion, as a poetics of ambient circling (à la Stein), and as a philosophical statement in proximity to Foucault (power) and Deleuze (the crease).

Her own commentary on the quote swerves, however, to evoke the sensory modalities of a parking lot: "Words meant to sketch the condition of high fashion, but which could just as easily be applied to oil-slicked asphalt, acres of grid-striped spaces approximating the breadth and presence of the compact car" (3). "Oil-slicked asphalt" evokes touch and smell, "grid-striped spaces" evokes sight, and all three senses enhance the sensory overload of the sonic recording, which Lu finally describes:

> Played back, the music emitted a low earthy growl, privileging bass-level amplitude over quasi-narrative pop disappointment. Stripped down to essentials, the noise had the pounding attitude of reverb without its inbred conservatism. As always, a tough-minded aesthetic kept our minimalist concept intact, while the lusciousness of the infinite loop made even the shoegazers smile. (3)

Lu accomplishes two things in this sonic description: she evokes ambient sound qualities of recorded music while also exposing the snobbery that infects her group of young audiophiles. The novel pursues both lines of inquiry, braiding absurd, hilarious delineations of a youth sensibility fixated by recorded sound with evocative portrayals of ambient adventures taking place within a series of parking lots.

Lu's exfoliation of a poetic novel from the milieu of the ambient audio file rhymes with the methods of one of the most accomplished pieces of twentieth-century performance art, *The Cave* (1993), by composer Steve Reich and video artist Beryl Korot.[14] Like Lu and Mackey, Reich and Korot weave words and music and ambient sounds into an unprecedented work. The cave in *The Cave* is the Cave of Machpelah in Hebron, the Cave of the Patriarchs where Abraham, Isaac, and Jacob are said to be buried. Korot conducted video interviews with Israelis, Palestinians, and Americans, asking them the same questions: Who, for you, is Abraham? Who, for you, is Sarah? Who, for you, is Hagar? Who, for you, is Isaac? Who, for you, is Ishmael? The answers of each group comprise one of the three acts of this video opera. As a composer, Reich scores the pitch of each verbal phrase included in the opera, sometimes doubling it with musical instruments and other times including choral responses, embellished with much repetition. At the political level, Israelis and Palestinians answer the questions in remarkably divergent ways: for an Israeli settler, Ishmael is the Arab in the street, while for a Palestinian woman, Hagar is a refugee. Thus, the realities of Arab/Israeli conflict are never distant for them, but "distance" is precisely what characterizes the responses of the Americans, for whom, as Korot notes in the booklet accompanying the CDs, "Abraham to some is Abraham Lincoln. Ishmael is the lonesome cowboy riding off into the sunset" (17). Bringing together these three variant responses to the same biblical stories, Reich and Korot offer something like the x, y, and z axes of a three-dimensional graph of one of the world's most intractable and consequential conflicts. The audio files created by Korot's interviews highlight the painful ironies in the self-enclosed interpretations surrounding foundational stories shared by Jews, Muslims, and Christians. Beyond the dense verbal and musical texture, though, at the end of Act 1, there is a moment of pure ambience that anchors the work. For four minutes and twenty-seven seconds, one hears the acoustical resonance inside the cave itself, whose key Reich identified as A minor and then used as the culminating key for acts 1 and 2 (14).

Poet, video, and theatrical artist Tan Lin, brother of artist Maya Lin, uses the concept of "ambient writing" to make explicit the connections discussed thus far between poetry and ambient music. In the essay "ambient stylistics," he offers a Zen-like definition of poetry: "The source of the poem is not the maker and genius behind the poem but the experience of the reader and what the reader does above all is become someone who listens. Now if poetry could inspire that state of just listening, that would be poetry. . . . The best poetry wouldn't even know that it was poetry as it was being listened to."[15] Lin advocates ambient poetry as a linguistic space in which to live, where content is of less importance than the listener's ability to move freely within the environment created, erasing boundaries between the act of writing and the act of reading. In a page from his book *Seven Controlled Vocabularies and Obituary 2004. The Joy of Cooking*, Lin writes,

> What are the forms of non-reading and what are the non-forms a reading might take? Poetry = wallpaper. Novel = design object. Text as ambient soundtrack? Dew-champ wanted to create works of art that were non-retinal. It would be nice to create works of literature that didn't have to be read but could be looked at, like placemats. The most exasperating thing at a poetry reading is always the sound of the poet reading.[16]

Refusing to privilege the poet's attempt to invest his words with his own personality and drama in "the sound of the poet reading," Lin urges his readers to ponder instead the "non-forms a reading might take" as well as "forms" that might occur in a "non-reading," entering an ordinary, ambient condition in which literature could be both functional and tell a story, "like placemats." In this fluid, undefined, humorous ("Dew-champ" = Duchamp), always open space, Lin arrives at the goal of his writing: "Text as ambient soundtrack."

POETRY & PROSE: INTIMATE OPPOSITION

10

Translation and Not-Understanding

Studying in 1970–1971 with Clayton Eshleman at California Institute of the Arts in Los Angeles, I learned much about what poetry could demand of a poet. To weed out dilettantes in his poetry writing course, Eshleman would prescribe Rilke's *Letters to a Young Poet* (1929), with its famous advice to the novice:

> Search for the reason that bids you write; find out whether it is spreading out its roots in the deepest places of your heart, acknowledge to yourself whether you would have to die if it were denied you to write. This above all—ask yourself in the stillest hour of your night: *must* I write? . . . If you may meet this earnest question with a strong and simple *I must*, then build your life according to this necessity.[1]

As one way to build a life of poetic intention commensurate with Rilke's sense of necessity, Eshleman offered a course on translation as a poetic endeavor. From his experience wrestling for years with the linguistically challenging, gut-wrenching verse of Peruvian modernist César Vallejo, Eshleman portrayed translation as a life-and-death struggle. He demonstrated, through examples of his own work and from the work of other poets, how devoting oneself to words and images in another language can open up unforeseen possibilities in one's own writing. A few years later, operating on this advice, I undertook to translate Federico García Lorca's most enigmatic book, *Poet in New York*.[2] It was ripe for translation because the version then available in English, by Ben Belitt, seemed more attuned to the style of the English Metaphysical poets than to the surrealist juxtapositions of Lorca's prophetic rendition of New York City, scarred by racial and sexual and financial violence.

When I began to translate Lorca, Robert Duncan volunteered to read and comment on drafts. Although I didn't know it at the time, he had begun reading *Poet in New York* when it was first published in Spanish in 1940 and it was a key work in his poetic lineage.[3] Duncan saw the book as defined by the flow of its imagery; the imaginative twists and turns, as one image gives way to the next, effect carefully calibrated transmutations within the urban nightmare. Every time I would bring him a new portion, Duncan would peer at it to see if I had changed the order of images in favor of an easier English comprehension, insisting I give up a felicitous turn of phrase if it meant preserving the exact pattern of Lorca's metamorphoses. This made for spiky and sometimes strange poetry in English, but it kept the focus on how the poet matched precisely the travails of his inner anguish to the soul-depleting travails of the United States at the outbreak of the Great Depression.

After completing the Lorca text and translating several other poets from Spanish, I began to see that Eshleman was right: translation is a perilous and rewarding way into poetry. Not only that, but its practice engenders an affinity for what at first seems most frustrating—the experience of not understanding, which takes many forms. For example, when faced with an unfamiliar combination of words in the original language, the first thing to determine is whether it is an existing idiom or something newly minted by the poet. Sometimes, this can be easily resolved, sometimes not. If you think about it, this also pertains to written texts from the past of one's native language. How do you know if a strange locution was a contemporary idiom or a new coinage by the writer? And if you have a sensitive ear, you notice that a work written fifty years ago does not align perfectly with how we speak today. There are always tones and idioms and implied references and modes of address that we no longer use or do not hear in the same way. Or, to take an example from the present, think of the ambiguity of communicating via text message. It is so easy to mistake the tone, and therefore the meaning, of a brief text—even from a friend or spouse. The conclusion I've come to is that we are always translating.[4]

From a literary perspective, the site of translation, where clarity and not-understanding vie for attention, resembles the meeting ground of poetry and prose. It's a place where the desire to grasp with language encounters the resolve to let go and dwell in incomprehension. In its attempts at grasping, prose would like to get things straight. By analogy, a practical translation would like to make the foreign comprehensible. A prose that faces poetry, though, like a nuanced translation, must dwell alongside poetry in not-understanding. Prose works such as Paul Auster's memoir *The Invention of Solitude* and his early fiction or the sentences of autobiographical poetry in Lyn Hejinian's *My Life*, for example, take place within a linguistic aura that resists resolution into a particular mode of understanding. Such works contest the divide between poetry and prose. They are multi-intentional, and reading them places one in a similar situation to embarking on the translation of a poem, for there is already too much meaning. If the translation adheres to one strand of intention—to carry across a chain of images, for instance, or to replicate a formal invention—then other threads are left behind, and this is true also of literary interpretation when faced with these sorts of liminal works. This may appear to leave the writer or translator or reader with a hopelessly tangled knot, or, alternatively, it may prompt an acknowledgment of an inherent quality of language: it says too much and points in too many directions at once. Within this plenitude is an incipience that haunts poetry. Something beyond understanding is calling. Will prose be able to hear it?

NOT-UNDERSTANDING

An Abecedary for Walter Benjamin

> *It is the task of the translator to release in his own language that pure language which is under the spell of another, to liberate the language imprisoned in a work by his re-creation of that work.*

> *In this pure language—which no longer means or expresses anything but is, as expressionless and creative Word, that which is meant in all languages—all information, all sense, and all intention finally encounter a stratum in which they are destined to be extinguished.*
>
> Walter Benjamin, "The Task of the Translator"[5]

A Not-understanding can be a distinct pleasure. One of the great pleasures of writing and reading.

B A positive experience of not-understanding occurs in a state of looseness, suppleness, openness, lack of control, inattention, day-dreaming, puzzlement. A sense that here certain ineffable nodes or connections may have found expression.

C Foreign, strange, uncanny, unknown, distant, opaque: words.

D When not understood, words appear at their most physical—dense, concrete, singular. And yet around each is an aura that we invest with feelings, desires, insights, which we yearn toward, hoping: may it be here, in this otherness, that a new sense of self comes forth.

E It may, if we allow ourselves to dwell in not-understanding. So that as understanding gradually unclouds its own confusion and attempts to dispel the aura—intolerant in its ardor for sharp distinctions—a certain resolute settling into not-understanding throws up a bridge for new content (for what we only hoped might be revealed in not-understanding) to enter our understanding.

F Surely an unstable procedure. For often, once our prized content is embodied in a particular understanding, the understanding itself becomes so imperious in grasping for resolution that our content slips away. We return to certain phrases like a string of beads, seeking a reaffirmation of this fugitive content, this key to apprehension, and find it fled, with only the palpably resistant dead weight of the fully analyzed understanding usurping the content's place.

G It is possible, however, for the content to re-enter these very vocables stripped by understanding of their strangeness, if we are able to relax once again the grip of understanding, to re-say, "all is possible here; no necessary distinctions are drawn beforehand; this writing is overfull." In this spirit of generosity, this trust in a meaning beyond present understanding, the content, nestled between oneself and the writing (which is therefore perceived as an aura around the writing), may return.

H The aura around the writing, available only through not-understanding, is experienced by the writer as well, for whom it appears as the sign of being joined in writing.

I While writing, the aura remains present, calling words and phrases out of their positions in the ordering of syntax. The aura beckons words to fit its inarticulate content and, upon relinquishing them back into the formative syntax, gives them its own direction. So that it leads the writing, ever at oblique angles, closer and closer to revealing what it promises.

J A poem, an essay, a book—is read and not fully understood. Years later one returns and finds that whispers of new meanings it promised have since announced themselves explicitly and have been assimilated. During the first reading or hearing the unsuccessful effort at comprehension launches one into the aura around the work, where profound but inarticulate connections are made. One comes away dissatisfied but slightly tremulous. Certain possibilities of barely acknowledged desires have announced themselves, ever so softly.[6]

K There is an erotic pleasure in the recognition of a beckoning strangeness. In this otherness-we-recognize can be found a new identity of our own, just arriving. Eroticism wells up in the tension between the strangeness and our yearning to identify with it. Once we have engulfed this otherness and thus disclosed a new identity, that particular tension is discharged.

L Language creates identity. And therefore otherness. At every sociolinguistic level, each of us, through each linguistic choice, is in the act of creating an identity that joins us to and separates us from others. Such choices might be silence or speech, English or French, men's or women's, subjunctive or indicative, professional or slang, southern or northern Californian, idiolect or dialect, vocal or sub-vocal, clean-shaven or bearded, tattooed or un-inked.

M Identities do not communicate (as though information to be delivered were primary) but rather translate. Translation is constant, necessary, impossible. We are constantly faced with expression we don't understand. In which we locate a necessity of our own for understanding. Whereby we identify with what we don't understand, appropriating difference. Thus obliterating otherness by an imposition of achieved identity—and losing something essential. Such has seemed the necessary impossibility of translation in our time.

N In other times and places freer sway has been given to the workings of not-understanding. One imagines this as a Taoist posture, which achieves its physical expression in the underwater-like motions of *T'ai Chi Ch'uan.* Paradoxically, the ritualized motion receives its energy from combat with an unseen opponent, to whom one spontaneously responds. Maximum attentiveness arises from relaxed receptivity.

O Socrates may mark the loss of this attitude in the West. His profession of not understanding (the knowledge that he knows nothing) operates as a verbal strategy for leading an interlocutor to the understanding Socrates hides. Underlying our elevation of science as the only rigorous method of knowing is a *will to understand.*

P In the figure of the "New Angel"—visible in *Angelus Novus,* the painting by Paul Klee he owned—Walter Benjamin saw a messenger who pulls the viewer "along with himself on that way into the future on which he came and which he knows so well that he traverses it without turning around and letting the one he has chosen out of view."[7] In this Orphic fable in reverse, where the road to the future involves bringing a new content back to the origin, we have an adequate narrative for how understanding derives from not understanding. In understanding, the lived past and the unique future come to meet in the path of return along which new content is carried.

Q "Coming to meeting" is essential to the dynamic of understanding. Speaking of interpersonal understanding, Maurice Merleau-Ponty tells of a perceptual meeting: "But successful communication [for which read 'understanding'] occurs only if the listener instead of following the verbal chain link by link, on his own account resumes the other's linguistic gesticulation and carries it further. The 'clarity' of language is of a perceptual order."[8]

R Elaborating on the perceptual quality of understanding, he notes, "one cannot mimic a person's voice without assuming something of his physiognomy and even his personal style. In the same way, the author's voice results in my assuming his thoughts."[9] It may be that writers whose thoughts I have the most difficulty assuming are those I find it hardest to mimic, and that as I gradually become able to "act as that person" or "think in that person's terms," difficulties in understanding begin to dissolve. Great mimicry—divine skill: the practice of the inspired translator.

S Benjamin quotes approvingly an injunction by Rudolf Pannwitz: "'Particularly when translating from a language very remote from his own he must go back to the primal elements of language itself and penetrate to the point where word, image, and tone converge.'"[10] Not-understanding is the moment in reading when word, image, and tone have not yet diverged, when the sense is only incipient, and when translative insights are most available to the reader. This is when what Benjamin calls "pure language" (the creative, structuring aspect of language, prior to its economic function as the coinage of communication) appears as a virtual presence, begging the reader to leave off the vain pursuit of an expressed meaning and revel in the creative potential of the word.

T Speaking of a poem written for a friend who had died suddenly, David Antin says he refused the genre of the elegy: "It was these questions and answers and attempts at definition, which is why I called it 'definitions for mendy.' An elegy is not like that. It's related to a social structure that I no longer participated in. The formal structure of grief is not something I had any part or faith in. It was more terrible than that. . . . For me to talk about emotions is to fill the thing with socially approved forms. That is, the vocabulary of emotion relates essentially to sociology and to courtly states. It fills up the vacuum, it fills up what is not understood, it fills up the unintelligible with false understanding. . . . It takes you on bridges past the cracks in the real, and I wanted to deal with the cracks."[11]

U As an alternative to understanding, with its ghostly image of a merging of identities, of two people standing on the same spot, Antin proposes the concept of "tuning."[12] This is another name for the "coming to meeting" spoken of by Benjamin and Merleau-Ponty. Tuning is something entities do when they walk along or sing together. It involves a voluntary meeting and then a common effort of harmonizing through pacing and continual adjustment and then a departure. Tuning takes place among two or more identities never seen as merging.

V What are the prerequisites for tuning? The first movement of George Steiner's four-part hermeneutics of translation in *After Babel* is Trust.[13] In order to walk along with you, first I must want to—but before that I have to trust there's a purpose in our walking together. Only to the extent that I trust you (or trust in what you're doing) will I allow myself to walk alongside you. Trust also determines how far I'll go and how much effort I'll apply. This trust is constantly being tuned: as you betray it, as I misapply it, etc.

W To the degree I trust, I'll walk with you. To the extent I walk with you, I can speak to others of our going together, of how we've come into tune and of the static between us. Poor critics can provoke irritation when they begin reading without trust, walk only a short way, and thus have no tuning to speak of.

X Benjamin's advice is to read each writer individually, not as part of "literature." If we read merely by locating external factors (predecessors, biography, social forces), then we forgo the encounter with "pure language." However, if we know nothing of externalities, then we cannot see the writer's activity as a translator. To reach pure language (as a reader), one must take that as the writer's goal. And then we see everything the writer makes use of (predecessors, ideas) and everything that makes use of the writer (biography, society) as vehicles carrying the writing toward pure language.

Y The reader, as translator, enters as fully as possible into a state of not-understanding that mirrors the writer's creative struggle with materials to reveal the pure language. Only by intensive, revelatory reading does this happen. One begins to see the tremendous effort required to lift up materials and place them in a clear light—and maybe the destination is the light.

Z In caring for not-understanding we rise above the narrow obsession with information and enter the ever-fluid, ever-alterable medium that language is.

11

Paul Auster's Solitude in the Room of the Book

"THE BOOK THAT WILL GO ON BEING WRITTEN FOR AS LONG AS HE STAYS IN THE ROOM"

Reading the novels of Paul Auster, I find myself called back again and again to his first prose text, *The Invention of Solitude* (1982), especially to its second half, "The Book of Memory."[1] In this meditative memoir, Auster confronts central obsessions, obsessions that return in various forms to animate subsequent novels.[2] One of the most resonant images from "The Book of Memory" is that of "the room of the book," a location where life and writing meet in an unstable, creative, hazardous encounter. I propose to enter the room of the book through three conceptual doorways: (1) a contest between prose and poetry; (2) a parthenogenic fantasy of masculine creativity; and (3) an obsession with Holocaust imagery. Unlike many writers of fiction, Auster's prose emerged out of a preoccupation with avant-garde poetry in French and English, which continued to make demands upon him. In his memoir and in early works of fiction, he frequently inquires into transactions between writing and identity, a concern of many young poets in the 1970s and 1980s. In Auster's case, though, this inquiry takes a further, more personal turn, becoming a confrontation with gender issues oriented around the father, as though a family tree could be constructed with only fathers and sons. Excavating issues of paternity gives rise to an investigation of Jewish approaches to memory and the ways it can be used to probe ruptures in contemporary life. Ultimately, the writing arrives at unspeakable memories of the Holocaust, as though in support of the truism that the postmodern is inescapably post-Holocaust. For Auster, the act of composition is haunted by existential, psychological, sexual, and historical dangers, all of which lurk in the room of the book.

There is an exemplary dramatization of the stakes in yoking "the room" to "the book" in *Ghosts* (1986), the second volume of *The New York Trilogy*, Auster's foray into meta-detective fiction. The protagonist of *Ghosts*, Blue, has recently completed an apprenticeship to a master detective, Brown, and the novel narrates Blue's first case, in which he looks to establish his credentials as self-sufficient agent. Blue has been hired by White to "keep an eye on" Black, a simple "tail job" that turns out to be much more demanding than Blue could have imagined. It's not that Black is difficult to follow; in fact, he hardly ever leaves his room. From his own room across the street, Blue, using binoculars, can see that Black spends most of his time writing in a notebook and reading. To record Black's activities, Blue takes out a notebook himself and begins to write, thus initiating the equation between the room and the book.

After tailing Black for nearly a year, following him on long walks and watching him read and write, Blue begins to find his lack of knowledge about Black, White, and the case unbearable. When he fails to precipitate an explanation from the ever-elusive White, Blue realizes that his perpetual spying on the nearly sedentary Black has rendered Blue a virtual prisoner in his own room. It dawns on him that Black and White may be in cahoots, and that in fact *he* may be the one under surveillance:

> If so, what are they doing to him? Nothing very terrible, finally—at least not in any absolute sense. They have trapped Blue into doing nothing, into being so inactive as to reduce his life to almost no life at all. Yes, says Blue to himself, that's what it feels like: like nothing at all. He feels like a man who has been condemned to sit in a room and go on reading a book for the rest of his life. This is strange enough—to be only half alive at best, seeing the world only through words, living only through the lives of others. But if the book were an interesting one, perhaps it wouldn't be so bad. He could get caught up in the story, so to speak, and little by little begin to forget himself. But this book offers him nothing. There is no story, no plot, no action—nothing but a man sitting alone in a room and writing a book. That's all there is, Blue realizes, and he no longer wants any part of it. But how to get out? How to get out of the room that is the book that will go on being written for as long as he stays in the room?[3]

Not an intellectual nor even much of a reader, Blue has been converted into a writer—that is, into someone who lives inside a book. Every other aspect of his life has been taken away—he has abandoned his fiancée, his mentor refuses to offer advice, and so on—and so he comes face-to-face with the terror of the writer: "There is no story, no plot, no action—nothing but a man sitting alone in a room and writing a book." The essential condition of the writer in a postgeneric age—imprisoned, facing a blank page without the scaffolding of story, plot, or action to support him—has become Blue's life, and he begins to suspect that Black (or White?) has planned it that way, willing this monstrous metamorphosis.

Blue's suspicion that his life has been captured by a book is confirmed during two visits to Black's room. In the second, Blue crosses the street one night when Black is out and steals a pile of papers stacked on Black's desk. When he begins to read them, Blue sees that they are his own weekly reports. This confirms that Black and White are the same person and also that, in some mysterious way, Blue and Black have been writing the same book. With these discoveries, Blue collapses into vertigo and remains in a state of irresolvable doubleness:

> For Blue at this point can no longer accept Black's existence, and therefore he denies it. Having penetrated Black's room and stood there alone, having been, so to speak, in the sanctum of Black's solitude, he cannot respond to the darkness of that moment except by replacing it with a solitude of his own. To enter Black, then, was the equivalent of entering himself, and once inside himself, he can no longer conceive of being anywhere else. But this is precisely where Black is, even though Blue does not know it. (NYT 226)

When Blue realizes that Black is his double, he also becomes aware that Black's room is the uncanny scene of writing, which Blue, who never thought of himself as a writer, had been afraid of entering all along. In confronting Black's solitude, he meets his own; in confronting Black's writing, he recovers his own and realizes what he has become. When he walks across the street to Black's room one more time, Blue finds out why Black/White has hired him. Upon his arrival, Blue sees Black pointing a revolver at him, intending to end both of their lives. In the ensuing dialogue, Blue, the bewildered detective, tries one more time to understand what has been happening:

> You're supposed to tell me the story. Isn't that how it's supposed to end? You tell me the story, and then we say good-bye.
>
> You know it already, Blue. Don't you understand that? You know the story by heart.
>
> Then why did you bother in the first place?
>
> Don't ask stupid questions.
>
> And me—what was I there for? Comic relief?
>
> No, Blue, I've needed you from the beginning. If it hadn't been for you, I couldn't have done it.
>
> Needed me for what?
>
> To remind me of what I was supposed to be doing. Every time I looked up, you were there, watching me, following me, always in sight, boring into me with your eyes. You were the whole world to me, Blue, and I turned you into my death. You're the one thing that doesn't change, the one thing that turns everything inside out. (NYT 230)

Black has turned Blue into his ideal reader, for whom every moment of Black's existence in a room writing a book is full of unfathomable meaning. And by allaying the writer's constant fear that the external world will dematerialize during his residence in the space of writing, Blue's gaze has "turn[ed] everything inside out" for Black, making his writing into a fateful, and ultimately fatal, act. Having created this external witness to his internal activity as writer, Black has also transformed his reader, Blue, into a double, into a writer himself. Black has kept Blue trapped in a room, with Blue's gaze fixed upon Black, as part of a successful effort to enclose himself in the space of writing until the demands of the book are met. And because Blue is also the writer of the book, its demands cannot be fulfilled until Blue comes to see that all along he has been author of his own fate. When Blue achieves this recognition, the story that Black is writing ends in death—but not quite as Black had planned. For Blue is now the author, and he overpowers Black and beats him, presumably to death, as though breaking an insufferable mirror that has kept him confined inside the room that is the book.

"THE BRIDGE BETWEEN WRITING POETRY AND WRITING PROSE"

For whom can it be said that entrapment within the room that is the book is intolerable? Certainly Blue, who has always thought of himself as a man of action rather than a reader, finds it so: "He feels like a man who has been condemned to sit in a room and go on reading a book for the rest of his life" (NYT 201–2). But through the character of Blue, Auster also paints a portrait of a type of writer about whom Blue knows nothing: the modern poet. The condition of modern (male) poet can be epitomized by the statement, "There is no story, no plot, no action—nothing but a man sitting alone in a room and writing a book" (NYT 202). David Antin has characterized the solipsism of the modern poet in derogatory terms:

> as a poet i was getting extremely tired of   what i considered
> an unnatural language act   going into a closet   so to
> speak   sitting in front of a typewriter   because   anything is possible
> and nothing is necessary   a closet is no place to address anybody[4]

Although Antin might accuse him of perversity, Auster is powerfully drawn to this "unnatural language act," for the image of the lonely poet trapped inside the room that is the book haunts his writing. From another perspective, though, Auster's unnatural language act could be seen as inviting the intrusion of poetry into narrative prose. His fiction and memoirs have remained remarkably porous to poetry and to poetic thinking, and this porosity creates unusual transactions in the prose that account for many of its salient characteristics.

Typically, if we call a novel "poetic," we mean that it has a "lyrical" quality, like André Gide's *L'Immoraliste* or Virginia Woolf's *The Waves*, or we mean that the words have been chosen with particular relish for their sound and exactitude, as in the stories of Guy Davenport or in Michael Ondaatje's *The*

English Patient. Auster's fiction, however, is not especially lyrical in rhythm or sound; indeed, its tone has the deliberate flatness of factual statement. The statements of fact contribute to dilemmas of understanding that require an exactitude of a phenomenological or hermeneutic sort but not a heightened verbal precision. In other words, the poetic element in Auster's fiction cannot be seen as "formal" in any sense. Instead, his poetic thinking engages with a range of fundamental issues for twentieth-century poetry: the materiality of language, the relations between words and objects, the commanding presence of silence, the impact of prose upon poetry, and the ways in which, as Marina Tsvetaeva puts it, "In this most Christian of worlds / all poets are Jews."[5]

Just as the identity of a writer hides in the character of Blue, these poetic issues hide among the more noticeable metafictional qualities of Auster's writing. Admittedly, a general overview of his fiction would make it hard to differentiate Auster's work from that of any number of postmodern novelists, for whom poetry would be the least of concerns. Such an overview would depict his books as allegories of the excruciatingly difficult task of writing and of the nearly insurmountable task of achieving identity—peopled by characters plagued by doubles who represent the unknowable self. These tasks take place in an irrational world, governed by chance and coincidence, whose author cannot be known. And then it would be easy to construct a map of precursors and sources in which to situate Auster's writing: the textual entrapments of Kafka, Beckett, Borges, Calvino, Ponge, Blanchot, Jabès, Celan, and Derrida; the psychological intensities of Poe, Hawthorne, Melville, Thoreau, Dickinson, Dostoevsky, and Freud; the paranoid occultisms of surrealism, magic, alchemy, and Kabbalah. However, this capsule description and list of elective affinities slights two determinative facets of Auster's writing: his extensive work as a poet and as a translator of French poetry, and the crucial encounter between poetry and the novel staged in his narrative prose.

Many novelists at the outset of their careers use poetry as a kind of finger exercise, but Auster experienced a curiously persistent vacillation. In an interview with Larry McCaffery and Sinda Gregory, he tells of dodging back and forth between verse and prose before a decisive plunge into fiction: "I had always dreamed of writing novels. My first published works were poems, and for ten years or so I published only poems, but all along I spent nearly as much time writing prose. I wrote hundreds and hundreds of pages, I filled up dozens of notebooks. It's just that I wasn't satisfied with it, and I never showed it to anyone" (AH 291). Reportedly, he stopped altogether in the mid-1970s, only composing and translating poetry and writing critical essays. The poems initially "resembled clenched fists; they were short and dense and obscure, as compact and hermetic as Delphic oracles" (AH 293), but during the later 1970s they began to unclench: "The breath became somewhat longer, the propositions became somewhat more discursive" (AH 294). Finally, though, at a time of acute emotional and financial distress, he reached an impasse: "There were moments when I thought I was finished, when I thought I would never write another word" (AH 294). Having touched bottom, as many of his characters do, Auster was primed for a breakthrough, which occurred when observing a dance rehearsal: "Something happened, and a whole world of possibilities suddenly opened up to me. I think it was the absolute fluidity of what I was seeing, the continual motion of the dancers as they moved around the floor. It filled me with immense happiness" (AH 294). The next day he began writing *White Spaces* (1980), his one work of what I call "poet's prose," which he describes as "an attempt on my part to translate the experience of that dance performance into words. It was a liberation for me, a tremendous letting go, and I look back on it now as the bridge between writing poetry and writing prose" (AH 295).[6]

Over the past two centuries, poets have attested to a sense of liberation when they begin to write poetry in prose. You might imagine this as freedom from the rigorous demands of meter and rhyme, but you'd be wrong. Instead, it's as if the poet comes up on the other side of a heavily fortified wall (outside the "closet"?), moving beyond the tiny social space accorded to verse and penetrating the vast discursive domain of prose. In Auster's case, his verse had "resembled clenched fists," while his poet's prose was "a tremendous letting go"—as if verse (often associated metaphorically with dance) were frozen stock still, while prose (usually thought of as plodding) were free to dance. *White Spaces* marks the moment when prose and poetry literally meet in Auster's writing. At this juncture, Auster's poetic project in prose emerges: the investigation of the scene of writing. It is an immense undertaking—a kind of detective assignment that may well follow him for the remainder of his career. In *White Spaces*, he records a primary discovery, at once phenomenological, mystical, and social: that writing takes place in a room. Here, he begins to explore it:

> I remain in the room in which I am writing this. I put one foot in front of the other. I put one word in front of the other, and for each step I take I add another word, as if for each word to be spoken there were another space to be crossed, a distance to be filled by my body as it moves through this space. It is a journey through space, even if I get nowhere, even if I end up in the same place I started. It is a journey through space, as if into many cities and out of them, as if across deserts, as if to the edge of some imaginary ocean, where each thought drowns in the relentless waves of the real. (*Disappearances* 107)

In his poet's prose, Auster insists on the physicality of writing. He makes this physicality graphic by welding together three distinct spaces: the room, the space in which writing takes place; the interior space within the writer where writing occurs; and the space on the page the words occupy. In *White Spaces,* as later in *Ghosts,* Auster represents the physicality of writing by an equation of the room with the book: "I remain in the room in which I am writing this," he says, as though he were occupying the "white spaces" of the page, the mind, and the room. Whichever way he turns in this symbolic architecture, the writer finds his physical body trapped: when he writes, it enters into the closed space of the book; when he gets up from the book, it paces the narrow confines of the room. This claustrophobic situation draws attention to what Antin might deplore as solipsism, a tendency explored from different vantage points in later sections of this essay. At this point, however, it is important to note that the outside world does manage to break through the self-inscribed mental sphere of Auster's fictional characters, imposing actual consequences upon their ruminations and conjectures. In the passage above, he acknowledges at least the idea of the interpenetration of mental and social worlds by locating, in the manner of Wallace Stevens or Marianne Moore, an "imaginary ocean, where each thought drowns in the relentless waves of the real."

"AT NO MOMENT DOES THE NOVELIST LISTEN TO THE PAGE, TO ITS WHITENESS AND SILENCE"

Auster is by no means the first writer to figure the book as allegorical scene of writing. In particular, two French poets who wrote extensively in prose, Stéphane Mallarmé and Edmond Jabès, have been for Auster important precursors. He has translated, for instance, Mallarmé's poetic fragments on the death of his young son, *A Tomb for Anatole* (1983), some of which appeared first in *The Invention of Solitude.*[7] Mallarmé's notion of a grand Book that includes the entire world also hovers in the background of Auster's explorations of the scene of writing. But even more pertinent to Auster's obsessions are those of Jabès, the Jewish Egyptian poet, whose seven volumes of meditative and oracular poet's prose, *The Book of Questions* (1963–1973), have had a shaping hand in Auster's poetic narratives.[8] Auster makes an explicit connection between Jabès and Mallarmé, linking Jewish themes of *The Book of Questions* to central issues animating modern French poetry:

> Although Jabès's imagery and sources are for the most part derived from Judaism, *The Book of Questions* is not a Jewish work in the same way that one can speak of *Paradise Lost* as a Christian work. . . . The Book is his central image—but it is not only the Book of the Jews (the spirals of commentary around commentary in the Midrash), but an allusion to Mallarmé's ideal Book as well (the Book that contains the world, endlessly folding in upon itself). Fi-

> nally, Jabès's work must be considered as part of the on-going French poetic tradition that began in the late nineteenth century. (AH 113–14)

In a subsequent interview with Auster, Jabès acknowledges residing within French poetic tradition but takes great pains to differentiate Mallarmé's notion of the book from his own: "Mallarmé wanted to put all knowledge into a book. He wanted to make a great book, the book of books. But in my opinion this book would be very ephemeral, since knowledge itself is ephemeral. The book that would have a chance to survive, I think, is the book that destroys itself. That destroys itself in favor of another book that will prolong it" (AH 164). Jabès favors a midrashic approach to the book over an idealist one, a text composed of questions rather than answers, a book from which one can at least provisionally escape.[9] Like midrashic commentary, Jabès's *Book of Questions* locates anomalies or paradoxes or gaps in understanding as precursors to further writing—as if it were necessary first to get lost in order to be found. This may sound like a deconstructive truism (and in fact Jabès influences Derrida and other French theorists), but there is also a desire for truth and wholeness at odds with deconstructive protocols, and Auster unashamedly espouses this desire as well. Jabès seeks a wholeness to be found in fragments. If one maintains an awareness of the entire book at each moment of writing, he claims, the whole can exert an irresistible pressure that determines the composition word-by-word:

> When I say there are many books in the book, it is because there are many words in the word. Obviously, if you change the word, the context of the sentence changes completely. In this way another sentence is born from this word, and a completely different book begins. . . . I think of this in terms of the sea, in the image of the sea as it breaks upon the shore. It is not the wave that comes, it is the whole sea that comes each time and the whole sea that draws back. It is never just a wave, it is always everything that comes and everything that goes. This is really the fundamental movement in all my books. Everything is connected to everything else. . . . At each moment, in the least question, it is the *whole* book which returns and the *whole* book which draws back. (AH 168)

This highly elaborated notion of the book as the poetic principle of writing—as that which holds open the space of writing—allows Jabès to make a radical distinction between the novel and the (poetic) book.[10] Although *The Book of Questions* has characters, dialogue, and an implicit story and is classified on the jacket of the English version as "fiction," Jabès vehemently rejects the novel's storytelling function as undermining the writer's fidelity to the book. For the book makes moment-to-moment demands that he believes should supersede the narrative thrust of a particular story. He complains,

> The novelist's high-handed appropriation of the book has always been unbearable to me. What makes me uneasy is his pretense of making the *space* of the book the space of the story he tells—making the subject of his novel the subject of the book. . . . Novelistic fiction, even when innovative, does not, from my point of view, take charge of the totality of [the risk involved in writing]. The book loses its autonomy. . . . A stranger to the book, its breath, its rhythm, the novelist imposes an exterior, exclusive speech: a life and a death, invented in the course of the story. For him the book is only a tool. At no moment does the novelist listen to the page, to its whiteness and silence.[11]

Born in a textual age, Jabès locates the space of poetry within the book, which has a life of its own. Aided by evidence that a vital Jewish imagination has been able to survive within the book for two millennia, he seeks to defend this space from incursions by those lesser poetic talents, the novelists, who impose the stories of their characters over the mysterious imperatives of the book. In his own investigations of "the space of the book," Auster takes seriously the challenge issued by Jabès, endeavoring to enter the room of the book by attending to its "whiteness and silence." Like Jabès in *The Book of Questions,* Auster writes a prose animated by the poetic imperative of listening to the "white spaces" of the book. Unlike Jabès, however, Auster also commits to the novel, and thus a tension erupts in the confrontation between narrative and book. At the beginning of his published prose, with *The Invention of Solitude* and *The New York Trilogy,* Auster's fidelity rests primarily with the book. This promotes flat characterization and dialogue that appears more like its surrounding descriptive prose than like the speech of discrete persons. Likewise, the narrative of his early novels seems wholly governed by plot. Over the course of four subsequent novels, *In the Country of Last Things, Moon Palace, The Music of Chance,* and *Leviathan,* Auster hones an ability to create more realistic characters and begins to elaborate narratives that unfold beyond the exigencies of plot.[12] Still, his explorations of the scene of writing in these works evoke a palpable friction between novel and book.

His first book of prose, *The Invention of Solitude,* contains a Jabèsian text, "The Book of Memory," in which he enters the space of writing with an obsessive attention to the book that nearly rivals the poetic fixation of Jabès. And yet Auster does not wholly eschew narrative, for the "Book of Memory" brims with anecdotes and little stories, and it is here Auster begins to create a fiction of the book. In his article on Jabès, he gives a summary description of *The Book of Questions* that applies equally to "The Book of Memory": "What happens in *The Book of Questions*, then, is the writing of *The Book of Questions*—or rather, the attempt to write it, a process that the reader is allowed to witness in all its gropings and hesitations" (AH 111). "The Book of Memory" begins with a literal enactment of the "listen[ing] to the page, its whiteness and silence" that Jabès recommends: "He lays out a piece of blank paper on the table before him and writes these words with his pen. It was. It will never be again" (IS 75). Then, we continue to "witness in all its gropings and hesitations" subsequent attempts to write the book:

> Later that same day he returns to his room. He finds a fresh sheet of paper and lays it out on the table before him. He writes until he has covered the entire page with words. Later, when he reads over what he has written, he has trouble deciphering the words. Those he does manage to understand do not seem to say what he thought he was saying. Then he goes out to eat his dinner.
>
> That night he tells himself that tomorrow is another day. New words begin to clamor in his head, but he does not write them down. He decides to refer to himself as A. He walks back and forth between the table and the window. He turns on the radio and then turns it off. He smokes a cigarette.
>
> Then he writes. It was. It will never be again. (IS 75)

As in *Ghosts*, Auster creates a scene of writing that is both book and room, for which the question of identity is inseparable from the writing of the book. "The Book of Memory" is a memoir, in which, unaccountably, the author "decides to refer to himself as A." To create enough distance to see himself, he places himself at a turning point ("It was. It will never be again"), which urges an interpretation of the present in terms of the past. He invokes memory as a kind of book that, in Jabès's terms, "destroys itself in favor of another book that will prolong it" (AH 164). "The Book of Memory" destroys memory by making it into a book. Likewise, the present sense of self is an enclosure erected anew each time the past is queried. In other words, the question Blue asks in *Ghosts*, "How to get out of the room that is the book that will go on being written for as long as he stays in the room?" (NYT 201–2), animates "The Book of Memory" as well. There are at least three ways that room and book are intertwined in "The Book of Memory": A. describes in obsessive detail the room in which he lives and writes (as well as a number of significant rooms in his past); as in the old art of memory, he portrays memory in architectural terms, composed of rooms in which contiguous impressions create chains of memory; in addition, A. explores the principles that determine such contiguity—chance, coincidence, free association.

"AS THOUGH HE WERE ENTERING THAT MAN'S SOLITUDE AND MAKING IT HIS OWN"

Like Thoreau and Melville, whose *Walden* and "Bartleby" are among the ghosts in *Ghosts*, Auster is fascinated by solitude.[13] Many recurrent images in "The Book of Memory" evoke solitary enclosure, such as references to Jonah in the whale, to Pinocchio in the shark, to Anne Frank in hiding, and to George Oppen's phrase "the shipwreck of the singular." Regardless of the imagery, enclosure within the room of writing conjures not just aloneness but claustrophobia: "It is as if he were being forced to watch his own disappearance, as if, by crossing the threshold of this room, he were entering another dimension, taking up residence inside a black hole" (IS 77). Ultimately, the poetic anxiety about the room of writing is revealed as a fear of death, a fear so acute that A. tries to evacuate his life in the present in order to observe it safely, albeit disembodied, from the future:

> Christmas Eve, 1979. His life no longer seemed to dwell in the present. Whenever he turned on his radio and listened to the news of the world, he would find himself imagining the words to be describing things that had happened long ago. Even as he stood in the present, he felt himself to be looking at it from the future, and this present-as-past was so antiquated that even the horrors of the day, which ordinarily would have filled him with outrage, seemed remote to him, as if the voice in the radio were reading from a chronicle of some lost civilization. Later, in a time of greater clarity, he would refer to this sensation as "nostalgia for the present." (IS 76)

Auster displaces the present in four different ways. He portrays A. as bouncing off the present and into the past or the future, first, hearing a report of present events as though it were referring to a distant past and, second, trying to imagine himself looking at the present from the future. Then, in the last sentence, he places a narrator at a future point, "Later," looking back upon A. in the "present" moment. Finally, he gives this alienated condition the paradoxical label "nostalgia for the present," which further congeals and reifies it. Here, Auster joins an extensive lineage of writers recounting extreme alienation—especially Jewish writers such as Kafka, Freud, Scholem, Benjamin, Celan, Jabès, Oppen, Barthes, Bruno Schulz, Anne Frank, Charles Reznikoff, and Henry Roth. In "The Book of Memory" he deploys the impact of alienation in a particularly active way he shares with a smaller circle of writers, such as Samuel Beckett and the John Ashbery of *Three Poems*, who create what I have called a translative prose, which enquires into identity and writing simultaneously.[14] At one point, Auster offers translation as an image for what occurs when one enters the room of the book:

> For most of his adult life, he has earned his living by translating the books of other writers. He sits at his desk reading the book in French and then picks up his pen and writes the same book in English. It is both the same book and not the same book, and the strangeness of this activity has never failed to impress him. Every book is an image of solitude. . . . A. sits down in his own room to translate another man's book, and it is as though he were entering that man's solitude and making it his own. (IS 136)

In the act of translation, identity is both found and lost. Rewriting the words of another develops a profoundly intimate transaction, in which the translator finds identities melting, mingling, or repelling one another. The translator invades the isolation of the space of writing, an intruder who never knows whether that violated solitude will fortify or weaken a sense of self. For Blue, in *Ghosts,* penetration into the aloneness of another results in a terrifying mise en abyme: "Having penetrated Black's room and stood there alone, having been, so to speak, in the sanctum of Black's solitude, he cannot respond to the darkness of that moment except by replacing it with a solitude of his own" (NYT 226). Like the fictional character Blue, "A. imagines himself as a kind of ghost of that other man, who is both there and not there, and whose book is both the same and not the same as the one he is translating" (IS 136).

Meditating on translation, though, offers A. a new sort of life: "It dawns on him that everything he is trying to record in The Book of Memory, everything he has written so far, is no more than the translation of a moment or two of his life—those moments he lived through on Christmas Eve, 1979, in his room at 6 Varick Street" (IS 136). Just as translation renders the writer a ghost confined to the room that is the book, it also provides a way out. The recognition that A.'s life and his writing have been on a collision course that eventuates in their complete merging—a recognition provoked when he sits down at his desk and writes, "It was. It will never be again." (IS 75)—also begins a translation of that moment out of itself. The only way to get out of the room that is the book is by writing the book, for writing translates the moment that inaugurates the book into an ongoing present that opens out of the memory of that moment. Auster makes explicit the notion of escape through the translation of memory by citing the famous example of Pascal's "Memorial," an ecstatic testimony sewn into the lining of the philosopher's clothing as a constant reminder of mystical illumination on the night of November 23, 1654 (IS 137). The memory of such a moment irradiates the space of writing, and as the writer dives into memory he can see a way of moving beyond his solitude and out into the world and, ultimately, into history:

> As he writes, he feels that he is moving inward (through himself) and at the same time moving outward (towards the world). What he experienced, per-

> haps, during those few moments on Christmas Eve, 1979, as he sat alone in his room on Varick Street, was this: the sudden knowledge that came over him that even alone, in the deepest solitude of his room, he was not alone, or, more precisely, that the moment he began to try to speak of that solitude, he had become more than just himself. Memory, therefore, not simply as the resurrection of one's private past, but an immersion in the past of others, which is to say: history—which one both participates in and is a witness to, is a part of and apart from. (IS 139)

The poet is trapped in narrative prose. The writer is trapped in the book. The "agent" Blue is trapped in the room. Can these figures use memory to come out into the world, into history? One way of resolving this conundrum would be to notice that for both Pascal and A., memory already includes simultaneously an inside and an outside. When Pascal writes up his memory and then sews it in his clothing, he gives it a double exteriority, which matches the way that A. moves both inward and outward by writing about what he remembers of Christmas Eve, 1979. But thinking of memory in this way offers a too-easy solution. Memory is not only interior and exterior but also the site where remembering and forgetting meet. For now, it is necessary to hold in abeyance Auster's affirmation that memory leads out of the room and into history until we have looked at what the text actively forgets.

"ROOM AND TOMB, TOMB AND WOMB, WOMB AND ROOM"

To think about the repressed in "The Book of Memory," it's time to invoke the second interpretive framework mentioned in the introduction to this essay, which is a parthenogenic fantasy of masculine creativity. Ostensibly a book of mourning, "The Book of Memory" follows on the recent death of A.'s father, and his grandfather dies during its composition. The first half of *The Invention of Solitude*, "Portrait of an Invisible Man," treats his father's death and Auster's discovery that his paternal grandfather was murdered by Auster's grandmother. Throughout "The Book of Memory," Auster thinks about fathers and sons, brooding on his own young son while reflecting on traumas and losses inscribed in the continuity of generations.[15] The mood is melancholy, veering between hopelessness, nostalgia, and obsessive self-regard, but its desperate goal is regeneration of a life through writing. Thus, the room of the book bears a set of figurative equivalents that differ in emphasis from those in *Ghosts*. In the latter, the room of the book is a cell where Blue is trapped and forcibly initiated into the brotherhood of writers. In "The Book of Memory," the room of the book is more often a void, a place of nothingness or meaninglessness, a site for confrontation with death. Auster offers a chain of rhyming words for this particular figuration of the room as scene of writing: "Room and tomb, tomb and womb, womb and room" (IS 159–60).

This chain of equivalents implies that the room of the book is a place where death transforms into rebirth. But this can happen only if meaninglessness is a first principle. By meaninglessness, Auster has a specific denial in mind, that of the motivated connection between any two factors:

> Like everyone else, he craves a meaning. Like everyone else, his life is so fragmented that each time he sees a connection between two fragments he is tempted to look for a meaning in that connection. The connection exists. But to give it a meaning, to look beyond the bare fact of its existence, would be to build an imaginary world inside the real world, and he knows it would not stand. At his bravest moments, he embraces meaninglessness as the first principle. (IS 147)

Thus enshrining meaninglessness, Auster strikes a blow against the conventions of the novel, which assume that meaningful connections between events can be mooted. Without this assumption, the ideological labor of the novel as guarantor of identity within a social world risks failure. Auster undermines this ideology by telling stories in which coincidences and other unmotivated connections are never sufficient to ensure identity.

He asserts the "principle" of meaninglessness particularly when discussing coincidence or chance. After telling a story about M., a friend who finds himself living in Paris in the exact same attic room where his father hid from the Nazis twenty years before, A. notes the further coincidence that he, too, lived in such a *chambre de bonne* and that it was where his own father had come to see him. These thoughts cause A. to "remember his father's death. And beyond that, to understand—this most important of all—that M.'s story has no meaning" (IS 81). In this passage, meaninglessness is associated directly with A.'s father's death, and beyond that with the equation of the room of the book with the tomb. From this void, however, comes A.'s impulse to write and to make his memorial book a site of regeneration, to be reborn within the act of mourning. Acknowledging that M.'s story is meaningless, A. counters,

> Nevertheless, this is where it begins. The first word appears only at a moment when nothing can be explained anymore, at some instant of experience that defies all sense. To be reduced to saying nothing. Or else, to say to himself: this is what haunts me. And then to realize, almost in the same breath, that this is what he haunts. (IS 81)

But what does haunt A. in this experience of nothingness? There is a clue in the chain of equivalents, "Room and tomb, tomb and womb, womb and room." They offer a glimpse behind the ostensible subject of mourning, into a repressed but significant motivation for writing: to bring the room and the tomb into equivalence with the womb injects gender considerations into a narrative otherwise exclusively masculine. Here, terms like "nothingness" and "meaninglessness" are gendered feminine, and women are figured as void and men as self-generating. Having projected so many desires upon the notion of nothingness, it's as though Auster takes the Buddhist image of the "pregnant void" and splits it in half, assigning the void to women and pregnancy to men. In "The Book of Memory," he attempts a kind of parthenogenesis, using the room as a womb to give birth to the book, without the intervention of woman.

In a discussion of Paris and of a composer he meets there, S., who becomes a father figure, A. gives a striking description of the room as a place at once claustrophobic (to the body) and infinitely generative (to the mind)—a masculine womb. He begins by noting, "These are his earliest memories of the city, where so much of his life would later be spent, and they are inescapably bound up with the idea of the room" (IS 89). Having highlighted the room's significance, A. goes on to describe first its claustrophobic quality: "S. lived in a space so small that at first it seemed to defy you, to resist being entered. The presence of one person crowded the room, two people choked it. It was impossible to move inside it without contracting your body to its smallest dimensions, without contracting your mind to some infinitely small point within itself." The claustrophobia affects both body and mind, as though the room were attempting to squeeze both down to nothingness. For the mind, however, this contraction gives way to its opposite, a sudden expansion, inaugurated by studying the room's contents:

> For there was an entire universe in that room, a miniature cosmology that contained all that is most vast, most distant, most unknowable. It was a shrine, hardly bigger than a body, in praise of all that exists beyond the body: the representation of one man's inner world, even to the slightest detail. S. had literally managed to surround himself with the things that were inside him. The room he lived in was a dream space, and its walls were like the skin of some second body around him, as if his own body had been transformed into a mind, a breathing instrument of pure thought. This was the womb, the belly of the whale, the original site of the imagination. (IS 89)

In this masculinist fantasy of self-generative creativity, the enwombing room is "like the skin of some second body around him," capable of giving birth to the works of the solitary artist, without female intercession—or even that of the body. In this male "hysteria," the wandering womb of the room takes on the generative qualities of the composer S.'s inner life.[16] Within "The Book of Memory," the masculine birth Auster depicts most fully is that of

Pinocchio, sculpted into being by his father. This image runs as a leitmotif throughout the text. Another striking masculinist image of self-generation, derived from the *Monadology* of Leibniz, also recurs at several points. For instance, further on in the same meditation that equates room with tomb and womb, A. imagines language "as a monadology," a transactional matrix of words that "functions as a kind of bridge that joins opposite and contrasting aspects of the world with each other":

> Language, then, not simply as a list of separate things to be added up and whose sum total is equal to the world. Rather, language as it is laid out in the dictionary: an infinitely complex organism, all of whose elements—cells and sinews, corpuscles and bones, digits and fluids—are present in the world simultaneously, none of which can exist on its own. For each word is defined by other words, which means that to enter any part of language is to enter the whole of it. (IS 160)

Like a Kabbalist, A. ascribes tremendous potency to language, imagining it as the matrix of being, as the genetic matter of the world. He sums up this apotheosis by invoking Leibniz directly: "Language, then, as a monadology, to echo the term used by Leibniz" (IS 160). Auster construes the "monadology" as the interconnected network of irreducible "monads" that compose the universe, such that, as Leibniz puts it, "'every body experiences everything that goes on in the universe'" (IS 160). After a long citation from Leibniz, Auster concludes, "Playing with words in the way A. did as a schoolboy, then, was not so much a search for the truth as a search for the world as it appears in language. Language is not truth. It is the way we exist in the world" (IS 161). To say that language "is the way we exist in the world" sounds like Heidegger or Wittgenstein, but A. takes this proposition in a different direction. He fantasizes that "language . . . is an infinitely complex organism" with "cells and sinews, corpuscles and bones, digits and fluids," as though language were not just a mode of existence *in the world* but a replacement for life *in the body*. When "it is possible for events in one's life to rhyme as well" (IS 161), then the "monadology" of language has seemingly taken over everything. At the end of this three-page meditation on the awesome power of language, A. arrives at the mysterious recognition that, in fact, everything is beginning to rhyme for him:

> What A. is struggling to express, perhaps, is that for some time now none of the terms has been missing for him. Wherever his eye or mind seems to stop, he discovers another connection, another bridge to carry him to yet another place, and even in the solitude of his room, the world has been rush-

> ing in on him at a dizzying speed, as if it were all suddenly converging in him and happening to him at once. Coincidence: to fall on with; to occupy the same place in time or space. The mind, therefore, as that which contains more than itself. As in the phrase from Augustine: "But where is the part of it which it does not itself contain?" (IS 162)

This sense of linkages snapping into place can result from a visionary heightening of consciousness, or, noticing that "the world has been rushing in on him at a dizzying speed," it may well be that A. is experiencing a moment of sheer paranoia. If this is paranoia, it may have a causal relation to A.'s masculinist notion of self-generation, of mind outside body in a room. In fact, A.'s imagining of the human mind as the entire universe of monads goes far beyond Leibniz, whom Auster quotes as cautioning, "A soul, however, can read in itself only what is directly represented in it; it is unable to unfold all at once all its folds; for these go on into infinity" (161). In his vision that everything has begun to rhyme, A. has taken something like Robert Duncan's poetic conceit that "the structure of rime" is "an absolute scale of resemblance and disresemblance" and inflated it into the fantasy of a wrinkle-free existence, in which every connection is available to the mind.[17]

"HE STORMED OUT OF THE ROOM AND WENT TO HIS SON'S BEDSIDE"

The gender implications of this fantasy of self-sufficient disembodiment become clear in a scene in which A., "for no particular reason," wanders into a topless bar in Manhattan. In a completely detached tone of voice, the narrator describes how A. "found himself sitting next to a voluptuously naked young woman," who invites him into the back room. "There was something so openly humorous and matter-of-fact about her approach, that he finally agreed to her proposition. The best thing, they decided, would be for her to suck his penis, since she claimed an extraordinary talent for this activity." At the moment of ejaculation, the Leibnizian monad is revealed as an image of masculine parthenogenesis:

> As he came in her mouth a few moments later, with a long and throbbing flood of semen, he had this vision, at just that second, which has continued to radiate inside him: that each ejaculation contains several billion sperm cells—or roughly the same number as there are people in the world—which means that, in himself, each man holds the potential of an entire world. And what would happen, could it happen, is the full range of possibilities: a spawn of idiots and geniuses, of the beautiful and the deformed, of saints, catatonics,

> thieves, stock brokers, and high-wire artists. Each man, therefore, is the entire world, bearing within his genes a memory of all mankind. Or, as Leibniz put it: "Every living substance is a perpetual living mirror of the universe." For the fact is, we are of the same stuff that came into being with the first explosion of the first spark in the infinite emptiness of space. Or so he said to himself, at that moment, as his penis exploded into the mouth of that naked woman, whose name he has now forgotten. (IS 114)

This passage makes explicit the conjunction of woman as nothingness with masculine parthenogenesis. The sexual function of the woman is located in the mouth, not in the womb, and absolutely no connection, aside from mechanical friction, takes place between the woman and the man. The woman is not nameless, but her name is actively erased by A.'s final qualification: "that naked woman, whose name he has now forgotten." There is a barb in that statement, which we will have to look at more closely. First, however, note the careful working out of the mechanics of parthenogenesis: the emotionless ejaculation is converted into a purely mental reverie—as though the phallus were the mind, capable of generating the entire world by its explosive satisfaction. The woman's role in this masculine self-generation is "effaced" (that is, she is rendered faceless), and as oral recipient of the exploding penis she becomes mute as well.

A few pages further in "The Book of Memory," A. makes a seemingly technical reference to "Solitude," a song recorded by Billie Holiday, whose vocal style unforgettably registers the many nuances of masculine aggression. Following the technical reference, A. notices that the mention of Billie Holiday and an immediately prior description of Emily Dickinson's room ("it was the room that was present in the poems and not the reverse" [IS 123]) constitute "First allusions to a woman's voice. To be followed by specific reference to several" (IS 123). But he does not deliver on this promise. Instead, he launches into an odd speculation: "For it is his belief that if there is a voice of truth—assuming there is such a thing as truth, and assuming this truth can speak—it comes from the mouth of a woman" (IS 123). This conjectured truth never arrives, but ironically, the only thing that "comes from the mouth of a woman" is A.'s penis. It's as though Billie Holiday and Emily Dickinson are invoked as powerful female artists only to be silenced. The question, then: why this desire to erase the female voice?

A clue appears in a passage describing A.'s relationship to the one other character who is denied a name—also a woman. A. is telling a story about his two-year-old son's sudden illness and resultant stay in the hospital. The fearful parents spend every waking hour with him:

> His wife, however, began to show the strain. At one point she walked out to A., who was in the adult sitting room, and said, "I give up, I can't handle him anymore"—and there was such resentment in her voice against the boy, such an anger of exasperation, that something inside A. fell to pieces. Stupidly, cruelly, he wanted to punish his wife for such selfishness, and in that one instant all the newly won harmony that had been growing between them for the past month vanished: for the first time in all their years together, he had turned against her. He stormed out of the room and went to his son's bedside. (108)

The woman-without-a-name in "The Book of Memory" is A.'s wife. In the passage above, his suppressed anger begins to leak out. One expects to hear from the mother of a two-year-old at least daily, "I give up, I can't handle him anymore," but its effect on A., who seems to have transferred his anger at his wife to an excessive doting upon his son (apparent in many passages), is to break through the shell of his repression. Rather than commiserate with her, "A. fell to pieces," that is, he became enraged: "Stupidly, cruelly, he wanted to punish his wife for such selfishness." What is "stupid" and "cruel" in the context of a marriage would be not the anger itself but its reported suppression for so many years: "For the first time in all their years together, he had turned against her." If these two characters have throttled conflict for so long, it's no wonder their marriage is falling apart or that A.'s anger toward women reaches a bizarre climax in attempting to exclude them completely from the room of the book. The parthenogenic fantasy running through "The Book of Memory" and the masculine genealogy of fathers and sons that Auster maps out in the entire *Invention of Solitude* must arise, at least in part, from the explosive potential of bottled-up anger. One important facet of this psychic economy is A.'s transforming his anger and sense of betrayal into a smothering identification with his son. He writes the mother out of the family romance, portraying his wife only as her son's betrayer and shifting the focus of the divorce drama onto the relationship of the parents to the son.

If this is a book of mourning, of confrontation with death, then the fatality that looms largest within it but is given least expression is the death of a marriage. At a "ghostly" level, this is a book of divorce, a book of memory born from the almost total erasure of the memories of marriage. A. allows his nameless wife very few appearances, and in none of them does she possess the regenerative qualities A. so desperately seeks. For instance, he figures their marriage as hopeless from its outset: "He remembers returning home from his wedding party in 1974, his wife beside him in her white dress, and taking the front door key out of his pocket, inserting the key in the lock, and then, as he turned his wrist, feeling the blade of the key snap off inside the lock" (IS 145). Rather than explore the interior landscape of his marriage to understand how what might be interpreted as a symbolic castration took place, A. retreats to a room and writes a book of self-renewal, in which he invents a masculine genealogy of creativity that will substitute for his father's emotional distance and will also mourn the father's recent death. The correlation between death and divorce provokes the most striking "coincidence" in the book: "Two months after his father's death (January 1979), A.'s marriage collapsed" (IS 101). In a misguided attempt to deny the consequences of his divorce—such as, an inability to participate in a mutually beneficial relationship—A. clutches the emotional bond with his son: "It was quite another thing for him to swallow the consequences it entailed: to be separated from his son. The thought of it was intolerable to him" (IS 101).

"SHE WROTE HER DIARY IN THIS ROOM"

In keeping with an exclusively masculine genealogy, all of A.'s hopes for regeneration reside in his son. His feelings toward him are more than those of a father protecting his son in potentially damaging circumstances, for they partake of an almost messianic desire for deliverance. Throughout *The Invention of Solitude*, the hope prevails that the son will rescue the father. Like Geppetto in the Pinocchio story, A. as father hides in the room of the book, parthenogenically creating a son as his savior.[18] Given the depiction in "Portrait of an Invisible Man" of Auster's own desperately wounded father (who witnessed his father's murder at the hands of his mother), this desire for the son to rescue the father is a painful patrimony. And the desire is not only a response to his father's baffling emotional distance, for it also corresponds to the need to rescue parents felt by children of Holocaust victims and survivors. The parallels between Auster's personal history and a post-Holocaust sensibility run throughout "The Book of Memory." Of all the scenes of hiding in a room, the most central thematically is that of Anne Frank, writing her own identity in a room of the book while hiding from the Nazis. "The Book of Memory" is shot through with post-Holocaust imagery, which provides the third interpretive framework for reading Auster's memoir.[19]

I say "post-Holocaust" because, as a Jewish writer born after the war, Auster's imagination has been infected by the Shoah. Although his secularity and his marked affinity for Protestant American writers, such as Poe, Hawthorne, Thoreau, and Melville, may mask the pervasive Jewish subtext, Auster provides a significant gauge of it in his essays, collected in *The Art of Hunger*. The title, of course, alludes to Kafka's story "The Hunger Artist," and of the nineteen essays, eleven discuss secular Jewish writers, all of whom have significantly influenced Auster: Laura Riding (2), Franz Kafka (2), Louis Wolfson, Charles Reznikoff, Paul Celan, Edmond Jabès (2), George Oppen, and Carl Rakosi. For Jews born after World War II, two paramount realities demand attention: the devastation of the Holocaust and the creation of the State of Israel. Auster makes mention of Israel in "The Book of Memory" only by reproducing an encyclopedia entry about a relative, Daniel Auster, who became the first mayor of Jerusalem after statehood (IS 85). Daniel is also the name of A.'s son (the only character given a full name in the text), and this coincidence ties his Israeli relative into the genealogy A. is constructing. Suggestively, the invocation of Israel takes place within the context of an extended meditation on Anne Frank. During this meditation, Auster identifies Frank's room directly with the room of the book, setting forth the post-Holocaust theme.

On a short trip to Amsterdam, ostensibly to look at art, A. finds himself confronted by traces of Frank. As when he enters the topless bar in Manhattan, A. goes to her house "for no particular reason." By this point in the narrative, it is clear that this phrase indicates not chance but overdetermination:

> For no particular reason (idly looking through a guide book he found in his hotel room) he decided to go to Anne Frank's house, which has been preserved as a museum. It was a Sunday morning, gray with rain, and the streets along the canal were deserted. He climbed the steep and narrow staircase inside the house and entered the secret annex. As he stood in Anne Frank's room, the room in which the diary was written, now bare, with the faded pictures of Hollywood movie stars she had collected still pasted to the walls, he suddenly found himself crying. Not sobbing, as might happen in response to deep inner pain, but crying without sound, the tears streaming down his cheeks, as if purely in response to the world. It was at that moment, he later realized, that the Book of Memory began. As in the phrase: "she wrote her diary in this room." (IS 82–83)

Anne Frank's room of the book, in which she wrote her diary, supplies a point of origin for "The Book of Memory." Entering this room, A. experiences not just a psychological but also an ontological pain, as if the condition of hiding imposed upon Frank by the threat of the Holocaust had now become the condition of being in the world. Two paragraphs later, A. imagines this claustrophobic ontology as "a solitude so crushing, so unconsolable, that one stops breathing for hundreds of years" (IS 83). It's as though every post-Holocaust experience of solitude, every self-encounter, were haunted by Anne Frank's absolute isolation. Looking out her window at children's toys in a yard, A. wonders "what it would be like to grow up in the shadow of Anne Frank's room" (IS 83), in the shadow of that breath-stopping solitude. In a figurative sense, all Jews after the war grow up within this shadow. Whenever Auster enters the room of the book, he seems to find it shrouded by this shadow, as if his writing were a repetition-compulsion brought about by the trauma of the Shoah. In an ironic juxtaposition, A. quotes another famous saying of Pascal: "All the unhappiness of man stems from one thing only: that he is incapable of staying quietly in his room" (IS 83). It's as if Frank's life in the room of the book were a reproach to the Christian monastic psychology of hiding and self-incarceration as a freely chosen way of life. Growing up figuratively in the shadow of Frank's room, A. feels trapped inside the room of the book. He *chooses* not his location but his identification with Anne Frank as writer, as though his unending task of mourning were given concretion and containment by her room and her book.

Not only does A. identify with Frank, but he also states, "Anne Frank's birthday is the same as his son's" (IS 83), thus placing her into the genealogical chain of fathers and sons, rather than opening up for her the vanishing space of the feminine. Following this avowal of a post-Holocaust kinship between Anne Frank, his son, and himself, A. quotes from "Israel Lichtenstein's Last Testament. Warsaw; July 31, 1942," in which one of the resistance fighters in the Warsaw Ghetto, knowing he is about to die, asks not "for gratitude, any monument, any praise. I want only a remembrance" (IS 84). Lichtenstein asks for remembrance of himself, of his wife, and especially of his preternaturally gifted daughter: "Margalit, 20 months old today. Has mastered Yiddish perfectly, speaks a pure Yiddish. . . . In intelligence she is on a par with 3- or 4-year old children. I don't want to brag about her. . . . I am not sorry about my life and that of my wife. But I am sorry for the gifted little girl. She deserves to be remembered also" (IS 84). Disasters of such magnitude—involving the obliteration of individuals, of communities, and, most poignantly for A., of marvelous children—are suffered not only by those who experience them. They are passed on to future generations as unfinished projects of mourning. Unbearable memories for the family (such as Auster's father witnessing his father's murder) and for the society (such as the Holocaust or American slavery or Indigenous genocide) are braided within the continuity of generations and preserve a virulent force that can yank a member of a succeeding generation out of the present and into its secret room. When A. imagines the continuity of generations, he does not call up a biblical plenitude within which to reside. Instead, the trauma displaces him into a realm of isolation, in which generations are squeezed into an individual body—itself incapable of inhabiting the present:

> When the father dies, he writes, the son becomes his own father and his own son. He looks at his son and sees himself in the face of the boy. He imagines what the boy sees when he looks at him and finds himself becoming his own father. Inexplicably, he is moved by this. It is not just the sight of the boy that moves him, nor even the thought of standing inside his father, but what he

> sees in the boy of his own vanished past. It is a nostalgia for his own life that he feels. . . . Inexplicably, he finds himself shaking at that moment with both happiness and sorrow, if this is possible, as if he were going both forward and backward, into the future and into the past. And there are times, often there are times, when these feelings are so strong that his life no longer seems to dwell in the present. (IS 81–82)

When transported out of the present by trauma, A. lives in a genealogical world in which time is sped up and fathers and children subsume one another: "Each time he saw a child, he would try to imagine what it would look like as a grown-up. Each time he saw an old person, he would try to imagine what that person had looked like as a child" (IS 87). Like Blake's "mental traveller" who moves back and forth in time, A.'s "life no longer seems to dwell in the present." This hallucinatory vision is at its most extreme when A. gazes at women:

> It was worst with women, especially if the woman was young and beautiful. He could not help looking through the skin of her face and imagining the anonymous skull behind it. And the more lovely the face, the more ardent his attempt to seek in it the encroaching signs of the future: incipient wrinkles, the later-to-be-sagging chin, the glaze of disappointment in the eyes. He would put one face on top of another: this woman at forty; this woman at sixty; this woman at eighty; as if, even as he stood in the present, he felt compelled to hunt out the future, to track down the death that lives in each one of us. (IS 87)

In this passage, the post-Holocaust haunting by death dovetails with A.'s inability to imagine regeneration through the feminine, such that dissolution and decay replace fertility and fecundity. A. ends this passage with a dispiriting quotation from Flaubert: "The sight of a naked woman makes me imagine her skeleton" (IS 87).

"THE SON SAVES THE FATHER"

Casting aside the feminine as a source of regeneration, A. turns to the hope that the son can rescue the father. When the father has suffered an unbearable wound, it is natural for the son to entertain the fantasy of rescuing his father. An impulse of this sort must be at work, for instance, in *Maus*, Art Spiegelman's brilliant graphic biography.[20] Foregrounding his difficult relationship with his father during the telling of Vladek's tale of surviving the Holocaust, Spiegelman subtly inscribes the son's desire to rescue the father. In "Portrait of an Invisible Man," Auster presents himself as trapped within trauma, incapable both of rescuing his father and of mourning him satisfactorily, for complete mourning would require some kind of acceptance, and this he is unable to provide: "There has been a wound, and I realize now that it is very deep. Instead of healing me as I thought it would, the act of writing has kept this wound open. At times I have even felt the pain of it concentrated in my right hand, as if each time I picked up the pen and pressed it against the page, my hand were being torn apart. Instead of burying my father for me, these words have kept him alive, perhaps more so than ever" (IS 32).

Attempting to mourn the father he imagines as unburied, A. goes into the room of the book and begins to write, seeking through writing to find his way back to the present: "The world has shrunk to the size of this room for him, and for as long as it takes him to understand it, he must stay where he is. Only one thing is certain: he cannot be anywhere until he is here. And if he does not manage to find this place, it would be absurd for him to think of looking for another" (IS 79). It sounds as though A. is setting himself a phenomenological project of learning to inhabit the room, as in the saying by Heidegger, "But we do not want to get anywhere. We would like only, for once, to get just where we are already."[21] But instead of registering his sense of location in phenomenological terms, A. turns figurative and remembers stories: "Life inside the whale. A gloss on Jonah, and what it means to refuse to speak. Parallel text: Geppetto in the belly of the shark (whale in the Disney version), and the story of how Pinocchio rescues him. Is it true that one must dive to the depths of the sea and save one's father to become a real boy?" (IS 79). Through the intertwined stories of Jonah and Pinocchio, A. tries to fathom what it means to live in the room of the book and how such dwelling might eventuate in rescuing his father. Thinking about Jonah inside the whale, A. notes that the whale "is by no means an agent of destruction. The fish is what saves him from drowning in the sea" (IS 125). Such confinement presents incarceration as salvation, a symbolic death that is "a preparation for new life, a life that has passed through death, and therefore a life that can at last speak" (IS 125).

The room of the book is an alchemical chamber, in which Auster hopes to make death speak life through the renewal of the father by the son's agency. In "The Book of Memory," alchemy makes its fullest appearance when A. meditates on *Pinocchio* as he reads the story to his young son. Noting, "the little boy never tired of hearing the chapter about the storm at sea, which tells of how Pinocchio finds Geppetto in the belly of the Terrible Shark" (IS 130), A. quotes Pinocchio's charged exclamation, "Oh, Father, dear Father! Have I found you at last? Now I shall never, never leave you again!" (IS 131). Initially, this exclamation gives expression to the feelings of these particular readers: "For A. and his son, so often separated from each other during the past year, there was something deeply satisfying in this passage of reunion" (IS 131). On another level, this exclamation reiterates A.'s desire to recover his own father and, beyond that, to reclaim a patrilineal heritage from the dead that will enable him to speak. In his own life, as in Pinocchio's, reunion with the father has become essential for the son's regeneration. As A. explains, the bulk of *Pinocchio* "tells the story of Pinocchio's search for his father—and Geppetto's search for his son. At some point, Pinocchio realizes that he wants to become a real boy. But it also becomes clear that this will not happen until he is reunited with his father" (IS 132).

When this reunion happens, however, the story is far from over. For full restitution to take place—for Pinocchio to become a "real boy," for A. to redeem his traumatized father—the boy has to emerge from the belly of the shark with his father upon his back. The boy created by parthenogenesis must give birth to himself out of the womb/tomb. This iconic image resides at the core of Auster's fantasy of regeneration through the room of the book, and he has A. contemplate it obsessively:

> The father on the son's back: the image evoked here is so clearly that of Aeneas bearing Anchises on his back from the ruins of Troy that each time A. reads the story aloud to his son, he cannot help seeing . . . certain clusters of other images, spinning outward from the core of his preoccupations: Cassandra, for example, predicting the ruin of Troy, and thereafter loss, as in the wanderings of Aeneas that precede the founding of Rome, and in that wandering the image of another wandering: the Jews in the desert, which, in its turn, yields further clusters of images: "Next year in Jerusalem," and with it the photograph in the Jewish Encyclopedia of his relative, who bore the name of his son. (IS 133)

In this swirling series of associations, Greco-Roman "master" civilization is brought into conjunction with "wandering" Jewish culture and with A.'s own family. Here, the Jewish son carries tradition upon his back, redeeming "Hebraism" in the face "Hellenism." The story of Pinocchio is so seductive for A. because it promises redemption of the fathers—and, proleptically, of the son.

For A.'s son, who spends an entire summer dressed as Superman, this fantasy of omnipotence and salvation is as irresistible as it is for his father:

> And for the little boy to see Pinocchio, that same foolish puppet who has stumbled his way from one misfortune to the next, who has wanted to be "good" and could not help being "bad," for this same incompetent little marionette, who is not even a real boy, to become a figure of redemption, the very being who saves his father from the grip of death, is a sublime moment of revelation. The son saves the father. This must be fully imagined from the

perspective of the little boy. And this, in the mind of the father who was once a little boy, a son, that is, to his own father, must be fully imagined. *Puer aeternus.* The son saves the father. (IS 134)

Through the mythical figure of the "eternal boy," the son gives birth to the father—and thus to himself as "a real boy." This represents the son's wish-fulfillment of overcoming the father's trauma, as well as the postwar Jew's fantasy of saving the victims of the Holocaust. The "incompetent little marionette," a mere simulacrum of a boy, can redeem the world of the fathers. At the same time, however, A. as father remains only too aware of his own son's vulnerability. In a meditation upon children who die before their fathers, A. muses upon an imaginary stack of photographs: "Mallarmé's son, Anatole; Anne Frank ('This is a photo that shows me as I should always like to look. Then I would surely have a chance to go to Hollywood. But now, unfortunately, I usually look different'). . . . The dead children. The children who will vanish, the children who are dead. Himmler: 'I have made the decision to annihilate every Jewish child from the face of the earth'" (IS 97–98). These are the children whose fathers were unable to rescue them. Their fate is sealed by Himmler's chilling antiredemptive vow: for if there are no children, there is no one to rescue and no one to do the rescuing.

"TO SAVOR THE CHAOS OF IT IN ALL ITS RAW AND URGENT SIMULTANEITY"

It is time to return for a final look at this essay's central question:
Q: What goes on inside the room of the book?
A: A Book of Memory is being written.

By shouldering this task, Auster follows a command reiterated throughout the Jewish Scriptures: *Remember!* The historian, Y. H. Yerushalmi, counts its iterations: "the verb *zakhar* [to remember] appears in its various declensions in the Bible no less than one hundred and sixty-nine times, usually with Israel or God as the subject, for memory is incumbent upon both."[22] Remembering is a primary function of Jewish culture, a form of commemoration that takes the place of priestly rituals (after the destruction of the Second Temple in 70 CE), sanctifying the present through linking it to the past. In the Passover *seder*, for instance, the celebrants are enjoined to insert themselves into biblical scenes of deliverance to remember that they are celebrating something done by God not for their ancestors but for themselves. As A. writes himself deeper and deeper into the room of the book, his relationship to memory undergoes a shift: when made active, memory need not be a means of hiding from the present by slipping into the past; instead, it can allow the past, with all its pain, to make the present more fully alive. "As he writes, he feels that he is moving inward (through himself) and at the same time moving outward (towards the world)" (IS 139).

Revealing that writing effects movement both inward and outward, A. posits a way for memory to lead him at least partway outside his confinement in the room of the book. To the extent that the memory of trauma can function as restorative—as, in Kabbalistic terms, *tikkun* (mending the broken vessels of creation)—writing that occurs in the room of the book might reimagine not only individual experience but also history. Taking this perspective, A. begins to realize that his initial entry into the room of the book ("He lays out a piece of blank paper on the table before him and writes these words with his pen. It was. It will never be again." [IS 75]) contained far greater potential than he knew:

> What he experienced, perhaps, during those few moments on Christmas Eve, 1979, as he sat alone in his room on Varick Street, was this: the sudden knowledge that came over him that even alone, in the deepest solitude of his room, he was not alone, or, more precisely, that the moment he began to try to speak of that solitude, he had become more than just himself. Memory, therefore, not simply as the resurrection of one's private past, but an immersion in the past of others, which is to say: history—which one both participates in and is a witness to, is a part of and apart from. . . . If there is any reason for him to be in this room now, it is because there is something inside him hungering to see it all at once, to savor the chaos of it in all its raw and urgent simultaneity. (IS 139)

A. believes that memory will never "make sense" of the past, but it is necessary for keeping the past alive in the present. When he inhabits the room of the book in this way, he writes as though his very life depends on it, for the broken world of the fathers constitutes a weight this latter-day Pinocchio must carry to become "a real boy." And when he writes this way, he can "savor the chaos" of the past interwoven with the present "in all its raw and urgent simultaneity."

As a post-Holocaust narrative, *The Invention of Solitude* takes the memory of disaster as groundless ground from which writing and life begin. The past cannot be possessed or made whole, but grief and memory can become generative forces. Thinking about Jabès's poetry as a response to the Shoah, Auster speaks of the writer's duties with respect to such memories: "What he must do, in effect, is create a poetics of absence. The dead cannot be brought back to life. But they can be heard, and their voices live in the Book" (AH 114). When the survivors emerged from hiding and from the death camps after World War

II, their nearly unanimous vow was expressed in two words: "Never again!" This meant: We must remember so that the moral revulsion created by these memories will prevent such deeds ever recurring. The last sentences of "The Book of Memory" seem to allude to this resolution: "It was. It will never be again. Remember" (IS 172). These words bring "The Book of Memory" full circle, repeating its inaugural phrases and adding to them the biblical command, "Remember." Can this injunction to remember trauma create the conditions for understanding history? In his famous image of the Angel in the "Theses on the Philosophy of History," Walter Benjamin invents a figure for history who stands openmouthed at the traumatic wreckage of events piling up at his feet without cessation.[23] This gesture bears a striking resemblance to the "crying without sound" that overcomes A. in Anne Frank's room, a reaction arising not only "in response to deep inner pain" but also "purely in response to the world. It was at that moment, he later realized, that the Book of Memory began" (IS 82–83).

As a writer, Auster makes use of the room of the book to interrogate the relationship of writing to history through an invocation of memory. With respect to "The Book of Memory," the question that remains is whether calling on memory affords a way to witness the world such that it releases him from confinement in the room of the book. On balance, I think the answer is negative, particularly in light of his refusal to remember divorce and to acknowledge anger toward women. But I applaud the seriousness of Auster's attempt to place issues of writing at the center of issues of living. Confronting head-on "a man sitting alone in a room and writing a book" (NYT 202), Auster makes of that situation an inexhaustibly fertile field for meditation, in which pressing intellectual, historical, and personal issues arise and ask to be heard. Auster's room of the book witnesses a mesmerizing struggle between the transactive tendencies of poetry and the narrative investment in fictional characters. It functions for the male writer both as a site of retreat from women and as an alchemical retort in which a parthenogenic theory of creativity bubbles up. And it becomes a space of hiding and torment, in which the irresolvable dilemmas of writing with respect to the Holocaust can be embodied. Within the room of the book, Auster compellingly stages persistent riddles of the writer, riddles that refuse to go away. To Blue's question, "How to get out of the room that is the book that will go on being written for as long as he stays in the room?" (NYT 202), the only decisive response would be to walk out. But for the writer, always susceptible to accusations of not living up to the moral claims of writing, to walk out of the room of the book would be impossible: it would mean to stop writing.[24]

12

Lyn Hejinian Becomes a Person on Paper

Since the 1980s, the work of Lyn Hejinian and other poets associated with Language poetry has grown and changed in many ways. In particular, the apotheosis of language in the early writing has been overtaken, in a kind of figure-ground shift, by concerns with perception, memory, and identity—issues that once seemed merely illustrative material for investigations of language. Hejinian's *My Life* (1980, 1987) has the unique status of keeping that figure-ground shift in process throughout its text, and thus the book has never gone out of date.[1] Standing squarely in the tradition of what I have called "poet's prose," especially that of John Ashbery's *Three Poems*, *My Life* has in turn inspired many subsequent prose experiments.[2] Hejinian's poetry shares several salient features with that of both Ashbery and David Antin: a phenomenological impulse to "put it all in" (in Ashbery's words)[3]; an engaging sense of playfulness, of trying things out; a pragmatist attempt to grasp in language the emergence of cognition and the undergoing of experience; and a reliance on Gertrude Stein as pragmatist mentor.

Even a cursory glance at her volume of essays, *The Language of Inquiry* (2000), reveals that Hejinian has designs to write a philosophical poetics. Her most-cited philosophical precursor is William James, and she seems comfortable in both the pragmatist and the phenomenological traditions. One of the philosophical concerns that drives her poetics is the question of identity, which informs not only her discursive prose but also her poetry (in verse and in prose). To discuss economically Hejinian's treatment of this question, I would like to consider her ambitious philosophy of "the person" as it appears both in some of her essays and in her autobiography in poetry, *My Life*. Across the forms of verse, prose poetry, and essay, Hejinian's writing maintains a remarkable continuity, both cognitive and stylistic. In all three forms she pursues a single, multifaceted lifework, in which the relationship between language and personhood is a major part of the inquiry.

In *My Life*, the interplay between person and language obtrudes immediately in the book's title, through the use of the possessive personal pronoun. At first glance, there is something embarrassingly "personal" about such a title, as though we were being given access to an intimate self-portrait that begs for the reader's indulgence. Paradoxically, however, many famous people have published autobiographies with just this title. My university library houses books called *My Life* by major figures in a variety of fields: Magic Johnson, Edith Piaf, Richard Wagner, George Sand, Golda Meir, Oskar Kokoschka, Marc Chagall, Havelock Ellis, Leon Trotsky, and Isadora Duncan. Given their status as public figures, these writers and their audiences feel no discomfort with a title that implicitly pairs "my (public) works" with "my life." Hejinian, though, is not a famous personage nor someone who maintains a discrete boundary between her life and works. Thwarting expectations provoked by its title, *My Life* gives a poetic text that is neither intimate like a diary nor an attempt to set the record straight by a public figure. The most direct way to read the title of *My Life* might be as warrant that the text contains those statements about personhood for which the author wishes to take responsibility.

At the beginning of another American philosophical autobiography, *Walden*, Thoreau makes an observation about the difference between personal and impersonal texts, implying that only the former take responsibility for what's being said: "In most books, the *I*, or first person, is omitted; in this it will be retained. . . . We commonly do not remember that it is, after all, always the first person that is speaking. I should not talk so much about myself if there were any body else whom I knew as well. Unfortunately, I am confined to this theme by the narrowness of my experience."[4] Like Hejinian, Thoreau speaks in the first person about things that concern everyone, and, like Hejinian too (as we shall see), he claims an epistemological necessity. He realizes that by using the first person he surrenders the impersonal authority that is normally invested in prose—an authority inherent in the respectable prose of such disciplines of fact as science, history, and law. But he also believes that his radical investigation must forsake depersonalized forms of writing to respond to the active challenge that language presents to a circumscribed self. In other words, wrestling with language becomes an essential endeavor for constructing an identity based upon experience.

Although concerned with identity, Thoreau and Hejinian in no way mean to imply that this first-person experience is in some way "special" or "unique." In this sense, Hejinian ironizes her own title by commenting in an essay: "Repeatedly I come upon the thought that everyone thinks, or wishes to think, of himself as unique. Often, one thinks that what one feels, what one experiences, is somehow **more** than what others feel or experience: **my** love, **my** suffering, **my** insight."[5] To investigate the connection between language and identity, Hejinian, like Thoreau, must take all of her statements personally, must measure herself against whatever she wishes to propose about human life and thought, without presuming to be an exceptional case. Both Marjorie Perloff and Craig Dworkin have noted how, in contrast to fetishizing uniqueness, Hejinian conjures up in *My Life* something closer to what Gertrude Stein calls *Everybody's Autobiography*.[6] She creates a work in which individual life is interwoven with language, perception, and social constructs, so that it is impossible to say where "Lyn Hejinian" leaves off and the world begins. Perloff finds the concept of identity in the book "less a property of a given character than a fluid state . . . that hence engages the reader to participate in its formation and deformation."[7] Speaking about identity in an essay, "The Person and Description," Hejinian describes herself as "always thinking about the unstable existence and recurrent or persistent experiences of a person, drawn into the world in and by perception, implicated by language, moving around in life, and unwilling to give up attempts at description."[8] Although this statement reflects her thinking about a poem called "The Person," it also speaks accurately for *My Life*, in which the relationship among perception, language, recurrent experience, and personhood is skillfully dramatized by a "descriptive" prose based grammatically in the first person.[9]

In other words, for Hejinian the first person is first a person, and her interest in autobiography lies in investigating personhood rather than in validating her experience or in claiming an exalted or representative status. In "The Person and Description," she enunciates what might be called a linguistic philosophy of the person, a philosophy that underlies much of her work. The essay begins with a statement and a question: "A person, alone or in groups of persons, has accompanied art throughout its history; it is assumed that a work of art is, at the very least a manifestation of his or her presence. But whose?" (LI 200). In attempting to answer that biographical or phenomenological question, Hejinian looks first to the "concept of some core reality at the heart of our sense of being," which she terms "the self" and which she defines as "an undemonstrable, but sensible entity on which each of us is somehow dependent, living off its truths, its heat, its energy" (LI 201). Uncomfortable with notions such as uniqueness or specialness, Hejinian casts into doubt the relation of such an essential self to the concept of the person, asking rhetorically, "But is it, the self, a person? And is art—including literary art—the work of a self?" (LI 201). Against the notion of the self as "the essence of each single human being, the sole and constant point from which the human being can truthfully and originally speak" (LI 202), Hejinian argues that the only experience one has is of being in a particular position in time and space and that "this sense of contingency is intrinsic to my experience of the self as a relationship rather than an essence" (LI 202). This contingent, relational sense of self is what she calls a "person": "The person . . . is a mobile (and mobilized) reference point; or, to put it another way, subjectivity is not an entity but a dynamic" (LI 203). For Hejinian, "person" is a linguistic and dramatic term that takes the place of an essential self. As such, the person is always constituted by experience in time and space: "There is no self undefiled by experience, no self unmediated in the perceptual situation; instead there is a world and the person is in it" (LI 203).

This active, contingent "person" must be recognized as a linguistic process because it consists of and is known by its descriptions of its own experiences. Hejinian first formulates this idea as, "The person is the described describer of what it knows by virtue of experience," but then she modifies her formulation to emphasize the unfinished character of the person as "the incompletely described incomplete describer."[10] Sounding like Ashbery, Stein, or Beckett, Hejinian declares that the duty of art is to replace the search for an essential and solipsistic self with a description of "the experience of experience" (LI 203). Ashbery elaborates on this goal by pairing the style of Stein's *Stanzas in Meditation* with that of Henry James's *The Golden Bowl*. The complexity and seeming unreadability of these works is a result of their imitating the "rhythm" of life, "its way of happening":

> Just as life is being constantly altered by each breath one draws, just as each second of life seems to alter the whole of what has gone before, so the endless process of elaboration which gives the work of these two writers a texture of bewildering luxuriance—that of a tropical rain-forest of ideas—seems to obey some rhythmic impulse at the heart of all happening.[11]

The insistent rhythm of repetition and variation, meant to invoke an awareness of awareness, has for these writers an epistemological force. As Hejinian puts it, borrowing the phrase "experience of experience," "I believe that the goal of the poem . . . is to provoke and sustain in both writer and readers an experience of experience; I believe too that this may suffice for knowledge."[12] The knowledge produced by the poem would not be primarily empirical or cultural but rather a pragmatist awareness of the situatedness of language, things, and persons: "Knowledge, like speaking or writing, is not an entity but a function—it would best be called 'knowing'—and the purpose of that function is to contextualize" (LI 223).

Knowledge performs its contextualizing function in writing by turning subjects into objects and objects into subjects. To accomplish this contextual metamorphosis, Hejinian employs a mode of inquiry that not only gauges the world but is simultaneously self-measuring, a mode such as that practiced by Thoreau or Robert Creeley. She calls it "constructivist introspection" ("Person" 170), a mode that "newly delineates and constantly shifts the boundary between subject and object" (LI 207). Again, what this shifty mode makes possible is the description of a person: "It establishes the relationship between self and other, between body and mind, and then transgresses the borders it has established . . . to describe the person." During this constant contextualizing, in which the boundaries of subject and object, self and other, are repeatedly transgressed, we cannot imagine that the person has any claim upon unity. Hejinian puts it succinctly: "The 'personal' is already a plural condition." As the pivot of a constructivist phenomenology, "the idea of the person enters poetics where art and reality, or intentionality and circumstance, meet. It is on the improvised boundary between art and reality, between construction and experience, that the person (or my person) in writing exists" (LI 207).

As demonstration of how "the person (or my person) in writing exists," *My Life* is particularly compelling. Using this book as exemplary poses problems, however, that should be acknowledged before proceeding. Analyzing a literary text usually involves breaking it down into units and then choosing a specific unit for extended commentary. In *My Life*, there are only two units smaller than the entire text: the two- or three-page "chapter"—which consists (in the 1987 version) of forty-five sentences and corresponds to a single year—and the individual sentence. Taking either unit as the basis for commentary is difficult because the one is too large and the other too small. A thorough analysis of an entire chapter of *My Life* would provide material for a much more extended essay, and commentary on a single sentence—although it can be pertinent to understanding the text and is a method often employed by critics—is not fully adequate precisely because of the contextual principle of knowledge that Hejinian values so highly. Single sentences are not just statements or propositions or commands or interjections; they also gain and change meaning by placement among nearby sentences, by relationship to other sentences within a chapter, and by repetition and permutation throughout the book. In other words, Hejinian has written a text that resists being broken into units for analysis because of the strong potential for metamorphosis that exists in any particular passage. She notes how the device of repetition works against the notion of discrete textual units and thus how it keeps meaning in flux:

> [I]n my book *My Life*, . . . certain phrases recur in the text, each time in a new context and with new emphasis. Sometimes the repetitions are literal, sometimes the phrases are emended in some way, but always they comment on and receive comment from the surrounding text. Since context is never the same and never stops, this device says that meaning is always in flux, always in the process of being created.[13]

As one reads and rereads *My Life*, the relationship of figure to ground remains in flux, causing sentences to emerge and recede with respect to other sentences around them. This perceptual flux mimes an epistemological flux, in which words and phrases act as both "subjects" and "objects," as both referential and material signifiers. Moreover, the requirement that the number of sentences in each chapter correspond to the years Hejinian has been alive means that when she published a new version of the book in 1987 she inserted seven extra sentences into each chapter from the 1980 version. Rather than add these sentences to the end of a chapter, she places them carefully within it, thus creating new contexts again.

Holding in mind this characteristic tendency for sentences to metamorphose in meaning, I want to look at a particular sentence (one that occurs only once in the book) that illustrates the ways in which language transforms subjects into objects and vice versa. This sentence, from the chapter corresponding to age five and the year 1946, runs: "I was sipping Shirley Temples wearing my Mary Janes" (19).[14] This sentence captures beautifully a little girl's glee at having an adult-looking drink while wearing the "right" shoes. It draws attention to the performative quality of a girl's identity and to the pleasure inherent in such performance. And for context, the two sentences that precede this one concern, not surprisingly, the subject of birthday parties and the observation, "But nothing could interrupt those given days." If we step aside, though, from the girl's world, where the terms "Shirley Temple" and "Mary Janes" refer, respectively, to a child's "cocktail" made of grenadine and Seven-Up (with the likely addition of a maraschino cherry impaled on a plastic sword) and to a simple but elegant girl's shoe style, we can see that these terms have their own fascination as linguistic objects. In this sentence, proper names become nouns, so that the name of a particular person, Shirley Temple, and the brand name constructed from a socially marked girl's name, Mary Janes, become objects in the world. In this linguistic transformation, subjects become objects, but there is also a sense in which the opposite is true. In keeping with Hejinian's philosophy of the person, there is a personifying activity within this sentence, in which nouns—things—are shown to be actually proper names. It's as though she were developing a theory of language in which each noun were a proper name and an epistemology in which each thing were a person. Another sentence in this chapter reinforces this personifying tendency: "The shape of who's to come" (19). Altering the cliché, "the shape of *things* to come," Hejinian equates things with persons, with "who's," as in the title of Dr. Seuss's *Horton Hears a Who!*.[15]

Several other sentences within this chapter look at the "personal" relationship between proper names and things. At one point Hejinian recalls, "While my mother shopped, I stood in *Produce* and ate raw peas" (19–20). "*Produce*" is an italicized name that stands for a place, the produce department, and yet saying it this way almost implies that the girl stood within a name, *Produce,* which gave her access to what it signifies—for example, "raw peas." In two other sentences, the relationship between names and persons is more directly interrogated: "My sister was named 'after' my aunt, the name not Murree but, like marriage, French, Marie. The first grade teacher, Miss Sly, was young and she might have been kind, but all the years that she had been named Sly so had made her" (20). Where does the name leave off and the "person" begin? What is the relationship of two persons with the same name? What is the difference between a name written and a name spoken? These are questions implicit in a child's fascination with language, but they are made explicit by Hejinian's investigation of the interdependence of names and persons.

For the remainder of this essay, I would like to move around within the text of *My Life*, stopping at a few locations where the relationship between person and text is considered. In the chapter for age six, one of the primary phrases of *My Life*, "a pause, a rose, something on paper," occurs in the context of two sentences related to the textual nature of the person: "I found myself dependent on a pause, a rose, something on paper. It is a way of saying, I want you, too, to have this experience, so that we are more alike, so that we are closer, bound together, sharing a point of view—so that we are 'coming from the same place'" (21–22). In this case, we hear an emphasis on paper and writing in the highly ambiguous "a pause, a rose, something on paper." Writing is described as an attempt to share experiences and points of view, and thus to create an identity, as though this first-person entity, "we," could be made of persons "coming from the same place." In the next chapter, Hejinian continues the emphasis on constructing an identity: "I was eventually to become one person, gathered up maybe, during a pause, at a comma" (25). Here, too, the advent of identity is textual, occurring at a comma, and echoing the earlier phrase by invoking the word "pause," upon which Hejinian had "found myself dependent." In the chapter for age ten and the year 1951, this process of constructing an identity, of becoming one person, is called into question: "Where I refer to 'a preliminary' I mean that until 1964 I regarded the world as a medium of recognition and I prepared for it to recognize me. A person does not look the same in a mirror as she does" (34). Expecting to find an identity by assembling the personal qualities the world reflects back, one is more likely to become disoriented than confirmed, for one's experience of a situation or one's description of it will never be echoed exactly by someone else's characterization of one's performance. Thus, the earlier statement, "I was eventually to become one person," begins to look suspect.

The textual quality of identity returns as an issue in the chapter for age seventeen, where Hejinian tries to understand her connection to lives that are led in books: "The lives of which I read seemed more real than my own, but I still seemed more real than the persons who had led them" (51). In Hejinian's pragmatist philosophy, what is most real is one's own experience, but to become aware of experience—to have "the experience of experience"—takes a degree of attention and skill that accomplished writers possess in greater abundance than seventeen-year-old girls. By age twenty-nine and 1970, Hejinian has come to identify her life much more closely with the text. Where Whitman proclaims the unity of the text and the person as fully accomplished, saying of *Leaves of Grass*, "Who touches this touches a man,"[16] Hejinian says much more conditionally about the process of writing, "And if I feel like a book, a person on paper, I will continue" (76). In this sentence, "something on paper," which earlier referred to writing, has metamorphosed into "a person on paper," and Hejinian makes her recognition of being such a person the condition for continuing to write. The uncertainty of being able to "feel like a book," and thus continue writing, comes up again two sentences later: "A fatigue in the cold, fear of finishing." But the intervening sentence, "What is the gender on paper," hints that, in 1970, gender considerations have disrupted Hejinian's sense of her relationship to the text. In another sentence in the same chapter, she declares, "Pronouns skirt the subject" (77). This sentence brilliantly encapsulates the uneasy interchange between gender and text: if pronouns "skirt the subject," in the sense of avoiding an implicit subject matter, then a gendered pronoun, such as "she," accomplishes this avoidance inadvertently when "she" becomes the subject of the sentence, thus putting a skirt on it. It's worth noting, too, that the verb "to skirt" also means to create a border or an edge or a margin, as in plowing a field or trimming upholstery, and so this gendering of the subject differentiates persons by creating margins and borders as well.

By age forty-one, 1982, Hejinian has become so identified with being a writer, so confident in her ability to construct a person in writing, that she no longer feels confined to a "skirted" subject. This expansion of the gendered person in writing becomes clear in a series of three sentences: "A sentence is a metaphor since when. I see it continually before me, it impatiently asks for my work. As such, a person on paper, I am androgynous" (105). The androgynous person on paper sums up her philosophy of identity at age forty-three in the following sentence: "As persons think so are they thoughts being things" (111). This interanimation of persons, thoughts, being, and things is not just an epistemological or ontological demonstration of what Hejinian knows; it is also part of a characterization of a person who, in her forties, has identified fully with writing. In her discussion of knowledge as a function, she remarks that it consists not only in "knowing *of* (which is experience *in potentia*) and knowing *that* (which generates propositions) but also knowing *how*" (LI 223). *My Life* is the autobiography of a person as writer who really knows *how*. As the issue of identity achieves resolution by the person becoming a writer, the text of the autobiography becomes not "the writing of a life" but rather the presentation of a "life as writing," for in Hejinian's philosophy of the person, an identity is arrived at by following the strict demands of writing. In *My Life*, writing takes place as a series of transactions within and between discontinuous sentences. Thus, Hejinian explores the essential building block of prose—the sentence—in order to release its full poetic potential, finding, "A sentence is a metaphor since when."

Epilogue

Teaching American Poetry

I first learned that poetry can be transactional through conversation with poets, both elders and peers. This insight has informed my work as a teacher, in the classroom and in bringing students to poetry readings and discussions with poets. Over the years, it has been both profound and amusing to watch students interact with poets in person. At Notre Dame, memorable moments occurred especially during the Sophomore Literary Festival, which used to take place each year in snowy February. Annually, Student Government would deposit a serious, though still limited, sum of money into the hands of sophomores, who planned and executed every facet of the week-long event. Their enthusiasm and naivete, charming and irresistible to writers, also had a humorous side. When they met with English Department faculty for coaching, for instance, they might learn their top choices were either exorbitantly expensive or no longer living. I can't tell you how many students were dying to extend an invitation to William Faulkner (d. 1962). But they did persuade many illustrious writers to come, and to stay often for the entire week, conversing in marathon sessions with students, faculty, and other writers. As the date of the festival neared, the organizers would turn with increasing desperation to their teachers for help in making contacts. In this way, poets whom I knew, but who may have been unfamiliar to students, were invited to campus. It was gratifying to see how thoroughly the writers gave themselves to the occasion and how much that meant to students.

Already a favorite of the organizers, Robert Creeley made a visit in the early 1980s. As I saw on many occasions, this poet whose verse many think of as exceptionally private was, in fact, intensely curious about others and nearly always engaged in animated interchange. This made him the perfect guest for the Literary Festival. When I picked him up at the South Bend Airport and drove him back to the Morris Inn on campus—a modest accommodation with a bare crucifix on the wall of each room—I let him know someone else was reading that evening, so there was no need to rush over to the library auditorium.

"OK, let's go."

After the reading and a reception, I ventured, "There's a party at a student house off-campus. But please, don't feel obligated."

"Onward!" he said.

As the evening wore on in the dingy student digs and the company was singing to a guitar, I found myself playing the spoons to keep the beat. Finally, I turned to Creeley and pleaded, "Bob, it's 2:00 a.m. and I have to teach in the morning! Would you like a ride back to the Morris Inn?"

"Oh no. One of the students will drop me off."

Hearing writers read and then speaking with them at parties, meals, and receptions was an undreamt of delight for students. Many recalled these encounters as determinative events in their collegiate careers. As recently as early 2017, when Claudia Rankine read from *Citizen* to a packed auditorium, students in my "Introduction to American Poetry" were struck by how she intercut the reading with slides of visual art. From her enthusiastic way of speaking about the images and the artists, they saw not only how alive the works are for her but also how she engages in transactional poetry all the time—not just when composing a poem.

Notwithstanding the excitement of bringing writers to campus, I have still found teaching American poetry a daunting assignment. There are few ready handholds to grasp when reading such demanding work, especially poetry that seems to invent the terms for its own reception. The only real option for encountering it is total immersion. When I was a freshman at Pomona College and Robert Duncan was there for a week as poet-in-residence, he made it clear that to seriously read a poet you have to learn to think like (maybe even to speak like or to breathe like) the poet. This involves finding out everything you can: reading all the poetry and essays, listening to or viewing readings (in person or on recordings), finding interviews, and then ranging out to texts and other art forms that compose the larger tradition the poet assembles. This method of reading began for me with Duncan himself, from whom I purchased a copy of *The Opening of the Field* that week. He inscribed it to me with a little sketch and it seemed such an intimate object, but making that stubbornly recalcitrant book "mine" in any real sense was a fierce challenge demanding years of effort.

This lengthy immersion in poetry does not easily take place in a university setting—especially at a school that requires five substantive courses per semester. As a teacher I have learned to see my main job as presenting artworks and ways of thinking that students would likely not encounter on their own, in order to provoke new perspectives—both in the present and for the future. Such works and modes of thought can appear difficult, weird, or even aggressive, but by confounding easy understanding they invite inventive thinking in turn. Which the best students thrive on. Because, really, what we already understand is boring. Artists challenge themselves and their audiences to enter situations not easy to resolve, daring us to generate new meanings. Not-understanding, I point out, is the posture of readiness in which new connections, insights, visions may come—a state familiar both to artists and to those who open themselves to a work of art. In other words, reading difficult poetry promotes creative experiences, which can in turn generate lasting enthusiasm.

However, students are not without resistances. In a course at Memorial Hospital in South Bend for doctors who wanted to write poetry, I assigned a portion from the *Selected Poems* of William Carlos Williams. America's greatest physician-poet would provide, I assumed, a perfect model for fruitful interchange between poetry and medicine. Meeting for a first discussion of Williams, we jumped into reading a poem and quickly reached an impasse at a line whose sense was not easy to parse.

The doctors were reluctant to offer thoughts, so, to get things started, I asked what they did when they came to this line in their own reading.

An emergency-room physician volunteered, "I turned the page."

"Why did you do that?"

"I'm a doctor: I'm supposed to understand things!"

Recognizing this impatience with not-understanding, I have worked with students to demonstrate how it can be a creative instigation rather than a source of self-accusation. As a way to forestall a self-imposed closure of horizons, and to provide entry to a variety of arts, I developed a course at Notre Dame called "American Culture as Collage" (a syllabus is provided below). Designed for English majors, it emphasizes the collage nature of representative works in many mediums: poetry, the essay, fiction, folk song, jazz, rock and roll, visual art, assemblage, and performance art. During this course, many opportunities arise to make visible the transactions between poetry and the other arts. By setting poetry within the contexts both of historical circumstances and of other artistic mediums, I can present it not as a self-enclosed form of writing but as an unendingly renewed invitation for engagement and conversation. The sense of what poetry can do expands from its commonly assigned modes of self-expression, commentary, or critique into its larger roles as direct participant and significant interlocutor in the making of American culture.

The course begins with a slide show of visual collage by artists such as Picasso and Schwitters and a discussion of why collage form is an apt artistic response to the lack of a grounding tradition in the United States. Simultaneously, I offer as a possible accompaniment to the course *A New Literary History of America*, a collage history of American culture (edited by Greil Marcus and Werner Sollors), which consists of two hundred articles of five pages, each focused around a date and events set into motion in American history at that time by cultural transactions. The first half of the course is anchored by Emerson's essays—especially "Circles," which provides a generative image and an intellectual rationale for a collage approach to American culture. In addition, we read "The Poet" for its founding of a poetry in the actual materials of American life and "Self-Reliance" for its posing of the shifting social and political dilemmas of the individual with respect to the collective. Walt Whitman picks up these dilemmas and the focus on diverse American materials in the first (1855) edition of *Leaves of Grass*, with its invention of free verse, its poetic catalogs, and its radical juxtaposition of images. We move into the twentieth century with Gertrude Stein's prose poetry in *Tender Buttons*, her verbal portraits of Matisse and Picasso, and her setting of African American vernacular in "Melanctha." Stein's notion of "composition," in which individual words bear equal weights (as do individual sentences), places her in active dialogue with cubist collage artists, such as Picasso and Gris. From this perspective, Pound's transactive participation as editor in the composition of Eliot's *Waste Land* highlights its collage technique—characterized by beginning over and over—rather than its pretensions to the status of a finished masterpiece. Pound's own selected poems and translations reveal a writer who, through the techniques of "luminous detail" and Imagist juxtaposition, assembles a collage poetry of transactions throughout his career—most insistently in *The Cantos*. At the end of the first half of the course, students write their own verbal collages, in verse or prose, along with a two-page commentary. We devote a class session to reading them aloud and discussing them, making apparent how the collage methods have seeped into our understanding of our own lives and times.

The second half of the course flows from Harry Smith's groundbreaking *Anthology of American Folk Music* (1952), which introduced blues, traditional country music, and other "folk" genres to a postwar audience. Smith is a transactional thinker whom many students initially find off-putting, both for his abrasive personality and for the seemingly bizarre songs juxtaposed in his carefully constructed assemblage. His rendition of American culture from the bottom up has an unmistakable aura of authenticity, and it becomes a lynchpin for building a tradition of vernacular imagery and collage forms in the arts of the second half of the twentieth century. For instance, Charles Reznikoff's *Testimony*, a collage history of the United States from 1885 to 1915 (composed from court testimony taken from legal books and rendered into verse), presents, like Smith's anthology, the depredations of American society as experienced by its least prestigious but in some ways its most expressive speakers. Langston Hughes's *Montage of a Dream Deferred* brings the simmering racial grievances of postwar Harlem into focus through a collage of poems and music. One of the main voices he foregrounds is that of bebop jazz, and we listen to major examples to hear the ways Hughes folds jazz into his verbal equivalent of cinematic montage. We move back to visual culture with class sessions devoted to the mid-century West Coast assemblage artists and poets included in the loose-leaf journal *Semina*, edited by artist Wallace Berman, and to the catalog for *The Art of Assemblage* exhibition at the Museum of Modern Art (1961). The second session takes place in Notre Dame's Snite Museum of Art, where we view some of the extensive holdings of collage and assemblage art. Later, we return to the Snite to view and discuss visual collages by the students in the context of museum works we have seen previously. The final three figures in the course unite poetry and music through a variety of collage techniques: Allen Ginsberg's "Howl" and other early poems; Bob Dylan's video of "Subterranean Homesick Blues," in which Ginsberg also appears, and his controversial 1966 performances in the United Kingdom; and Laurie Anderson's songs and videos that attempt to measure the imperial demise of the United States at the present moment.

From what I can gather from verbal comments and written feedback, it appears the course has some success in accomplishing its main task: showing American poetry as residing at the center of the arts, and thus at the heart of American culture, by demonstrating its many generative transactions.

ENGLISH 40761: AMERICAN CULTURE AS COLLAGE

Stephen Fredman • Spring 2017 • TuTh 12:30–1:45 • Office Hours: MW 1:30–3:00

Texts to Own

T. S. Eliot, *The Waste Land*, Norton Critical Edition

Ralph Waldo Emerson, *The Selected Writings*, Signet

Allen Ginsberg, *Howl and Other Poems*, City Lights

Ezra Pound, *New Selected Poems and Translations*, New Directions

Gertrude Stein, *Three Lives and Tender Buttons*, Signet

Walt Whitman, *Leaves of Grass (1855 Edition)*, Penguin

Marcus & Sollors, eds., *A New Literary History of America*, Harvard University Press (Recommended)

Other audio and texts on PennSound and in Library Reserve; videos on UbuWeb and YouTube

Requirements

1. Active participation in discussion, giving evidence of thorough preparation for each session. Participation includes each student taking class notes twice. Other students are urged not to take notes but to speak and listen. The notes are due to me by the next morning for distribution.

2. Class participation will be graded (20%).

3. A research paper of 8–10 pages (30%). Topic and annotated bibliography due February 28, essay due April 13.

4. Two creative assignments: a written collage (verse or prose) with two-page commentary, due March 21; a visual collage with two-page commentary, due April 25 (20%).

5. A take-home final exam, due at beginning of scheduled exam time for course (30%).

Objectives

One of the remarkable aspects of American culture is that we make it up as we go along, with no historical or traditional or divine road map we all agree to follow. Without a map, American artists and thinkers have often resorted to collage for representing American culture, creating new forms to contain our marvelous odds and ends. We will trace this urge to capture American culture through the medium of collage in R. W. Emerson's essays, Walt Whitman's *Leaves of Grass,* T. S. Eliot's *The Waste Land,* Gertrude Stein's *Tender Buttons* and "Melanctha," Ezra Pound's poetry and translations, Harry Smith's *Anthology of American Folk Music,* Charles Reznikoff's *Testimony,* Langston Hughes's *Montage of a Dream Deferred,* Bebop Jazz, Assemblage Art of the 1950s and 1960s, Allen Ginsberg's *Howl,* Bob Dylan's songs, and Laurie Anderson's performance art of the 1980s. Students will learn to think in large terms about American culture, to read demanding literary works, and to relate works of art in different mediums to one another.

Course Schedule

Jan. 17	Introduction (Collage & Tradition)
Jan. 19	R. W. Emerson, "The Poet"
Jan. 24	R. W. Emerson, "Self-Reliance"
Jan. 26	R. W. Emerson, "Circles," "Experience"; Jan. 26, 7:30 PM: See Claudia Rankine & Solmaz Sharif, McKenna Auditorium
Jan. 31	Walt Whitman, *Leaves of Grass,* Editor's Introduction, "Song of Myself"; discuss poetry reading
Feb. 2	Walt Whitman, *Leaves of Grass,* "Song of Myself"
Feb. 7	Walt Whitman, *Leaves of Grass,* "Song of Myself"

Feb. 9	Walt Whitman, *Leaves of Grass*, "A Song for Occupations," "The Sleepers"
Feb. 14	Walt Whitman, *Leaves of Grass*, "I Sing the Body Electric," "There Was a Child Went Forth," Whitman's Introduction
Feb. 16	Gertrude Stein, *Tender Buttons*, "Objects," 245–62; listen to "Matisse" and "If I Told Him"
Feb. 21	Gertrude Stein, "Melanctha," 71–205
Feb. 23	T. S. Eliot, *The Waste Land*, the poem, 1–26; look at "sources," 29–66
Feb. 28	T. S. Eliot, *The Waste Land*, Eliot's commentary, excerpts from essays, 112–21, 128–30; familiarize yourself with *The Waste Land: A Facsimile*; essay topic and annotated bibliography due
Mar. 2	Ezra Pound, *New Selected*, xi–xxi; "A Pact," "In a Station of the Metro," 39; *Cathay*, 55–68; poems, 81–85; *Hugh Selwyn Mauberly*, 109–23; view documentary, *Voices and Visions: Ezra Pound*
Mar. 7	Ezra Pound, *New Selected*, *The Cantos*, 125–64
Mar. 9	Ezra Pound, *New Selected*, *The Cantos*, 172–75, 184–85, 203–10, 224–30
Mar. 11–19	[Midsemester Break]
Mar. 21	Written Collage (verse or prose), with two-page commentary due
Mar. 23	Harry Smith, *Anthology of American Folk Music*, Selections from Programs 1, 2, 3; Greil Marcus, "The Old Weird America"
Mar. 28	Harry Smith, *Anthology of American Folk Music*, Selections from Programs 4, 5, 6; Stephen Fredman, "Forms of Visionary Collage"
Mar. 30	Charles Reznikoff, from *Testimony*
Apr. 4	Langston Hughes, *Montage of a Dream Deferred*
Apr. 6	Langston Hughes, *Montage of a Dream Deferred*; listen to Bebop jazz
Apr. 11	Assemblage: Duncan and McKenna, *Semina Culture*; Stephen Fredman, "Surrealism Meets Kabbalah"
Apr. 13	Assemblage: William Seitz, "The Collage Environment"; meet in Snite Museum of Art for Collage Tour; Research Paper due
Apr. 18	Allen Ginsberg, "Howl," "Footnote to Howl," "Sunflower Sutra," "America"; listen to poems
Apr. 20	Bob Dylan, video of "Subterranean Homesick Blues"; listen to *Live 1966*
Apr. 25	Visual Collage, with two-page commentary due; meet in Snite Museum to display and discuss student collages

Apr. 27	Laurie Anderson, listen to *Strange Angels*; watch *Home of the Brave*; read *Stories from the Nerve Bible*, 132–35, 150–51, 157–58, 174–81, 208–17, 222–25
May 2	Laurie Anderson, watch *Collected Videos*; read *Stories from the Nerve Bible*, 85–86, 155, 168–71, 203–4, 240–43, 252–56

Notes

Introduction

1. "The Structure of Rime, II," in Robert Duncan, *The Collected Later Poems and Plays*, ed. Peter Quartermain (Berkeley: University of California Press, 2014), 9.

2. James Maynard, *Robert Duncan and the Pragmatist Sublime* (Albuquerque: University of New Mexico Press, 2018), 32.

3. David Antin, *Radical Coherency: Selected Essays on Art and Literature, 1966 to 2005* (Chicago: University of Chicago Press, 2011), 149.

4. Stephen Fredman, *Poet's Prose: The Crisis in American Verse*, 2nd ed. (Cambridge: Cambridge University Press, 1990).

5. Walter Benjamin, "The Task of the Translator," in *Illuminations*, ed. Hannah Arendt, trans. Harry Zohn (New York: Schocken, 1969). George Steiner, *After Babel: Aspects of Language and Translation* (New York: Oxford University Press, 1975).

Chapter 1

1. Stephen Fredman, ed., *A Concise Companion to Twentieth-Century American Poetry* (Malden, MA: Blackwell, 2005).

2. Ezra Pound, *The Spirit of Romance* (New York: New Directions, 1968).

3. Maurice Tuchman, ed., *The Spiritual in Art: Abstract Painting, 1890–1985* (New York: Abbeville, 1986), 17–61.

4. Quoted in Demetres Tryphonopoulos, *The Celestial Tradition: A Study of Ezra Pound's "The Cantos"* (Waterloo, Ontario: Wilfred Laurier University Press, 1992), 25.

5. Leon Surette and Demetres Tryphonopoulos, eds., *Literary Modernism and the Occult Tradition* (Orono, ME: National Poetry Foundation, 1996), xvii.

6. Ezra Pound, *The Cantos of Ezra Pound* (New York: New Directions, 1970), 258.

7. John Ferguson, *Encyclopedia of Mysticism and Mystery Religions* (New York: Crossroad, 1982), 52–54.

8. Guy Davenport, "Persephone's Ezra," *The Geography of the Imagination* (San Francisco: North Point, 1981), 141–64.

9. Ezra Pound, *Personae: The Collected Shorter Poems of Ezra Pound* (New York: New Directions, 1926), 3.

10. Charles Olson, *The Collected Poems of Charles Olson: Excluding the Maximus Poems*, ed. George Butterick (Berkeley: University of California Press, 1997), 96–101.

11. Duncan, *The Collected Later Poems and Plays*, 56–63.

12. Ezra Pound, *Selected Prose, 1909–1965* (New York: New Directions, 1973), 53.

13. See Cleo McNally Kearns, *T. S. Eliot and Indic Traditions: A Study in Poetry and Belief* (Cambridge: Cambridge University Press, 1987).

14. T. S. Eliot, *The Complete Poems and Plays, 1909–1950* (New York: Harcourt, 1971), 50.

15. Timothy Materer, *Modernist Alchemy: Poetry and the Occult* (Ithaca, NY: Cornell University Press, 1995), xiv.

16. H.D. (Hilda Doolittle), *Collected Poems, 1912–1944*, ed. Louis Martz (New York: New Directions, 1983), 552.

17. Walt Whitman, *Leaves of Grass*, ed. Sculley Bradley and Harold Blodgett (New York: Norton, 1973), 252–53.

18. Robert Duncan, *The H.D. Book*, ed. Michael Boughn and Victor Coleman (Berkeley: University of California Press, 2011), 125–26.

19. Gershom Scholem, *Major Trends in Jewish Mysticism* (New York: Schocken, 1954).

20. Robert Duncan, *The Collected Early Poems and Plays*, ed. Peter Quartermain (Berkeley: University of California Press, 2012), 633–77.

21. David Meltzer, ed., *The Secret Garden: An Anthology in the Kabbalah* (1976; repr. Barrytown, NY: Station Hill, 1998), x.

22. Charles Olson, *Collected Prose*, ed. Donald Allen and Benjamin Friedlander (Berkeley: University of California Press, 1997), 262–63.

23. Charles Olson, *The Maximus Poems*, ed. George Butterick (Berkeley: University of California Press, 1983), 33.

24. Charles Olson, *The Special View of History*, ed. Ann Charters (Berkeley: Oyez, 1970), 20.

25. Kent Johnson and Craig Paulenich, eds., *Beneath a Single Moon: Buddhism in Contemporary American Poetry* (Boston: Shambhala, 1991), 8.

26. *The Wisdom Anthology of North American Buddhist Poetry*, edited by Andrew Schelling (Boston: Wisdom, 2005), includes a number of Asian American poets, alongside some Euro-American poets missing from the earlier Johnson-Paulenich anthology.

27. John Cage, *Silence* (Middletown, CT: Wesleyan University Press, 1961).

28. John Cage, *Indeterminacy: New Aspect of Form in Instrumental and Electronic Music* (New York: Folkways, 1959), 2 sound discs.

29. John Cage, *Diary: How to Improve the World (You Will Only Make Matters Worse)* (Los Angeles: Siglio, 2015).

30. Jack Kerouac, *Dharma Bums* (New York: Viking, 1958).

31. Gary Snyder, *No Nature: New and Selected Poems* (New York: Pantheon, 1992), 54.

32. Rick Fields, *How the Wild Swans Came to the Lake: A Narrative History of Buddhism in America*, rev. ed. (Boston: Shambhala, 1986), 210.

33. Allen Ginsberg, *Collected Poems, 1947–1980* (New York: Harper, 1984), 398.

34. This is the thesis of Kearns, *T. S. Eliot and Indic Traditions*.

35. Eloise Knapp Hay, *T. S. Eliot's Negative Way* (Cambridge, MA: Harvard University Press, 1982), 174–75.

36. See Fanny Howe, *The Wedding Dress: Meditations on Word and Life* (Berkeley: University of California Press, 2003).

37. Fanny Howe, *Selected Poems* (Berkeley: University of California Press, 2000), 138.

38. Albert Gelpi, ed., *Denise Levertov: Selected Criticism* (Ann Arbor: University of Michigan Press, 1993), 262.

39. Paul A. Lacey and Anne Dewey, eds., *The Collected Poems of Denise Levertov* (New York: New Directions, 2013), 172–73.

40. Robert Bertholf and Albert Gelpi, eds., *The Letters of Robert Duncan and Denise Levertov* (Stanford: Stanford University Press, 2004), 561.

Chapter 2

1. Jerome Rothenberg, ed., *Technicians of the Sacred: A Range of Poetries from Africa, America, Asia, Europe & Oceania*, 3rd ed. (Berkeley: University of California Press, 2017), xviii.

2. Robert Duncan, "Rites of Participation," in *The H.D. Book*, 153–99.

3. Jerome and Diane Rothenberg, eds., *Symposium of the Whole: A Range of Discourse Toward an Ethnopoetics* (Berkeley: University of California Press, 1983), xii.

4. "Featuring Robert Duncan," *Audit/Poetry* 4.3 (1967): 49.

5. For considerations of the notion of derivation in Duncan's poetry, see Michael André Bernstein, "Bringing It All Back Home: Derivations and Quotations in Robert Duncan and the Poundian Tradition," *Sagetrieb* 1, no. 2 (1982): 176–89; and Stephen Collis and Graham Lyons, eds., *Reading Duncan Reading* (Iowa City: University of Iowa Press, 2012).

6. Duncan, *The Collected Later Poems and Plays*, 298.

7. Barry Alpert, ed., *Vort* 3, no. 1: "David Antin—Jerome Rothenberg," (1975): 101.

8. Ekbert Faas titles the chapter of *Young Robert Duncan: Portrait of the Poet as Homosexual in Society* (Santa Barbara, CA: Black Sparrow, 1983) that treats this period "The Shaman Poet" (81–92); and James Maynard discusses "Toward the Shaman" in relation to surrealism in *Robert Duncan and the Pragmatist Sublime* (59–72). Drawing on the scholarship of Mircea Eliade, Peter O'Leary uses the figure of the shaman as a central interpretive device in his lengthy exploration of Duncan's poem "My Mother Would Be a Falconress" in *Gnostic Contagion: Robert Duncan and the Poetry of Illness* (Middletown: Wesleyan University Press, 2002), 130–32, 144–51, 160–67.

9. Mircea Eliade, *Shamanism: Archaic Techniques of Ecstasy*, trans. Willard Trask, Bollingen Series 76 (New York: Pantheon, 1964).

10. Harry Smith, ed., *Anthology of American Folk Music* (1952; reissue, Smithsonian Folkways 2951-3, 1997). Rothenberg acknowledges Smith as helpful, xxxviii.

11. Rothenberg invokes in this commentary the poetics of juxtaposition he shared early in his career with Robert Bly, Robert Kelly, and other "Deep Image" poets. Deep Image builds on Ezra Pound's ideogrammic method and the nonrational juxtaposition found in surrealism.

12. William Blake, letter to Butts, November 22, 1802, *The Letters of William Blake*, ed. Geoffrey Keynes (Cambridge, MA: Harvard University Press, 1968), 59–63.

13. Jerome Rothenberg, *Pre-Faces & Other Writings* (New York: New Directions, 1981), 31.

14. Jonathan N. Barron and Eric Murphy Selinger, eds., *Jewish American Poetry: Poems, Commentary, and Reflections* (Hanover, NH: Brandeis University Press, 2000), 144–45.

15. Robert Duncan, Notebook 41, August 1, 1969, Robert Duncan Archive, Poetry /

Rare Books Collection, University at Buffalo. Thanks to Robert Kaufman for email conversations about Duncan's reactions to Rothenberg and *Technicians* in his notebooks.

16. Robert Farris Thompson, *African Art in Motion* (1974; new ed., Berkeley: University of California Press, 1979). Thompson was mentor to David Byrne, leader of the band Talking Heads, one of the first popular musicians of the 1980s to incorporate African rhythms. Byrne produced an ethnographic film about Candomblé (Brazil's Afro-Catholic religion), *Ilé Aiyé: The House of Life* (1989), and directed the film *True Stories* (1986), one of whose strands follows a voodoo advisor, played by Roebuck (Pops) Staples, who cobbles together many of the African motifs explored by Thompson.

17. Wai Chee Dimock, *Through Other Continents: American Literature Across Deep Time* (Princeton, NJ: Princeton University Press, 2006), 3.

18. Yuval Noah Harari, *Sapiens: A Brief History of Humankind* (New York: Harper, 2015); Robert Bellah, *Religion in Human Evolution: From the Paleolithic to the Axial Age* (Cambridge, MA: Harvard University Press, 2011); David Lewis-Williams, *The Mind in the Cave: Consciousness and the Origins of Art* (New York: Thames & Hudson, 2002); Agustín Fuentes, *The Creative Spark: How Imagination Made Humans Exceptional* (New York: Dutton, 2017).

19. David Abram, *The Spell of the Sensuous: Perception and Language in a More-Than-Human World* (New York: Random House, 1996). David Abram, *Becoming Animal: An Earthly Cosmology* (New York, Random House, 2010).

Chapter 3

1. Jonathan Curley and Burt Kimmelman, eds., *The Poetry and Poetics of Michael Heller: A Nomad Memory* (Madison, NJ: Roman and Littlefield / Fairleigh Dickinson University Press, 2015), 9.

2. Michael Heller, *This Constellation Is a Name: Collected Poems, 1965–2010* (Callicoon, NY: Nightboat, 2012). For some earlier instances of critical attention to Heller's work, see the articles in *Talisman* 11 (Fall 1993): 48–112, and Norman Finkelstein, *Not One of Them in Place: Modern Poetry and Jewish American Identity* (Albany, NY: State University of New York Press, 2001), 142–55. Finkelstein's review of *This Constellation* (*Notre Dame Review* 35 [Winter/Spring 2013]: 186–95) provides an excellent introduction to Heller's work. See also the collection of essays by Curley and Kimmelman, for which my piece was written.

3. Michael Heller, *Eschaton* (Jersey City, NJ: Talisman House, 2009). Reprinted in *Constellation*, 385–466.

4. For an extensive treatment of this subject, see Stephen Fredman, *A Menorah for Athena: Charles Reznikoff and the Jewish Dilemmas of Objectivist Poetry* (Chicago: University of Chicago Press, 2001).

5. Michael Heller, *Conviction's Net of Branches: Essays on the Objectivist Poets and Poetry* (Carbondale: Southern Illinois University Press, 1985); Michael Heller, ed., *Carl Rakosi: Man and Poet* (Orono, ME: National Poetry Foundation, 1993).

6. Michael Heller, "Encountering Oppen: A Memoir," *Speaking the Estranged: Essays on the Work of George Oppen* (Cambridge, UK: Salt, 2008), 124–35. Heller supplements this memoir with a reflection on his correspondence with Oppen, "'Glad You've

Initiated This Correspondence . . . ,'" in *The Oppens Remembered: Poetry, Politics, and Friendship*, ed. Rachel Blau DuPlessis (Albuquerque: University of New Mexico Press, 2015), 44–53.

7. Stephen Paul Miller and Daniel Morris, eds., *Radical Poetics and Secular Jewish Culture* (Tuscaloosa: University of Alabama Press, 2010), 16.

8. Charles Bernstein, *Shadowtime* (Los Angeles: Green Integer, 2005). Heller, too, has written the libretto for an opera about Benjamin, *Constellations of Waking* (Loveland, OH: Dos Madres, 2019).

9. DuPlessis's ongoing long poem, *Drafts*, has appeared in multiple volumes: *Drafts 1–38, Toll* (Middletown, CT: Wesleyan University Press, 2001); *Drafts 39–57, Pledge* (Cambridge, UK: Salt, 2004); *Torques: Drafts 58–76* (Cambridge, UK: Salt, 2007); *Pitch: Drafts 77–95* (Cambridge, UK: Salt, 2010); *Surge: Drafts 96–114* (Cambridge, UK: Salt, 2013).

10. Rothenberg, too, has been writing the lost works of Jewry for decades. Three major books of this poetry, *Poland 1931*, *Khurbn*, and *The Burning Babe* are collected in *Tryptich* (New York: New Directions, 2007), and he edited, with Harris Lenowitz and Charles Doria, *A Big Jewish Book: Poems and Other Visions of the Jews from Tribal Times to Present* (Garden City, NY: Doubleday, 1978).

11. Heller, "Remains of the Diaspora: A Personal Meditation," in *Radical Poetics and Secular Jewish Culture*, ed. Miller and Morris, 171.

12. I have discussed at length the ways American Jewish intellectuals, especially the Objectivist poets, have responded to the Hebraism/Hellenism dichotomy in *A Menorah for Athena*.

13. Michael Heller, *Living Root: A Memoir* (Albany, NY: State University of New York Press, 2000).

14. Robert Duncan, *The Truth and Life of Myth: An Essay in Essential Autobiography* (1969), repr. in *Collected Essays and Other Prose*, ed. James Maynard (Berkeley: University of California Press, 2014), 139–94; Duncan, *The H.D. Book*.

15. Rodger Kamenetz, *The Jew in the Lotus: A Poet's Rediscovery of Jewish Identity in Buddhist India* (San Francisco: HarperSanFrancisco, 1994).

16. Gary Snyder, "Introduction," in *Beneath a Single Moon*, ed. Kent Johnson and Craig Paulenich, 8.

17. Michael Heller, "Rethinking Rilke," in *Uncertain Poetries* (Cambridge, UK: Salt, 2005), 54.

Chapter 4

1. Lawrence Rainey, *Institutions of Modernism: Literary Elites and Public Culture* (New Haven, CT: Yale University Press, 1998), 10–41.

2. Barry Ahearn, ed., *Pound/Zukofsky: Selected Letters of Ezra Pound and Louis Zukofsky* (New York: New Directions, 1987), 42–73.

3. George F. Butterick, ed., *Charles Olson and Robert Creeley: The Complete Correspondence*, vols. 1 and 2 (Santa Barbara, CA: Black Sparrow, 1980).

4. Reprinted in L. S. Dembo and Cyrena N. Pondrom, eds., *The Contemporary Writer: Interviews with Sixteen Novelists and Poets* (Madison: University of Wisconsin

Press, 1972). In their introduction, the editors state, "It was in the spring of 1968 that we had the extreme good fortune of bringing to the Madison campus, separately, the so-called 'Objectivist' poets, Louis Zukofsky, George Oppen, Carl Rakosi, and Charles Reznikoff, each enjoying not so much a revival as a re-efflorescence. A serial interview of these writers would, we surmised, clarify an important trend in the history of modern poetry" (x).

5. Donald M. Allen, ed., *The New American Poetry, 1945–1960* (New York: Grove, 1960; repr., Berkeley: University of California Press, 1999). In an afterword to the 1999 edition, Allen states he had initially planned to include recent work by Williams, H.D., cummings, Moore, Pound, and Stevens, as well as "a few poems by Kenneth Rexroth, Kenneth Patchen, and Louis Zukofsky," before moving on to "a larger selection of poems by twenty-four of the 'new' poets." Olson objected vehemently, arguing, "I wouldn't myself add either of those two units, either the 'aunties' or the grandpas. If the thing we are now in is it is just in its own character, and there isn't any one of us who isn't bound together in that way, than by any of those older connections." Ultimately, selections by the "older connections" were excised and forty-four of the "new," postwar poets were included (448).

6. Hugh Kenner, *A Homemade World: The American Modernist Writers* (New York: William Morrow, 1975), 169.

7. Dennis Young, "Conversation with Mary Oppen," *Iowa Review* 18, no. 3 (1988): 37.

8. Oppen's newly discovered book is *21 Poems*, ed. David B. Hobbs (New York: New Directions, 2017).

9. John Felstiner, *Paul Celan: Poet, Survivor, Jew* (New Haven: Yale University Press, 1995), xvi. George Oppen, *New Collected Poems*, ed. Michael Davidson (New York: New Directions, 2002), 99. Kristen Prevallet performs a beautiful meditation on the impact of the war on Oppen's poetry in "One among the Rubble: George Oppen and World War II," in *Thinking Poetics: Essays on George Oppen*, ed. Steve Shoemaker (Tuscaloosa: University of Alabama Press, 2009), 131–42.

10. Peter Nicholls offers the fullest account of Oppen's philosophical engagements, especially those with Heidegger, in *George Oppen and the Fate of Modernism* (Oxford: Oxford University Press, 2007).

11. For a direct comparison of Oppen and Celan, see "Forum: Two Poems Entitled 'Psalm' by George Oppen and Paul Celan," ed. Henry Weinfield, *Religion and Literature* 48, no. 1 (Spring 2017): 159–91, with essays by Weinfield, Robert Baker, Carsten Dutt, Kevin Hart, and Peter Nicholls. Earlier, Anthony Rudolf placed Oppen in the company of European writers such as Celan, Primo Levi, Yves Bonnefoy, and Vaclav Havel in *Wine from Two Glasses* (London: Adam Archive Publications, 1991), and Michael Heller brings Oppen, Celan, and Olson into a fruitful meditation about the materiality of language in "The Voice of the Impersonal: Oppen and Celan," in his *Speaking the Estranged: Essays on the Work of George Oppen* (Cambridge, UK: Salt, 2008), 106–23. Finally, Eliot Weinberger compares Oppen and Celan in the first paragraph of his preface to Oppen's *New Collected Poems*: "[Oppen] had an aura about him, that of the honorable man trying to speak in the roar of history, much like the aura that has now gathered posthumously around Paul Celan" (vii).

12. Kevin Power, *Where You're At: Poetics and Visual Art* (Berkeley, CA: Poltroon, 2011), 78–79.

13. Olson, *Collected Prose,* 174.

14. Charles Olson, *Muthologos: Lectures and Interviews,* rev. 2nd ed., ed. Ralph Maud (Vancouver, BC: Talonbooks, 2010), 132.

15. George Oppen, *Selected Letters,* ed. Rachel Blau DuPlessis (Durham, NC: Duke University Press, 1990), 115.

16. Peter Nicholls also points to a coincidence (or possible influence of Olson upon Oppen) in the use of the term "human universe," which is the title of one of Olson's best-known essays. For Olson, the human universe avoids the "universe of discourse" but dwells alongside the "universe of things." Oppen also concerns himself with "the human vision which creates the human universe" through relationship to the phenomenal world. Nicholls rightly emphasizes their shared commitment to phenomenology (49).

17. Olson, *The Collected Poems of Charles Olson,* 46.

18. David Herd finds Olson newly relevant for thinking about America's seemingly endless wars and the abrogation of rights and mass migrations such wars have set in motion. Herd finds crucial political insights in Olson's poetry and essays: "What he evolves in the writing of *The Maximus Poems* are forms of thought that speak directly to the states of political exclusion and exception that were the legacy of the Second World War, and that have once again become definitive of where we find ourselves." David Herd, "Open Field Poetics and the Politics of Movement," in *Contemporary Olson,* ed. David Herd (Manchester, UK: Manchester University Press, 2015), 275. See also David Herd, "'From Him Only Will the Old State-Secret Come': What Charles Olson Imagined," *English* 59, no. 227 (2010): 375–95. The term "state of exception," for the power gained by a government through the suspension of rights in a time of emergency, was coined by Giorgio Agamben in *State of Exception,* trans. Kevin Attell (Chicago: University of Chicago Press, 2005). Susan Thackrey has recourse to Agamben's critique of the contemporary reduction of human experience in her discussion of Oppen's use of language in his late poetry. Susan Thackrey, *George Oppen: A Radical Practice* (San Francisco: O, 2001), 69–70.

19. George F. Butterick, *A Guide to "The Maximus Poems" of Charles Olson* (Berkeley: University of California Press, 1978), 495–96.

20. George Oppen, "Three Poets," in *Selected Prose, Daybooks, and Papers,* ed. Stephen Cope (Berkeley: University of California Press, 2007), 24–25.

21. John Crawford, "Since My Distances Became My Home," in *The Oppens Remembered: Poetry, Politics, Friendship,* ed. Rachel Blau DuPlessis (Albuquerque: University of New Mexico Press, 2015), 79. The Olson quote is from *The Maximus Poems* (367).

22. Robert Duncan, *Collected Later Poems and Plays,* ed. Peter Quartermain (Berkeley: University of California Press, 2014), 295.

23. Michael Davidson discusses the "poem-as-notebook" in great detail in his classic essay "Palimtexts: Postmodern Poetry and the Material Text," reprinted in *Thinking Poetics,* ed. Shoemaker, 23–44. He compares Oppen and Olson on pages 36–38.

24. Louis Zukofsky, *Prepositions +: The Collected Critical Essays* (Middletown, CT: Wesleyan University Press, 2000), 12.

Chapter 5

1. *Poetry* 100, no. 5 (1962): 332, repr. in George Oppen, *Selected Prose, Daybooks, and Papers*, 27.

2. Butterick, *A Guide to "The Maximus Poems" of Charles Olson*, 495–96.

3. Joel Dinerstein explores the historical and stylistic features of cool in *The Origins of Cool in Postwar America* (Chicago: University of Chicago Press, 2017). Compare John Leland's account of the development of "hipness" in American culture in *Hip: The History* (New York: HarperCollins, 2004).

4. Olson read Freud as early as 1939–1940, and he continued to refer to Freud as a touchstone in a number of circumstances. See Ralph Maud, *Charles Olson's Reading: A Biography* (Carbondale: Southern Illinois University Press, 1996), 37, 256. Olson had much more extensive transactions with Jung's psychology, as documented and discussed by Charles Stein in *The Secret of the Black Chrysanthemum: The Poetic Cosmology of Charles Olson and His Use of the Writings of C. G. Jung* (Barrytown, NY: Station Hill, 1987).

5. Mary Oppen, *Meaning a Life: An Autobiography* (Santa Barbara, CA: Black Sparrow, 1978), 201–2.

6. Ralph Maud, ed., *Poet to Publisher: Charles Olson's Correspondence with Donald Allen* (Vancouver, BC: Talonbooks, 2003), 34, 40.

7. Michael Rumaker, *Black Mountain Days: A Memoir* (2003; repr., New York: Spuyten Duyvil, 2012), 174–75.

8. Thanks to Henry Weinfield for drawing my attention to Williams as one source for the term "isolate."

9. Herman Melville, *Moby-Dick*, ed. Harrison Hayford and Hershel Parker, Norton Critical Edition (New York: Norton, 1967), 108.

10. Stephen Fredman, *The Grounding of American Poetry: Charles Olson and the Emersonian Tradition* (Cambridge: Cambridge University Press, 1993).

11. Olson, *The Maximus Poems*, 16. The asymmetry of "men and girls" lies at the heart of the feminist critiques of Olson. See below for a discussion of such critiques by Michael Davidson and Rachel Blau DuPlessis.

12. A. Walton Litz and Christopher MacGowan, eds., *The Collected Poems of William Carlos Williams*, vol. 1, *1909–1939* (New York: New Directions, 1986), 217.

13. In *Black Mountain Days*, Rumaker testifies, "Incongruously, or perhaps not so, the scene from the 1954 movie *The Wild One*, the rebel motorcycle gang movie starring Marlon Brando, that's had a powerful impact on a number of the young males at the college" (551). The era engaged by "The Lordly and Isolate Satyrs" also contains two other films about motorcyclists that made a significant impact on the larger culture: *Roustabout* (1964), starring Elvis Presley, and *Easy Rider* (1969), starring Dennis Hopper and Jack Nicholson.

14. Michael Davidson, *Guys Like Us: Citing Masculinity in Cold War Poetics* (Chicago: University of Chicago Press, 2004), 208.

15. DuPlessis's interpretation of the poem first appeared in "Manhood and Its Poetic Projects: The Construction of Masculinity in the Counter-Cultural Poetry of the U.S. 1950s," *Jacket* 31 (October 2006), http://jacketmagazine.com/31/duplessis-manhood.html, accessed 22 August 2011. A revised version of this essay is chapter 4 of her *Purple Passages* (Iowa City: University of Iowa Press, 2012). The passage cited is from page 111.

16. *Evergreen Review* 1, no. 4 (1957 copyright, Spring 1958 issue): 5–8. Charles Olson, *Selected Letters*, ed. Ralph Maud (Berkeley: University of California Press, 2000), 273.

17. Kenneth Rexroth, "San Francisco Letter," *Evergreen Review* 1, no. 2 (1957): 5.

18. Donald M. Allen, ed., *The New American Poetry, 1945–1960* (New York: Grove, 1960; repr., Berkeley: University of California Press, 1999), 2–39, 386–400. For a detailed discussion of the making of Allen's anthology, see Alan Golding, "*The New American Poetry* Revisited, Again," *Contemporary Literature* 39, no. 2 (1998): 180–211. The other books of Olson's that Allen published include: *The Distances* (1960), *Maximus from Dogtown* (1961), *A Bibliography on America for Ed Dorn* (1964), *Human Universe and Other Essays* (1965), *Proprioception* (1965), *Stocking Cap* (1966), *In Cold Hell, In Thicket* (1967), *Causal Mythology* (1969), *Poetry and Truth* (1971), *Additional Prose* (1974), *The Post Office: A Memoir of His Father* (1975), *The Fiery Hunt and Other Plays* (1977), and *Muthologos.*

19. Olson, *Muthologos*, 164–65.

20. Robert Frank, *The Americans* (Paris: Robert Delpire, 1958; New York: Grove, 1959).

21. Maud, ed., *Poet to Publisher*, 33.

22. William Blake, *The Marriage of Heaven and Hell* (London: Oxford University Press, 1975), plate 11. For an account of Blake's influence on postwar American arts, see Stephen Eisenman, ed., *William Blake and the Age of Aquarius* (Princeton, NJ: Princeton University Press, 2017).

23. Olson, *Collected Prose*, 246.

24. In *The Black Mountain Book: A New Edition* (Rocky Mount: North Carolina Wesleyan College Press, 1991), Fielding Dawson recounts a conversation with Olson at Black Mountain College in which Dawson identified "the leader's woman" as "(in tone and context as well as image), [Raymond] Chandler's woman, a truth he acknowledged, and enjoyed" (77).

25. DuPlessis discusses the relationship between homosexuality and the one woman in the poem. She contends that Olson evokes "male-male love and eroticism without homosexuality. This is bliss indeed; enacted in Olson's relationships, it may well explain his electric power for men. Indeed, the only function of this one female figure in the poem, is as a token guarantor of normative sexual desire. She provides the right outlet for all the almost taboo eros of the poem, and has only one other function—to be inferior" (175).

26. Dawson also comments on Olson's awed appreciation of truck drivers, whom he characterized in terms of a phallic potency similar to that of the motorcyclists: "He . . . told us in commuting from D.C. he and Connie stopped at truckstops for coffee, and listened, as he loved to do, to the drivers, Connie smiled, eager in their recent memory, enjoyed his pleasure—'Those guys!' he breathed. 'In their big rigs'" (76).

27. Kenneth Anger, dir., *Scorpio Rising*, 28 mins., color (1964). Behind Anger's sadomasochistic depiction of motorcyclists is Cocteau's use of them as minions of death in his 1950 *Orphée*. Both Anger and Cocteau portray these hooded, motorized figures as menacing and deadly, where Olson seems to concentrate solely on erotic and heroic valences. Thanks to Richard Berengarten for reminding me of Cocteau's motorcyclists.

28. Allen Ginsberg, *Collected Poems, 1947–1997* (New York: HarperCollins, 2006), 134, 136. Another gay poet, Thom Gunn, also portrayed motorcyclists as cultural icons in his poetry, most famously in "On the Move" (1957). Using Marlon Brando in *The Wild One* as his model, Gunn sees the cyclists as representing continuous movement: "At worse, one is in motion; and at best, / Reaching no absolute, in which to rest, / One is always nearer by not keeping still" (Thom Gunn, *Selected Poems*, ed. August Kleinzahler [New York: Farrar, Straus and Giroux, 2009], 8). Olson, contrarily, insists on their monumental solidity.

Chapter 6

1. Laurie Anderson, At the Kelly Writers House, University of Pennsylvania, March 24–25, 2003, http://writing.upenn.edu/wh/people/fellows/anderson.html.

2. Allen Ginsberg, *Howl and Other Poems* (San Francisco: City Lights, 1956); David Antin, *How Long Is the Present: Selected Talk Poems of David Antin*, ed. Stephen Fredman (Albuquerque: University of New Mexico Press, 2014); Rothenberg, ed., *Technicians of the Sacred*; Claudia Rankine, *Don't Let Me Be Lonely: An American Lyric* (Minneapolis: Graywolf, 2004); Laura Mullen, *Murmur* (New York: Futurepoem, 2007); and Nathaniel Mackey, *Whatsaid Serif* (New York: New Directions, 1998).

3. Laurie Anderson, *All the Things I Lost in the Flood: Essays on Pictures, Language and Code* (New York: Rizzoli/Electa, 2017), 10.

4. Laurie Anderson, *Strange Angels* (Warner Brothers, 1989), audio.

5. Henry Sayre, *The Object of Performance: The American Avant-Garde since 1970.* (Chicago: University of Chicago Press, 1989), 147. See also Marjorie Perloff, *Poetry On & Off the Page: Essays for Emergent Occasions* (Evanston, IL: Northwestern University Press, 1998), 11–15; and Michael Davidson, *Ghostlier Demarcations: Modern Poetry and the Material Word* (Berkeley: University of California Press, 1997), 213–18.

6. Laurie Anderson, *Stories from the Nerve Bible: A Retrospective, 1972–1992* (New York: HarperCollins, 1994), 150.

7. Benjamin, "Theses on the Philosophy of History," in *Illuminations*, 255–66.

8. Tony Kushner, *Angels in America: A Gay Fantasia on National Themes* (New York: Theatre Communications Group, 1995).

9. Harold Bloom, *Omens of Millennium: The Gnosis of Angels, Dreams, and Resurrection* (New York: Riverhead, 1996).

10. Roselee Goldberg, *Laurie Anderson* (New York: Harry Abrams, 2000), 25.

11. R. M. Rilke, *Selected Poetry of Rainer Maria Rilke*, trans. Stephen Mitchell (New York: Vintage, 1989), 201, 199.

12. Patti Smith, *Just Kids* (New York: Ecco, 2010).

13. Laurie Anderson, "Some Thoughts on the *Live in New York* Recording," liner notes for *Live at Town Hall* (New York: Nonesuch, 2002), compact disc.

Chapter 7

1. In addition to an octavo edition of 2,500, *Numbers* was printed in a larger format (27 × 20 inches) as loose sheets in a case, in a run of 275. There were also twenty-five bound and signed copies, one of which resides in the Hesburgh Library.

2. A symposium to celebrate the acquisition of Creeley's library and the publication of his *Selected Letters* (Rod Smith, Peter Baker, and Kaplan Harris, eds. [Berkeley: University of California Press, 2014]) was held at the University of Notre Dame, Department of Rare Books and Special Collections, on February 7, 2014. Lectures by Penelope Creeley, Steve Clay, Kaplan Harris, and a panel of graduate students can be viewed at https://www.youtube.com/user/UNDEnglishDept.

3. Steve Clay, publisher of Granary Books, recounts in conversation with Kyle Schlesinger his essential role as book dealer in the meticulous description of Creeley's library. He also discusses in detail the materials housed in Creeley's copy of *Presences*, photocopies of which can be found in the appendix to the new edition. See Steve Clay, "Robert Creeley's Library," *Mimeo Mimeo* 5 (Fall 2011): 33–46.

4. Penelope Creeley, "Robert and Books" (unpublished manuscript), 5. One of Creeley's close associates, Susan Howe, composed *The Midnight* (New York: New Directions, 2003), a biography of her mother, Mary Manning, largely by examining the materials found in books in the family library, such as Robert Louis Stevenson's *The Master of Ballantrae* and W. B. Yeats's *Later Poems*.

5. For critical interpretations of *Presences*, see Michael Davidson, "The Presence of the Present: Morality and the Problem of Value in Robert Creeley's Recent Prose," in "Robert Creeley: A Gathering," ed. William Spanos, *Boundary 2*, 6–7 (Spring–Fall 1978): 545–64; William Sylvester, "Is That a Real Statue or Did Marisol Just Make It Up? Affinities with Creeley's *Presences*," in *Robert Creeley: The Poet's Workshop*, ed. Carroll F. Terrell (Orono, ME: National Poetry Foundation, 1984), 275–87; Stephen Fredman, "'A Life Tracking Itself': Robert Creeley's *Presences: A Text for Marisol*," in *Poet's Prose*, 57–100; Douglas Gunn, "Inappropriate Literary Performances: The Unstable Texts of Robert Creeley's *Mabel: A Story and Other Prose*," *Review of Contemporary Fiction* 15, no. 3 (Fall 1995): 141–53; John Yau, "Active Participant: Robert Creeley and the Visual Arts," in *In Company: Robert Creeley's Collaborations*, ed. Amy Cappellazzo and Elizabeth Licata (Niagara Falls, NY, and Greensboro, NC: Castellani Art Museum of Niagara University and Weatherspoon Art Gallery, University of North Carolina at Greensboro, 1999), 45–82; Jeffrey Twitchell-Waas, "Robert Creeley," *Review of Contemporary Fiction* 24, no. 2 (Summer 2004): 7–54; and Barbara Montefalcone, "'Celebrating the Instant': Robert Creeley and Marisol Escobar's *Presences*," in *USA: Identities, Cultures, and Politics in National, Transnational and Global Perspectives*, ed. Marina Camboni et al. (Macerata, Italy: Eum Edizioni Università di Macerata, 2009), 127–38.

6. For general discussions of Creeley's collaborations with artists, see Cappellazzo and Licata; Barbara Montefalcone, "The 'Eye' and the 'Company': Robert Creeley's Col-

laborations, 1953–2004" (Diss. Université Lumière Lyon 2, 2006); and Barbara Montefalcone and Anca Cristofovici, eds., *The Art of Collaboration: Poets, Artists, Books* (Victoria, TX: Cuneiform Press, 2015). The quote by Creeley is from the latter book, page 27.

7. Marisol Letter to Creeley, May 1972, Robert Creeley Collection, Hesburgh Library, University of Notre Dame.

8. Robert Creeley, *Mabel: A Story and Other Prose* (London: Marion Boyars, 1976), 5–6.

9. Robert Creeley and Robert Indiana, *Numbers*, ed. Dieter Honisch, trans. Klaus Reichert (Stuttgart: Edition Domberger, 1968).

10. Creeley, interview with Elizabeth Licata, November 21, 1998 (*In Company*, 15).

11. William Katz, telephone conversation with Stephen Fredman, January 18, 2015, and email correspondence, July 16, 2016.

12. *Io* 14 (Summer 1972): 183–226. Dates that accompany many of the prose units identify the time of composition as December 1, 1971, to April 12, 1972. The dates were dropped in the Scribner's edition.

13. Robert Creeley and R. B. Kitaj, *A Day Book* (Berlin: Graphis, 1971); Robert Creeley and Jim Dine, *Mabel: A Story* (Paris: Editions Crommelynck, 1977).

14. Letter to Marjorie Kinsey, October 23, 1976, Robert Creeley Collection, Hesburgh Library, University of Notre Dame.

15. Because of the early interest in her work by the Albright-Knox Art Gallery, Marisol bequeathed her estate to it upon her death in 2016.

16. José Ramón Medina, *Marisol*, photographs by Jack Mitchell (Caracas: Ediciones Armitano, 1968).

17. Although folk art has always been considered a crucial element in Marisol's art, it has recently been given new prominence in the work of Johns and Rauschenberg by Thomas Crow in *The Long March of Pop: Art, Music, and Design, 1930–1995* (New Haven, CT: Yale University Press, 2014).

18. Cécile Whiting, *A Taste for Pop: Pop Art, Gender, and Consumer Culture* (Cambridge: Cambridge University Press, 1997), 188.

19. Exceptions to the exclusion of sculptures of public figures would be *The Generals, Portrait of Sydney Janis Selling a Portrait of Sidney Janis, Henry* [Geldzahler], *The Band*, and *Father Damien*.

20. Quoted in Leon Shulman, *Marisol* (Worcester, MA: Worcester Art Museum, 1971), n.p.

21. Robert Creeley, *The Collected Essays of Robert Creeley* (Berkeley: University of California Press, 1989), 561.

22. Power, *Where You're At*, 114.

23. For a consideration of the shared preoccupation with assemblage among postwar artists and poets, see my *Contextual Practice: Assemblage and the Erotic in Postwar Poetry and Art* (Stanford, CA: Stanford University Press, 2010).

24. For a discussion of *Baby Girl* within the context of Marisol's depictions of family relationships, see Marina Pacini, "Marisol's Families," in *Marisol: Sculptures and Works on Paper*, ed. Marina Pacini, 73–96 (New Haven, CT: Memphis Brooks Museum of Art and Yale University Press, 2014).

25. Federico García Lorca, *Collected Poems*, ed. Christopher Maurer (New York: Farrar, Strauss and Giroux, 2002), 112.

Chapter 8

1. David Antin, *talking at the boundaries* (New York: New Directions, 1976); *tuning* (New York: New Directions, 1984); *what it means to be avant-garde* (New York: New Directions, 1993).

2. David Antin, *How Long Is the Present.*

3. For a meditation on how Antin's talk poems fit within a spectrum between poetry and prose (including what I call "poet's prose"), see my *Poet's Prose*, 137–42, 156–61.

4. John Dewey, *Art as Experience*, in *The Later Works, 1925–1953*, vol. 10, *1934*, ed. Jo Ann Boydston (Carbondale: Southern Illinois University Press, 1987).

5. Examples of audio versions of Antin's talk poems can be found at http://writing.upenn.edu/pennsound/x/Antin.php.

6. Antin, *Radical Coherency*.

7. David Antin, *Definitions* (New York: Caterpillar, 1967); *Autobiography* (New York: Something Else, 1967); *Code of Flag Behavior* (Los Angeles: Black Sparrow, 1968); *Meditations* (Los Angeles: Black Sparrow, 1971); *Talking* (1972; repr., Champlain, IL: Dalkey Archive, 2001).

8. Peter Middleton applies Antin's insight to a general view of the poetry reading: "The poet *performs* authorship, becoming in the process a divided subject by reproducing language constructed into a poem at some time prior to the reading, while reading aloud as if it were a spontaneous speech act arising in the present." Peter Middleton, *Distant Reading: Performance, Readership, and Consumption in Contemporary Poetry* (Tuscaloosa: University of Alabama Press, 2005), 33.

9. Marjorie Perloff devotes a chapter to Cage, Antin, and performance poetry in *The Poetics of Indeterminacy: Rimbaud to Cage* (1981; repr., Evanston, IL: Northwestern University Press, 1999), 288–339.

10. To gain a measure of Antin's engagement with Wittgenstein, see his review of Marjorie Perloff's *Wittgenstein's Ladder* in his *Radical Coherency*, "Wittgenstein among the Poets," 305–30.

11. Ralph Waldo Emerson, "The American Scholar," in *Essays and Lectures* (New York: Library of America, 1983), 63.

12. Henry Sayre discusses issues of orality and narrative in Antin's work in *The Object of Performance*, 177–79, 201–10.

13. A. W. Plumstead and Harrison Hayford, eds., *The Journals and Miscellaneous Notebooks of Ralph Waldo Emerson*, vol. 7, *1838–1842* (Cambridge, MA: Harvard University Press, 1969), 265.

14. David Antin, *john cage uncaged is still cagey* (San Diego: Singing Horse, 2005).

15. Jerome Rothenberg, ed., with commentaries, *Technicians of the Sacred: A Range of Poetries from Africa, America, Asia, & Oceania* (Garden City, NY: Doubleday, 1968). Henry Sayre discusses relationships between Antin and Rothenberg and ethnopoetics in *The Object of Performance*, 177–92. For another generous assessment of the two

poets in conjunction, see Hank Lazer, *Opposing Poetries*, vol. 1, *Issues and Institutions* (Evanston, IL: Northwestern University Press, 1996), 91–125. In "The Oral Impulse in Contemporary American Poetry," *Boundary 2*, 3, no. 3 (1975), editor William Spanos combines interviews with both poets, new poetry, and essays by critics. In his book, *In Search of the Primitive: Rereading David Antin, Jerome Rothenberg, and Gary Snyder* (Baton Rouge: Louisiana State University Press, 1986), Sherman Paul reads three principal poets of ethnopoetics.

16. David Antin, *i never knew what time it was* (Berkeley: University of California Press, 2005).

17. Stanley Cavell, *Little Did I Know: Excerpts from Memory* (Stanford: Stanford University Press, 2010).

18. David Antin and Charles Bernstein, *A Conversation with David Antin* (New York: Granary, 2002).

19. Bob Perelman, *Modernism the Morning After* (Tuscaloosa: University of Alabama Press, 2017), 189–91. For a contemporaneous account of the incident Perelman refers to—a talk poem Antin delivered at 80 Langton Street in 1978—see *The Poetry Reading: A Contemporary Compendium on Language & Performance*, ed. Stephen Vincent and Ellen Zweig (San Francisco: Momo's, 1981), particularly Zweig's "Where Is the Piece?" (174–86) and Antin's response (187–91). Earlier, in 1975, Barry Alpert put on display the sometimes uneasy relationship between Antin and the West Coast avant-garde in *Vort* 3, no. 1, an issue of criticism, interviews, and poetry devoted to Antin and Rothenberg.

20. Hank Lazer, ed., "David Antin Issue," *Review of Contemporary Fiction* 21, no. 1, (Spring 2001).

21. Kathy Acker, *Hannibal Lecter, My Father*, ed. Sylvère Lotringer (New York: Semiotext(e), 1991), 3.

22. Caroline Bergvall, Review of *A Conversation with David Antin*, *Jacket* 22 (Online, 2003), http://jacketmagazine.com/22/bergv-antin.html.

23. David Shields, *Reality Hunger: A Manifesto* (New York: Knopf, 2010).

24. David Antin, "The Theory and Practice of Postmodernism: A Manifesto," in John D'Agata, *The Next American Essay* (St. Paul, MN: Graywolf, 2003), 11–22.

Chapter 9

1. http://www.writing.upenn.edu/pennsound/.

2. http://www.ubu.com.

3. Mark Prendergast, *Ambient Century: From Mahler to Trance; The Evolution of Sound in the Electronic Age* (New York: Bloomsbury, 2001), xi.

4. Quoted in John T. Lysaker, *Brian Eno's "Ambient 1: Music for Airports"* (Oxford: Oxford University Press, 2018), 1.

5. See, for example, the CDs accompanying Paul D. Miller aka DJ Spooky that subliminal kid, *Rhythm Science* (Boston: MIT Press, 2004), and Paul D. Miller, ed., *Sound Unbound: Sampling Digital Music and Culture* (Boston: MIT Press, 2008).

6. There is an entire field, sound studies, which uses sound rather than sight to describe the lived environments of human beings across time and space. Poetics took

account relatively early of this reordering of the senses, as evidenced by two excellent anthologies of essays, *Sound States: Innovative Poetics and Acoustical Technologies*, ed. Adalaide Morris (Chapel Hill: University of North Carolina Press, 1997), and *Close Listening: Poetry and the Performed Word*, ed. Charles Bernstein (New York: Oxford University Press, 1998).

7. Ulla Dydo, ed., *A Stein Reader* (Evanston, IL: Northwestern University Press, 1993), 464–66.

8. Philip Glass, *Words Without Music* (New York: Liveright, 2015), 293.

9. Philip Glass, *Music by Philip Glass*, ed. Robert T. Jones (New York: Harper and Row, 1987), 64.

10. John Taggart, *Loop* (Los Angeles: Sun and Moon, 1991), 216.

11. The first three volumes are collected in *From a Broken Bottle Traces of Perfume Still Emanate* (New York: New Directions, 2010), followed by *Bass Cathedral* (New York: New Directions, 2008) and *Late Arcade* (New York: New Directions, 2017).

12. Brian Eno, *Ambient 1: Music for Airports* (Virgin, 1978).

13. Pamela Lu, *Ambient Parking Lot* (Chicago: Kenning, 2011).

14. Steve Reich and Beryl Korot, *The Cave* (New York: Nonesuch Records, 1995).

15. Tan Lin, "ambient stylistics," in Mark Wallace and Steven Marks, eds., *Telling It Slant: Avant-Garde Poetics of the 1990s* (Tuscaloosa: University of Alabama Press: 2002), 342–43.

16. Tan Lin, *Seven Controlled Vocabularies and Obituary 2004. The Joy of Cooking: [AIRPORT NOVEL MUSICAL POEM PAINTING FILM PHOTO HALLUCINATION LANDSCAPE]* (Middletown, CT: Wesleyan University Press, 2010), 16.

Chapter 10

1. R. M. Rilke, *Letters to a Young Poet*, trans. M. D. Herter Norton (Rev. ed., New York: W. W. Norton, 1954), 18–19.

2. Federico García Lorca, *Poet in New York*, trans. Stephen Fredman (San Francisco: Fog Horn, 1975).

3. For a discussion of Duncan's tangled relationship to Lorca's book, see Fredman, *Contextual Practice*, 141–45. For a broader consideration of Lorca's impact on American poetry, see Jonathan Mayhew, *Apocryphal Lorca: Translation, Parody, Kitsch* (Chicago: University of Chicago Press, 2009).

4. In *Transgressive Circulation: Essays on Translation* (n.p.: Noemi, 2018), Johannes Göransson portrays translation as an activity of ceaseless circulation, in which the norms for poetry in a specific language at a specific time are always being overturned by incoming acts of translation from elsewhere.

5. Benjamin, "The Task of the Translator," in *Illuminations*, 80.

6. Or, as Friedrich Schlegel puts it: "A classical text must never be entirely comprehensible. But those who are cultivated and who cultivate themselves must always want to learn more from it." (*Critical Fragment* 20, quoted by Schlegel in "On Incomprehensibility," in *Classic and Romantic German Aesthetics*, ed. J. M. Bernstein (Cambridge: Cambridge University Press, 2003), 306.

7. Benjamin's original meditation on the angel is in "Theses on the Philosophy

of History," in *Illuminations,* 259–60. This quotation by Benjamin is taken from Gershom Scholem, *On Jews and Judaism in Crisis: Selected Essays,* ed. Werner Dannhauser (New York: Schocken, 1976), 207.

8. Maurice Merleau-Ponty, *The Prose of the World,* ed. Claude Lefort, trans. John O'Neill (Evanston, IL: Northwestern University Press, 1973), 28–29.

9. Merleau-Ponty, *The Prose of the World,* 12.

10. Benjamin, *Illuminations,* 81.

11. Barry Alpert, "David Antin—An Interview," in Barry Alpert, ed., *Vort* 3, no. 1: "David Antin—Jerome Rothenberg" (1975): 16.

12. See the talk poem "tuning" in *How Long Is the Present,* 181–223.

13. Steiner, *After Babel,* 296–97.

Chapter 11

1. Paul Auster, *The Invention of Solitude* (1982; repr., New York: Penguin, 1988). Hereafter abbreviated as IS.

2. In "Paul Auster, or the Heir Intestate," in Dennis Barone, ed., *Beyond the Red Notebook: Essays on Paul Auster* (Philadelphia: University of Pennsylvania Press, 1995), Pascal Bruckner also makes a strong case for the centrality of *The Invention of Solitude* to Auster's oeuvre.

3. *The New York Trilogy* (1985, 1986, 1986; repr., New York: Penguin, 1990), 201–2. Hereafter abbreviated as NYT.

4. Antin, *How Long Is the Present,* 31–32.

5. Quoted by Auster in *The Art of Hunger* (New York: Penguin, 1993), 114. Hereafter abbreviated as AH.

6. Paul Auster, *White Spaces,* in *Disappearances: Selected Poems* (Woodstock, NY: Overlook, 1988), 101–10.

7. Stéphane Mallarmé, *A Tomb for Anatole,* trans. Paul Auster (San Francisco: North Point, 1983).

8. Edmond Jabès, *The Book of Questions,* vols. 1 and 2, in *From the Book to the Book: An Edmond Jabès Reader,* trans. Rosmarie Waldrop (Middletown, CT: Wesleyan University Press, 1991). On the back cover of *From the Book to the Book,* Auster writes: "I first read *The Book of Questions* twenty years ago, and my life was permanently changed. I can no longer think about the possibilities of literature without thinking of the example of Edmond Jabès. He is one of the great spirits of our time, a torch in the darkness." For a short consideration of Auster's relationship to Jabès, see Norman Finkelstein, "In the Realm of the Naked Eye: The Poetry of Paul Auster," in Barone, ed., *Beyond the Red Notebook,* 48–49. For more extended discussions of Jewish elements in Auster's work, see Finkelstein, *Not One of Them in Place,* 48–53, and Derek Rubin, "'The Hunger Must Be Preserved at All Cost': A Reading of *The Invention of Solitude,*" in Barone, *Beyond the Red Notebook,* 60–70.

9. When Jabès speaks of a "book that would have a chance to survive," he means also a book whose reader would have a chance of surviving *it.* For a fascinating meditation, via Jabès and Levinas, on the creative necessity of an escape from the book, see Marc-Alain Ouaknin, *The Burnt Book: Reading the Talmud,* trans. Llewellyn Brown (1986; Princeton: Princeton University Press, 1995).

10. This insight about the book as a fundamental creative concept underlies the massive anthology, *A Book of the Book: Some Works & Projections about the Book & Writing* (New York: Granary, 2000), edited by Jerome Rothenberg and Steve Clay. Here, the radical notions of the book put forth by Mallarmé and Jabès are starting points for an anthology of verbal, artistic, and critical works that project the book as a habitable space.

11. Edmond Jabès, *From the Desert to the Book: Dialogues with Marcel Cohen*, trans. Pierre Joris (Barrytown, NY: Station Hill, 1990), 101.

12. Paul Auster, *In the Country of Last Things* (New York: Viking Penguin, 1987); *Moon Palace* (New York: Viking Penguin, 1989); *The Music of Chance* (New York: Viking Penguin, 1990); and *Leviathan* (New York: Viking Penguin, 1992).

13. Thanks to Fred Rush for reminding me how much the notion of the room of the book owes to Melville's "Bartleby, the Scrivener" (1853) and also for noticing that *The Art of Hunger* alludes to Kafka's story "The Hunger Artist."

14. Perloff argues strongly for the contribution of Beckett to contemporary poet's prose. There is a discussion of Ashbery's "translative prose" in Fredman, *Poet's Prose*, 101–35.

15. For an application of notions of genealogy to Auster's *Moon Palace*, see Steven Weisenburg, "Inside *Moon Palace*," Barone, *Beyond the Red Notebook*, 130–42.

16. In many ways, Auster's fantasy of masculine self-generation is similar to Melville's in *Moby-Dick*—an appropriate analogy in light of A.'s characterization of S.'s room as "the womb, the belly of the whale." In chapter 95 of *Moby-Dick* (350–51), a character also wears "the skin of some second body around him," namely the "pelt," or outer covering, of the whale's penis. Having skinned and dried it, the "mincer" wears the sheath to protect himself from boiling blubber. Melville presents this investiture as a form of primitive phallus-worship—and then, as often in *Moby-Dick*, jeeringly compares the "primitive" with the Christian: "What a candidate for an archbishoprick, what a lad for a Pope were this mincer!" [351]). By turning the phallus into a sheath, the mincer has, in effect, invaginated it.

17. "The Structure of Rime," one of Duncan's two open-ended poetic sequences, first appears in *The Opening of the Field*. Although Duncan calls the Structure of Rime "*an absolute scale of resemblance and disresemblance [that] establishes measures that are music in the actual world*" (*The Collected Later Poems and Plays*, 9), he does not allow the mind to imagine itself as privy to this "absolute scale." He ascribes this knowledge, instead, to a feminine presence, whom he designates in "Often I Am Permitted to Return to a Meadow" as the "Queen Under the Hill / whose hosts are a disturbance of words within words / that is a field folded" (3). As in Leibniz, interconnectedness remains for Duncan "folded within all thought."

18. In crafting a Jewish interpretation of the Pinocchio story, Auster strangely makes nothing of the puppet's embarrassingly prominent nose. See Sander Gilman, *The Jew's Body* (New York: Routledge, 1991), especially chapter 7, "The Jewish Nose," for reflections on the stigma of the nose and the history of the "nose job."

19. Auster's meditation on Anne Frank's room as a scene of writing has many parallels in the work of artist Rachel Lichtenstein. *Rodinsky's Room* (London: Granta, 1999), written by Lichtenstein and Iain Sinclair, chronicles her multiyear project of

reconstructing the lost world of David Rodinsky, a Polish immigrant to London's Jewish East End, who wrote on the walls of his room in a magical language. Thanks to Anthony Rudolf for alerting me to its similarities to the rooms Auster evokes.

20. Art Spiegelman, *Maus: A Survivor's Tale,* vols. 1 and 2 (New York: Random House, 1986, 1991).

21. Martin Heidegger, *Poetry, Language, Thought,* trans. Albert Hofstadter (New York: Harper, 1971), 190.

22. Yosef Hayim Yershalmi, *Zakhor: Jewish History and Jewish Memory* (1982; New York: Schocken, 1989), 5.

23. Benjamin, *Illuminations,* 259.

24. Through the medium of cinema, Auster was given an opportunity to walk out of the room and yet continue writing. In the midst of shooting *Smoke* (1995), for which he wrote the screenplay, Auster, the director, Wayne Wang, and one of the actors, Harvey Keitel, were having so much fun they decided to improvise another film. Auster outlined the screenplay on the fly and even took over directing the resulting movie, *Blue in the Face* (1995), when Wang was sick for two days. In the midst of recounting the joy of working with actors such as Keitel, Michael J. Fox, Roseanne Barr, Lou Reed, Jim Jarmusch, Lily Tomlin, and Madonna, Auster was asked if he planned to direct or write screenplays again. He answered in the negative but noted a signal benefit: "It was a great experience, it got me out of my room" (Kenneth Chanko, "'Smoke' Gets in Their Eyes," *Entertainment Weekly* 281/282 [June 30 / July 7, 1995]: 15).

Chapter 12

1. Lyn Hejinian, *My Life* (Providence, RI: Burning Deck, 1980); (Los Angeles: Sun & Moon, 1987).

2. For instance, see Juliana Spahr's assessment in *Everybody's Autonomy: Connective Reading and Collective Identity* (Tuscaloosa: University of Alabama Press, 2001): "*My Life* has been an interesting influence on younger writers who are using its concerns and intents to discuss race more directly, such as Pamela Lu in *Pamela: A Novel,* Renee Gladman in *Arlem* and *Not Right Now,* and Summi Kaipa in *The Epics*" (81).

3. John Ashbery, *Three Poems* (New York: Viking, 1972), 3.

4. Henry David Thoreau, *Walden and Civil Disobedience,* ed. Owen Thomas (New York: Norton, 1966), 1.

5. Lyn Hejinian, "Variations: A Return of Words," *In the American Tree,* ed. Ron Silliman (Orono, ME: National Poetry Foundation, 1986), 503.

6. Craig Douglas Dworkin, "Penelope Reworking the Twill: Patchwork, Writing, and Lyn Hejinian's *My Life,*" *Contemporary Literature* 36 (1995): 64–65; Marjorie Perloff, *The Dance of the Intellect: Studies in the Poetry of the Pound Tradition* (Cambridge: Cambridge University Press, 1985), 225.

7. Marjorie Perloff, *Radical Artifice: Writing Poetry in the Age of Media* (Chicago: University of Chicago Press, 1991), 166.

8. Lyn Hejinian, *The Language of Inquiry* (Berkeley: University of California Press, 2000), 204. Hereafter abbreviated as LI.

9. Lyn Hejinian, "The Person," in *The Cold of Poetry* (Los Angeles: Sun & Moon, 1994), 143–81.

10. Because these phrases have been edited out of *The Language of Inquiry*, I have returned to an earlier version of the essay in "The Person and Description," *Poetics Journal* 9 (1991): 166–70. The quotation is from page 167.

11. John Ashbery, "The Impossible," *Selected Prose*, ed. Eugene Richie (Ann Arbor: University of Michigan Press, 2004), 12.

12. Lyn Hejinian, "The Quest for Knowledge in the Western Poem," in *Disembodied Poetics: Annals of the Jack Kerouac School*, ed. Anne Waldman and Andrew Schelling (Albuquerque: University of New Mexico Press, 1994), 179–80.

13. Lyn Hejinian, "The Rejection of Closure," in *Writing/Talks*, ed. Bob Perelman (Carbondale: Southern Illinois University Press, 1985), 273.

14. The purpose of calling attention to the coordinates of age and year that mark each chapter is not to assert a causal or narrative continuity. In my view, these coordinates act as part of the implicit grid-structure of a chapter. My thanks to Lynn Keller for seeking this clarification. See Spahr, *Everybody's Autonomy*, chapter 2, for a detailed discussion of autobiographical issues in *My Life*.

15. Dr. Seuss (Theodor Geisel), *Horton Hears a Who!* (New York: Random House, 1954).

16. Whitman, *Leaves of Grass*, 505.

Bibliography

Abram, David. *Becoming Animal: An Earthly Cosmology*. New York: Random House, 2010.

———. *The Spell of the Sensuous: Perception and Language in a More-Than-Human World*. New York: Random House, 1996.

Acker, Kathy. *Hannibal Lecter, My Father*. Edited by Sylvère Lotringer. New York: Semiotext(e), 1991.

Agamben, Giorgio. *State of Exception*. Translated by Kevin Attell. Chicago: University of Chicago Press, 2005.

Ahearn, Barry, ed. *Pound/Zukofsky: Selected Letters of Ezra Pound and Louis Zukofsky*. New York: New Directions, 1987.

Allen, Donald M., ed. *The New American Poetry, 1945–1960*. Berkeley: University of California Press, 1999. First published 1960 by Grove (New York).

Alpert, Barry, ed. "David Antin—Jerome Rothenberg." *Vort* 3, no. 1 (1975).

Anderson, Laurie. *All the Things I Lost in the Flood: Essays on Pictures, Language and Code*. New York: Rizzoli/Electa, 2017.

———. At the Kelly Writers House, University of Pennsylvania, March 24–25, 2003. http://writing.upenn.edu/wh/people/fellows/anderson.html.

———, dir. *Home of the Brave*. Warner Brothers, 1986. Film.

———. "Some Thoughts on the *Live in New York* Recording." Liner notes for *Live at Town Hall*. New York: Nonesuch, 2002. CD.

———. *Stories from the Nerve Bible: A Retrospective, 1972–1992*. New York: HarperCollins, 1994.

———. *Strange Angels*. Warner Brothers, 1989. Audio.

———. *United States Live*. Warner Brothers, 1984. Audio.

Anger, Kenneth, dir., *Scorpio Rising*. 28 mins. Color. 1964.

Antin, David. *Autobiography*. New York: Something Else, 1967.

———. *Code of Flag Behavior*. Los Angeles: Black Sparrow, 1968.

———. *Definitions*. New York: Caterpillar, 1967.

———. *How Long Is the Present: Selected Talk Poems of David Antin*. Edited by Stephen Fredman. Albuquerque: University of New Mexico Press, 2014.

———. *i never knew what time it was*. Berkeley: University of California Press, 2005.

———. *john cage uncaged is still cagey*. San Diego: Singing Horse, 2005.

———. *Radical Coherency: Selected Essays on Art and Literature 1966 to 2005*. Chicago: University of Chicago Press, 2011.

———. *Talking*. 1972. Reprint, Champlain, IL: Dalkey Archive, 2001.

———. *talking at the boundaries*. New York: New Directions, 1976.

———. *tuning*. New York: New Directions, 1984.

———. *what it means to be avant-garde*. New York: New Directions, 1993.

Antin, David, and Charles Bernstein. *A Conversation with David Antin*. New York: Granary, 2002.

Artaud, Antonin. *The Theater and Its Double*. Translated by Mary Caroline Richards. New York: Grove, 1958.

Ashbery, John. "The Impossible." In *Selected Prose*, edited by Eugene Richie, 11–14. Ann Arbor: University of Michigan Press, 2004.

———. *Three Poems*. New York: Viking, 1972.

Auster, Paul. *The Art of Hunger*. New York: Penguin, 1993.

———. *Disappearances: Selected Poems*. Woodstock, NY: Overlook, 1988.

———. *In the Country of Last Things*. New York: Viking Penguin, 1987.

———. *The Invention of Solitude*. 1982. Reprint, New York: Viking Penguin, 1988.

———. *Leviathan*. New York: Viking Penguin, 1992.

———. *Moon Palace*. New York: Viking Penguin, 1989.

———. *The Music of Chance*. New York: Viking Penguin, 1990.

———. *The New York Trilogy*. 1985, 1986, 1986. New York: Viking Penguin, 1990.

———, ed. *The Random House Book of Twentieth-Century French Poetry*. New York: Random House, 1982.

Barone, Dennis, ed. *Beyond the Red Notebook: Essays on Paul Auster*. Philadelphia: University of Pennsylvania Press, 1995.

Barron, Jonathan N., and Eric Murphy Selinger, eds. *Jewish American Poetry: Poems, Commentary, and Reflections*. Hanover, NH: Brandeis University Press, 2000.

Bellah, Robert. *Religion in Human Evolution: From the Paleolithic to the Axial Age*. Cambridge, MA: Harvard University Press, 2011.

Benjamin, Walter. *Illuminations*. Edited by Hannah Arendt. Translated by Harry Zohn. New York: Schocken, 1969.

Bergvall, Caroline. Review of *A Conversation with David Antin*. *Jacket* 22 (Online, 2003). http://jacketmagazine.com/22/bergv-antin.html.

Bernstein, Charles, ed. *Close Listening: Poetry and the Performed Word*. New York: Oxford University Press, 1998.

———. *Shadowtime*. Los Angeles: Green Integer, 2005.

Bernstein, Michael André. "Bringing It All Back Home: Derivations and Quotations in Robert Duncan and the Poundian Tradition." *Sagetrieb* 1, no. 2 (1982): 176–89.

Bertholf, Robert, and Albert Gelpi, eds. *The Letters of Robert Duncan and Denise Levertov*. Stanford: Stanford University Press, 2004.

Blake, William. *The Marriage of Heaven and Hell*. London: Oxford University Press, 1975.

Bloom, Harold. *Omens of Millennium: The Gnosis of Angels, Dreams, and Resurrection*. New York: Riverhead, 1996.

Butterick, George F., ed. *Charles Olson and Robert Creeley: The Complete Correspondence*. Vols. 1 and 2. Santa Barbara, CA: Black Sparrow, 1980.

———. *A Guide to "The Maximus Poems" of Charles Olson*. Berkeley: University of California Press, 1978.

Byrne, David, dir. *Ilé Aiyé: The House of Life*. Plexifilm, 1989.

———. *True Stories*. Warner Bros., 1986.

Cage, John. *Diary: How to Improve the World (You Will Only Make Matters Worse)*. Los Angeles: Siglio, 2015.

———. *Indeterminacy: New Aspect of Form in Instrumental and Electronic Music*. New York: Folkways, 1959. 2 sound discs.

———. *Silence*. Middletown, CT: Wesleyan University Press, 1961.

Cappellazzo, Amy, and Elizabeth Licata, eds. *In Company: Robert Creeley's Collaborations*. Niagara Falls, NY, and Greensboro, NC: Castellani Art Museum of Niagara University and Weatherspoon Art Gallery, University of North Carolina at Greensboro, 1999.

Cavell, Stanley. *Little Did I Know: Excerpts from Memory*. Stanford: Stanford University Press, 2010.

Chanko, Kenneth. "'Smoke' Gets in Their Eyes." *Entertainment Weekly* 281/282 (June 30/July 7, 1995): 14–15.

Clay, Steve. "Robert Creeley's Library." *Mimeo Mimeo* 5 (Fall 2011): 33–46.

Collis, Stephen, and Graham Lyons, eds. *Reading Duncan Reading*. Iowa City: University of Iowa Press, 2012.

Creeley, Penelope. "Robert and Books." Unpublished manuscript.

Creeley, Robert. *The Collected Essays of Robert Creeley*. Berkeley: University of California Press, 1989.

———. Letter to Marjorie Kinsey, October 23, 1976. Robert Creeley Collection. Hesburgh Library, University of Notre Dame.

———. *Mabel: A Story and Other Prose*. London: Marion Boyars, 1976.

———. "Presences." *Io* 14 (Summer 1972): 183–226.

———. *Presences: A Text for Marisol*. New York: Scribner's, 1976.

———. *Selected Letters*. Edited by Rod Smith, Peter Baker, and Kaplan Harris. Berkeley: University of California Press, 2014.

Creeley, Robert, and Jim Dine. *Mabel: A Story*. Paris: Editions Crommelynck, 1977.

Creeley, Robert, and Robert Indiana. *Numbers*. Edited by Dieter Honisch. Translated by Klaus Reichert. Stuttgart: Edition Domberger, 1968.

Creeley, Robert, and R. B. Kitaj. *A Day Book*. Berlin: Graphis, 1971.

Crow, Thomas. *The Long March of Pop: Art, Music, and Design, 1930–1995*. New Haven, CT: Yale University Press, 2014.

Curley, Jonathan, and Burt Kimmelman, eds. *The Poetry and Poetics of Michael Heller: A Nomad Memory*. Madison, NJ: Roman and Littlefield/Fairleigh Dickinson University Press, 2015.

D'Agata, John. *The Next American Essay*. St. Paul, MN: Graywolf, 2003.

Davenport, Guy. *The Geography of the Imagination*. San Francisco: North Point, 1981.

Davidson, Michael. *Ghostlier Demarcations: Modern Poetry and the Material Word*. Berkeley: University of California Press, 1997.

———. *Guys Like Us: Citing Masculinity in Cold War Poetics*. Chicago: University of Chicago Press, 2004.

———. "The Presence of the Present: Morality and the Problem of Value in Robert

Creeley's Recent Prose." In "Robert Creeley: A Gathering," edited by William Spanos, *Boundary 2*, 6–7 (Spring–Fall 1978): 545–64.

Dawson, Fielding. *The Black Mountain Book: A New Edition*. Rocky Mount: North Carolina Wesleyan College Press, 1991.

Dembo, L. S., and Cyrena N. Pondrom, eds. *The Contemporary Writer: Interviews with Sixteen Novelists and Poets*. Madison: University of Wisconsin Press, 1972.

Dewey, John. *Art as Experience*. In *The Later Works, 1925–1953*, vol. 10, *1934*, edited by Jo Ann Boydston. Carbondale: Southern Illinois University Press, 1987.

Dimock, Wai Chee. *Through Other Continents: American Literature Across Deep Time*. Princeton, NJ: Princeton University Press, 2006.

Dinerstein, Joel. *The Origins of Cool in Postwar America*. Chicago: University of Chicago Press, 2017.

Duncan, Robert. *The Collected Early Poems and Plays*. Edited by Peter Quartermain. Berkeley: University of California Press, 2012.

———. *Collected Essays and Other Prose*. Edited by James Maynard. Berkeley: University of California Press, 2014.

———. *The Collected Later Poems and Plays*. Edited by Peter Quartermain. Berkeley: University of California Press, 2014.

———. *The H.D. Book*. Edited by Michael Boughn and Victor Coleman. Berkeley: University of California Press, 2011.

———. Notebook 41, July 14, 1968–December 30, 1970. Robert Duncan Archive, Poetry/Rare Books Collection, University at Buffalo.

———. "Rites of Participation." In *The H.D. Book*, edited by Michael Boughn and Victor Coleman, 153–99. Berkeley: University of California Press, 2011.

DuPlessis, Rachel Blau. *Drafts 1–38, Toll*. Middletown, CT: Wesleyan University Press, 2001.

———. *Drafts 39–57, Pledge*. Cambridge, UK: Salt, 2004.

———. *Torques: Drafts 58–76*. Cambridge, UK: Salt, 2007.

———. *Pitch: Drafts 77–95*. Cambridge, UK: Salt, 2010.

———. *Surge: Drafts 96–114*. Cambridge, UK: Salt, 2013.

———. "Manhood and Its Poetic Projects: The Construction of Masculinity in the Counter-Cultural Poetry of the U.S. 1950s." *Jacket* 31 (October 2006). http://jacketmagazine.com/31/duplessis-manhood.html.

———, ed. *The Oppens Remembered: Poetry, Politics, Friendship*. Albuquerque: University of New Mexico Press, 2015.

———. *Purple Passages*. Iowa City: University of Iowa Press, 2012.

Dworkin, Craig Douglas. "Penelope Reworking the Twill: Patchwork, Writing, and Lyn Hejinian's *My Life*." *Contemporary Literature* 36 (1995): 58–81.

Dydo, Ulla, ed. *A Stein Reader*. Evanston, IL: Northwestern University Press, 1993.

Eisenman, Stephen, ed. *William Blake and the Age of Aquarius*. Princeton, NJ: Princeton University Press, 2017.

Eliade, Mircea. *Shamanism: Archaic Techniques of Ecstasy*. Translated by Willard Trask. Bollingen Series 76. New York: Pantheon, 1964.

Eliot, T. S. *The Complete Poems and Plays, 1909–1950*. New York: Harcourt, 1971.

Emerson, Ralph Waldo. "The American Scholar." In *Essays and Lectures*, 51–71. New York: Library of America, 1983.

Eno, Brian. *Ambient 1: Music for Airports*. Virgin, 1978.

Evergreen Review 1, no. 2 (1957).

Evergreen Review 1, no. 4 (1957 copyright, Spring 1958 issue).

Faas, Ekbert. *Young Robert Duncan: Portrait of the Poet as Homosexual in Society*. Santa Barbara, CA: Black Sparrow, 1983.

"Featuring Robert Duncan." *Audit/Poetry* 4.3 (1967).

Felstiner, John. *Paul Celan: Poet, Survivor, Jew*. New Haven: Yale University Press, 1995.

Ferguson, John. *Encyclopedia of Mysticism and Mystery Religions*. New York: Crossroad, 1982.

Fields, Rick. *How the Wild Swans Came to the Lake: A Narrative History of Buddhism in America*. Rev. ed. Boston: Shambhala, 1986.

Finkelstein, Norman. *Not One of Them in Place: Modern Poetry and Jewish American Identity*. Albany, NY: State University of New York Press, 2001.

———. Review of Michael Heller, *This Constellation Is a Name*. *Notre Dame Review* 35 (Winter/Spring 2013): 186–95.

Frank, Robert. *The Americans*. New York: Grove, 1959. First published 1958 by Robert Delpire (Paris).

Fredman, Stephen. *Contextual Practice: Assemblage and the Erotic in Postwar Poetry and Art*. Stanford, CA: Stanford University Press, 2010.

———. *The Grounding of American Poetry: Charles Olson and the Emersonian Tradition*. Cambridge: Cambridge University Press, 1993.

———. *A Menorah for Athena: Charles Reznikoff and the Jewish Dilemmas of Objectivist Poetry*. Chicago: University of Chicago Press, 2001.

———. *Poet's Prose: The Crisis in American Verse*. 2nd ed. Cambridge: Cambridge University Press, 1990.

———, ed. *A Concise Companion to Twentieth-Century American Poetry*. Malden, MA: Blackwell, 2005.

Fuentes, Agustín. *The Creative Spark: How Imagination Made Humans Exceptional*. New York: Dutton, 2017.

García Lorca, Federico. *Collected Poems*. Edited by Christopher Maurer. New York: Farrar, Strauss and Giroux, 2002.

———. *Poet in New York*. Translated by Stephen Fredman. San Francisco: Fog Horn, 1975.

Gelpi, Albert, ed. *Denise Levertov: Selected Criticism*. Ann Arbor: University of Michigan Press, 1993.

Gilman, Sander. *The Jew's Body*. New York: Routledge, 1991.

Ginsberg, Allen. *Collected Poems, 1947–1980*. New York: Harper, 1984.

———. *Collected Poems, 1947–1997*. New York: HarperCollins, 2006.

———. *Howl and Other Poems*. San Francisco: City Lights, 1956.

Glass, Philip. *Music by Philip Glass*. Edited by Robert T. Jones. New York: Harper and Row, 1987.

———. *Words Without Music*. New York: Liveright, 2015.

Goldberg, Roselee. *Laurie Anderson*. New York: Harry Abrams, 2000.

Golding, Alan. "*The New American Poetry* Revisited, Again." *Contemporary Literature* 39, no. 2 (1998): 180–211.

Göransson, Johannes. *Transgressive Circulation: Essays on Translation*. N.p.: Noemi, 2018.

Gunn, Douglas. "Inappropriate Literary Performances: The Unstable Texts of Robert Creeley's *Mabel: A Story and Other Prose*." *Review of Contemporary Fiction* 15, no. 3 (Fall 1995): 141–53.

Gunn, Thom. *Selected Poems*. Edited by August Kleinzahler. New York: Farrar, Straus and Giroux, 2009.

Harari, Yuval Noah. *Sapiens: A Brief History of Humankind*. New York: Harper, 2015.

Hay, Eloise Knapp. *T. S. Eliot's Negative Way*. Cambridge, MA: Harvard University Press, 1982.

H.D. (Hilda Doolittle). *Collected Poems, 1912–1944*. Edited by L. Martz. New York: New Directions, 1983.

Heidegger, Martin. *Poetry, Language, Thought*. Translated by Albert Hofstadter. New York: Harper, 1971.

Hejinian, Lyn. *The Language of Inquiry*. Berkeley: University of California Press, 2000.

———. *My Life*. Providence, RI: Burning Deck, 1980.

———. *My Life*. Los Angeles: Sun & Moon, 1987.

———. "The Person." In *The Cold of Poetry*, 143–81. Los Angeles: Sun & Moon, 1994.

———. "The Person and Description." *Poetics Journal* 9 (1991): 166–70.

———. "The Quest for Knowledge in the Western Poem." In *Disembodied Poetics: Annals of the Jack Kerouac School*, edited by Anne Waldman and Andrew Schelling, 171–89. Albuquerque: University of New Mexico Press, 1994.

———. "The Rejection of Closure." In *Writing/Talks*, edited by Bob Perelman, 270–91. Carbondale, IL: Southern Illinois University Press, 1985.

———. "Variations: A Return of Words." In *In the American Tree*, edited by Ron Silliman. Orono, ME: National Poetry Foundation, 1986.

Heller, Michael. *Constellations of Waking*. Loveland, OH: Dos Madres, 2019.

———. *Conviction's Net of Branches: Essays on the Objectivist Poets and Poetry*. Carbondale: Southern Illinois University Press, 1985.

———. *Eschaton*. Jersey City, NJ: Talisman House, 2009.

———. "'Glad You've Initiated This Correspondence . . .'" In *The Oppens Remembered: Poetry, Politics, and Friendship*, edited by Rachel Blau DuPlessis, 44–53. Albuquerque: University of New Mexico Press, 2015.

———. *Living Root: A Memoir*. Albany: State University of New York Press, 2000.

———. *This Constellation Is a Name: Collected Poems, 1965–2010*. Callicoon, NY: Nightboat, 2012.

———. *Speaking the Estranged: Essays on the Work of George Oppen*. Cambridge, UK: Salt, 2008.

———. *Uncertain Poetries*. Cambridge, UK: Salt, 2005.

———, ed. *Carl Rakosi: Man and Poet*. Orono, ME: National Poetry Foundation, 1993.

Herd, David, ed. *Contemporary Olson*. Manchester, UK: Manchester University Press, 2015.

———. "'From Him Only Will the Old State-Secret Come': What Charles Olson Imagined." *English* 59, no. 227 (2010): 375–95.

Higgins, Hannah. *Fluxus Experience*. Berkeley: University of California Press, 2002.

Howe, Fanny. *Selected Poems*. Berkeley: University of California Press, 2000.

———. *The Wedding Dress: Meditations on Word and Life*. Berkeley: University of California Press, 2003.

Howe, Susan. *The Midnight*. New York: New Directions, 2003.

Jabès, Edmond. *From the Book to the Book: An Edmond Jabès Reader*. Translated by Rosmarie Waldrop. Middletown, CT: Wesleyan University Press, 1991.

———. *From the Desert to the Book: Dialogues with Marcel Cohen*. Translated by Pierre Joris. Barrytown, NY: Station Hill, 1990.

Johnson, Kent, and Craig Paulenich, eds. *Beneath a Single Moon: Buddhism in Contemporary American Poetry*. Boston: Shambhala, 1991.

Kamenetz, Rodger. *The Jew in the Lotus: A Poet's Rediscovery of Jewish Identity in Buddhist India*. San Francisco: HarperSanFrancisco, 1994.

Kearns, Cleo McNally. *T. S. Eliot and Indic Traditions: A Study in Poetry and Belief*. Cambridge: Cambridge University Press, 1987.

Kenner, Hugh. *A Homemade World: The American Modernist Writers*. New York: William Morrow, 1975.

Kerouac, Jack. *Dharma Bums*. New York: Viking, 1958.

Keynes, Geoffrey, ed. *The Letters of William Blake*. Cambridge, MA: Harvard University Press, 1968.

Kushner, Tony. *Angels in America: A Gay Fantasia on National Themes*. New York: Theatre Communications Group, 1995.

Lacey, Paul A., and Anne Dewey, eds. *The Collected Poems of Denise Levertov*. New York: New Directions, 2013.

Lazer, Hank. *Opposing Poetries*. Vol. 1, *Issues and Institutions*. Evanston, IL: Northwestern University Press, 1996.

———, ed. "David Antin Issue." *Review of Contemporary Fiction* 21, no. 1 (Spring 2001).

Leland, John. *Hip: The History*. New York: HarperCollins, 2004.

Lewis-Williams, David. *The Mind in the Cave: Consciousness and the Origins of Art*. New York: Thames & Hudson, 2002.

Lichtenstein, Rachel, and Iain Sinclair. *Rodinsky's Room*. London: Granta, 1999.

Lin, Tan. *Seven Controlled Vocabularies and Obituary 2004. The Joy of Cooking: [AIRPORT NOVEL MUSICAL POEM PAINTING FILM PHOTO HALLUCINATION LANDSCAPE]*. Middletown, CT: Wesleyan University Press, 2010.

Lu, Pamela. *Ambient Parking Lot*. Chicago: Kenning, 2011.

Lysaker, John T. *Brian Eno's "Ambient 1: Music for Airports."* Oxford: Oxford University Press, 2018.

Mackey, Nathaniel. *Bass Cathedral*. New York: New Directions, 2008.

———. *From a Broken Bottle Traces of Perfume Still Emanate*. New York: New Directions, 2010.

———. *Late Arcade*. New York: New Directions, 2017.

———. *Whatsaid Serif*. New York: New Directions, 1998.

Mallarmé, Stéphane. *A Tomb for Anatole*. Translated by Paul Auster. San Francisco: North Point, 1983.

Materer, Timothy. *Modernist Alchemy: Poetry and the Occult*. Ithaca, NY: Cornell University Press, 1995.

Maud, Ralph. *Charles Olson's Reading: A Biography*. Carbondale: Southern Illinois University Press, 1996.

———, ed. *Poet to Publisher: Charles Olson's Correspondence with Donald Allen*. Vancouver, BC: Talonbooks, 2003.

Mayhew, Jonathan. *Apocryphal Lorca: Translation, Parody, Kitsch*. Chicago: University of Chicago Press, 2009.

Maynard, James. *Robert Duncan and the Pragmatist Sublime*. Albuquerque: University of New Mexico Press, 2018.

Medina, José Ramón. *Marisol*. Photographs by Jack Mitchell. Caracas: Ediciones Armitano, 1968.

Meltzer, David, ed. *The Secret Garden: An Anthology in the Kabbalah*. 1976. Reprint, Barrytown, NY: Station Hill, 1998.

Melville, Herman. *Moby-Dick*. Edited by Harrison Hayford and Hershel Parker. Norton Critical Edition. New York: Norton, 1967.

Merleau-Ponty, Maurice. *The Prose of the World*. Edited by Claude Lefort. Translated by John O'Neill. Evanston, IL: Northwestern University Press, 1973.

Middleton, Peter. *Distant Reading: Performance, Readership, and Consumption in Contemporary Poetry*. Tuscaloosa: University of Alabama Press, 2005.

Miller, Paul D. *Rhythm Science*. Boston: MIT Press, 2004.

———, ed. *Sound Unbound: Sampling Digital Music and Culture*. Boston: MIT Press, 2008.

Miller, Stephen Paul, and Daniel Morris, eds. *Radical Poetics and Secular Jewish Culture*. Tuscaloosa: University of Alabama Press, 2010.

Montefalcone, Barbara. "'Celebrating the Instant': Robert Creeley and Marisol Escobar's *Presences*." In *USA: Identities, Cultures, and Politics in National, Transnational and Global Perspectives*, edited by Marina Camboni et al., 127–38. Macerata, Italy: Eum Edizioni Università di Macerata, 2009.

———. "The 'Eye' and the 'Company': Robert Creeley's Collaborations, 1953–2004." Dissertation Université Lumière Lyon 2, 2006.

Montefalcone, Barbara, and Anca Cristofovici, eds. *The Art of Collaboration: Poets, Artists, Books*. Victoria, TX: Cuneiform, 2015.

Morris, Adalaide, ed. *Sound States: Innovative Poetics and Acoustical Technologies*. Chapel Hill: University of North Carolina Press, 1997.

Mullen, Laura. *Murmur*. New York: Futurepoem, 2007.

Nicholls, Peter. *George Oppen and the Fate of Modernism*. Oxford: Oxford University Press, 2007.

O'Leary, Peter. *Gnostic Contagion: Robert Duncan and the Poetry of Illness*. Middletown, CT: Wesleyan University Press, 2002.

Olson, Charles. *The Collected Poems of Charles Olson: Excluding the Maximus Poems*. Edited by George Butterick. Berkeley: University of California Press, 1997.

———. *Collected Prose*. Edited by Donald Allen and Benjamin Friedlander. Berkeley: University of California Press, 1997.

———. *The Maximus Poems*. Edited by George Butterick. Berkeley: University of California Press, 1983.

———. *Muthologos: Lectures and Interviews*. Rev. 2nd ed. Edited by Ralph Maud. Vancouver, BC: Talonbooks, 2010.

———. *Selected Letters*. Edited by Ralph Maud. Berkeley: University of California Press, 2000.

———. *The Special View of History*. Edited by Ann Charters. Berkeley: Oyez, 1970.

Oppen, George. *New Collected Poems*. Edited by Michael Davidson. New York: New Directions, 2002.

———. *Selected Letters*. Edited by Rachel Blau DuPlessis. Durham, NC: Duke University Press, 1990.

———. *Selected Prose, Daybooks, and Papers*. Edited by Stephen Cope. Berkeley: University of California Press, 2007.

———. *21 Poems*. Edited by David B. Hobbs. New York: New Directions, 2017.

Oppen, Mary. *Meaning a Life: An Autobiography*. Santa Barbara, CA: Black Sparrow, 1978.

Ouaknin, Marc-Alain. *The Burnt Book: Reading the Talmud*. 1986. Translated by Llewellyn Brown. Princeton: Princeton University Press, 1995.

Pacini, Marina, ed. *Marisol: Sculptures and Works on Paper*. New Haven, CT: Memphis Brooks Museum of Art and Yale University Press, 2014.

Paul, Sherman. *In Search of the Primitive: Rereading David Antin, Jerome Rothenberg, and Gary Snyder*. Baton Rouge: Louisiana State University Press, 1986.

Perelman, Bob. *Modernism the Morning After*. Tuscaloosa: University of Alabama Press, 2017.

Perloff, Marjorie. *The Dance of the Intellect: Studies in the Poetry of the Pound Tradition*. Cambridge: Cambridge University Press, 1985.

———. *The Poetics of Indeterminacy: Rimbaud to Cage*. 1981. Evanston, IL: Northwestern University Press, 1999.

———. *Poetry On & Off the Page: Essays for Emergent Occasions*. Evanston: Northwestern University Press, 1998.

———. *Radical Artifice: Writing Poetry in the Age of Media*. Chicago: University of Chicago Press, 1991.

Plumstead, A. W., and Harrison Hayford, eds. *The Journals and Miscellaneous Notebooks of Ralph Waldo Emerson*. Vol. 7, *1838–1842*. Cambridge, MA: Harvard University Press, 1969.

Pound, Ezra. *The Cantos of Ezra Pound*. New York: New Directions, 1970.

———. *Personae: The Collected Shorter Poems of Ezra Pound*. New York: New Directions, 1926.

———. *Selected Prose, 1909–1965*. New York: New Directions, 1973.

———. *The Spirit of Romance*. New York: New Directions, 1968.

Power, Kevin. *Where You're At: Poetics and Visual Art*. Berkeley, CA: Poltroon, 2011.

Prendergast, Mark. *Ambient Century: From Mahler to Trance; The Evolution of Sound in the Electronic Age*. New York: Bloomsbury, 2001.

Rainey, Lawrence. *Institutions of Modernism: Literary Elites and Public Culture.* New Haven, CT: Yale University Press, 1998.

Rankine, Claudia. *Don't Let Me Be Lonely: An American Lyric.* Minneapolis: Graywolf, 2004.

Reich, Steve, and Beryl Korot. *The Cave.* New York: Nonesuch Records, 1995.

Rilke, R. M. *Letters to a Young Poet.* Translated by M. D. Herter Norton. Rev. ed. New York: W. W. Norton, 1954.

———. *Selected Poetry of Rainer Maria Rilke.* Translated by Stephen Mitchell. New York: Vintage, 1989.

Rothenberg, Jerome. *Poetics and Polemics, 1980–2005.* Tuscaloosa: University of Alabama Press, 2008.

———. *Pre-Faces & Other Writings.* New York: New Directions, 1981.

———. *Tryptich.* New York: New Directions, 2007.

———, ed., with commentaries. *Technicians of the Sacred: A Range of Poetries from Africa, America, Asia, & Oceania.* Garden City, NY: Doubleday, 1968.

———, ed., with commentaries. *Technicians of the Sacred: A Range of Poetries from Africa, America, Asia, Europe & Oceania.* 2nd ed. Berkeley: University of California Press, 1985. Third edition published 2017.

Rothenberg, Jerome, and Steve Clay, eds. *A Book of the Book: Some Works & Projections about the Book & Writing.* New York: Granary, 2000.

Rothenberg, Jerome, and Diane Rothenberg, eds., with commentaries. *Symposium of the Whole: A Range of Discourse Toward an Ethnopoetics.* Berkeley: University of California Press, 1983.

Rothenberg, Jerome, Harris Lenowitz, and Charles Doria, eds. *A Big Jewish Book: Poems and Other Visions of the Jews from Tribal Times to Present.* Garden City, NY: Doubleday, 1978.

Rudolf, Anthony. *Wine from Two Glasses.* London: Adam Archive, 1991.

Rumaker, Michael. *Black Mountain Days: A Memoir.* 2003. Reprint, New York: Spuyten Duyvil, 2012.

Sayre, Henry. *The Object of Performance: The American Avant-Garde since 1970.* Chicago: University of Chicago Press, 1989.

Schelling, Andrew, ed. *The Wisdom Anthology of North American Buddhist Poetry.* Boston: Wisdom, 2005.

Schlegel, Friedrich. "On Incomprehensibility." In *Classic and Romantic German Aesthetics,* edited by J. M. Bernstein, 297–307. Cambridge: Cambridge University Press, 2003.

Scholem, Gershom. *Major Trends in Jewish Mysticism.* New York: Schocken, 1954.

———. *On Jews and Judaism in Crisis: Selected Essays.* Edited by Werner Dannhauser. New York: Schocken, 1976.

Seuss, Dr. (Theodore Geisel). *Horton Hears a Who!* New York: Random House, 1954.

Shields, David. *Reality Hunger: A Manifesto.* New York: Knopf, 2010.

Shoemaker, Steve, ed. *Thinking Poetics: Essays on George Oppen.* Tuscaloosa: University of Alabama Press, 2009.

Shulman, Leon. *Marisol.* Worcester, MA: Worcester Art Museum, 1971.

Smith, Harry, ed. *Anthology of American Folk Music*. 1952. Reissue, Smithsonian Folkways 2951-3, 1997.

Smith, Patti. *Just Kids*. New York: Ecco, 2010.

Snyder, Gary. *No Nature: New and Selected Poems*. New York: Pantheon, 1992.

Spahr, Juliana. *Everybody's Autonomy: Connective Reading and Collective Identity*. Tuscaloosa: University of Alabama Press, 2001.

Spanos, William, ed. "The Oral Impulse in Contemporary American Poetry." *Boundary 2*, 3, no. 3 (1975).

Spiegelman, Art. *Maus: A Survivor's Tale*. Vols. 1 and 2. New York: Random House, 1986, 1991.

Stein, Charles. *The Secret of the Black Chrysanthemum: The Poetic Cosmology of Charles Olson and His Use of the Writings of C. G. Jung*. Barrytown, NY: Station Hill, 1987.

Steiner, George. *After Babel: Aspects of Language and Translation*. New York: Oxford University Press, 1975.

Surette, Leon, and Demetres Tryphonopoulos, eds. *Literary Modernism and the Occult Tradition*. Orono, ME: National Poetry Foundation, 1996.

Sylvester, William. "Is That a Real Statue or Did Marisol Just Make It Up? Affinities with Creeley's *Presences*." In *Robert Creeley: The Poet's Workshop*, edited by Carroll F. Terrell, 275–87. Orono, ME: National Poetry Foundation, 1984.

Taggart, John. *Loop*. Los Angeles: Sun and Moon, 1991.

Talisman 11 (Fall 1993).

Thackrey, Susan. *George Oppen: A Radical Practice*. San Francisco: O, 2001.

Thompson, Robert Farris. *African Art in Motion*. 1974. New ed., Berkeley: University of California Press, 1979.

Thoreau, Henry David. *Walden and Civil Disobedience*. Edited by Owen Thomas. Norton Critical Edition. New York: Norton, 1966.

Tuchman, Maurice, ed. *The Spiritual in Art: Abstract Painting, 1890–1985*. New York: Abbeville, 1986.

Tryphonopoulos, Demetres. *The Celestial Tradition: A Study of Ezra Pound's "The Cantos."* Waterloo, ON: Wilfred Laurier University Press, 1992.

Twitchell-Waas, Jeffrey. "Robert Creeley." *Review of Contemporary Fiction* 24, no. 2 (Summer 2004): 7–54.

Vincent, Stephen, and Ellen Zweig, eds. *The Poetry Reading: A Contemporary Compendium on Language & Performance*. San Francisco: Momo's, 1981.

Wallace, Mark, and Steven Marks, eds. *Telling It Slant: Avant-Garde Poetics of the 1990s*. Tuscaloosa: University of Alabama Press, 2002.

Weinfield, Henry, ed. "Forum: Two Poems Entitled 'Psalm' by George Oppen and Paul Celan." *Religion and Literature* 48, no. 1 (Spring 2017): 159–91.

Wenders, Wim, dir. *Wings of Desire*. Road Movies Filmproduktion, 1987.

Whiting, Cécile. *A Taste for Pop: Pop Art, Gender, and Consumer Culture*. Cambridge: Cambridge University Press, 1997.

Whitman, Walt. *Leaves of Grass*. Edited by Sculley Bradley and Harold Blodgett. Norton Critical Edition. New York: Norton, 1973.

Williams, William Carlos. *The Collected Poems of William Carlos Williams*. Vol. 1, *1909–*

1939. Edited by A. Walton Litz and Christopher MacGowan. New York: New Directions, 1986.

Yerushalmi, Yosef Hayim. *Zakhor: Jewish History and Jewish Memory*. 1982. New York: Schocken, 1989.

Young, Dennis. "Conversation with Mary Oppen." *Iowa Review* 18, no. 3 (1988): 18–47.

Zukofsky, Louis. *Prepositions +: The Collected Critical Essays*. Middletown, CT: Wesleyan University Press, 2000.

Index

Page numbers in italics refer to figures.